Eliphalet Nott

Counsels to Young Men on the Formation of Character,

and the principles which lead to success and happiness in life; being addresses principally delivered at the anniversary commencements in Union college

Eliphalet Nott

Counsels to Young Men on the Formation of Character,
and the principles which lead to success and happiness in life; being addresses principally delivered at the anniversary commencements in Union college

ISBN/EAN: 9783337311742

Printed in Europe, USA, Canada, Australia, Japan

Cover: Foto ©Thomas Meinert / pixelio.de

More available books at **www.hansebooks.com**

COUNSELS TO YOUNG MEN

ON THE

FORMATION OF CHARACTER,

AND

THE PRINCIPLES WHICH LEAD TO SUCCESS AND HAPPINESS IN LIFE;

BEING

ADDRESSES

PRINCIPALLY DELIVERED AT THE ANNIVERSARY COMMENCEMENTS IN UNION COLLEGE.

BY ELIPHALET NOTT, D.D.,

PRESIDENT OF UNION COLLEGE.

NEW YORK:
HARPER & BROTHERS, PUBLISHERS,
329 & 331 PEARL STREET,
FRANKLIN SQUARE.
1860.

Entered, according to Act of Congress, in the year 1840, by
HARPER & BROTHERS,
In the Clerk's Office of the Southern District of New-York.

PUBLISHERS' ADVERTISEMENT.

THE great experience of the venerable author of these addresses as an instructer and guardian of youth, gives a value to his counsels which can be best appreciated by those whose happiness it has been to be trained to knowledge and virtue under his paternal guidance and care. To those, and the number is not small, who have gone forth from the halls of Union to honour their *alma mater* by their conduct in life, this volume must be peculiarly acceptable. Nor will the discourses it contains be read with scarcely less interest by others; being replete with sound moral and religious instruction, and written with all the originality, earnestness, and eloquence so characteristic of their able and excellent author. By young men, especially, they may be made of invaluable use, in directing them to the adoption of such principles as will lead to prosperity and happiness in this world, to the favour of God, and the assurance of a better inheritance in the world to come.

A few of the discourses in the series, although delivered on special occasions, and differing from the others in their leading design, will be found full of important information and the most striking views, in relation to subjects deeply interesting to every Christian mind. The publishers would also state, that, by permission of the author, a brief table of contents has been prefixed to each discourse for the convenience of the reader.

H. & B.

New-York, October, 1840

CONTENTS.

I.

Sanguine Anticipations of the Young.—Education should be the Business of Life.—Duty of controlling and subjugating the Passions.—Of cultivating and cherishing the Sympathies of our Nature.—Of practising Justice, and adhering scrupulously to Truth.—Religion inseparable from our Nature.—Christianity: its Character, Effects, Objects, Encouragements, and Rewards . . . . . . Page 13

II.

Nature of Man threefold: Sensitive, Intellectual, and Moral.—Pleasures of Sense: lawful and innocent in themselves, and forbidden and pernicious only when sinfully and excessively indulged.—Intellectual Pleasures: their elevated, refined, and durable Character.—Man's Moral Nature, and the Responsibilities derived from it.—Virtue alone leads to Happiness.—The duty of judging charitably of others: of avoiding Slander.—Claims of Parents upon their Children . . . 26

III.

The Young require to be specially cautioned against the predominant Vices of the Day.—Spirit of mutual Injury, Recrimination, and Revenge, characteristic of the Times.—Definition of Revenge, and its wicked and odious Character described.—Private Revenge forbidden by the Divine Law, and Vengeance declared to belong to God alone.—Under what circumstances, and how far we may resist personal Injuries.—False and true Honour.—The Practice of Duelling, its sinfulness and awful consequences.—Christian Treatment of Enemies.—An arrogant, ambitious, and revengeful Disposition in the last degree hateful in a Christian Minister.—The Character of the Saviour, his Precepts, and perfect Example, teach us how we should at all times act under Injuries . 43

IV.

Two opposite Systems offered to our Acceptance, the one founded on *Human Reason*, the other on *Divine Revelation*.—Man, by his own Wisdom, never has, nor ever can have a true and proper Conception of God.—Contradictory, false, and unworthy Notions entertained by the wisest of the Ancients in regard to the Nature and Attributes of the Supreme Being, their confused and erroneous Ideas as to Virtue and Vice, and the gross Immorality of their Lives.—The Appearance of Christianity in the World dispelled the Darkness and Delusion that had before universally prevailed, and brought in a new Era of Light, and Hope, and of pure and perfect Morals.—The Simplicity and Purity of the Christian System soon corrupted by being incorporated with the Errors of the ancient Philosophy.—Modern Infidelity, and the pernicious and absurd Doctrines on which it is founded.—Skeptical System of Hume (see Note).—Infidelity and Christianity, in their Character, Moral Effects, and ultimate Results, contrasted.—The Christian alone can have Hope in Death, and Assurance of a blessed Immortality . . . . Page 64

V.

Painful Feelings of Teachers in parting from their Pupils.—Responsibility of Teachers.—Constant Succession of Actors on the Stage of Life.—Motives held out to the Young to act their part well.—Discouragements to an honourable Ambition removed.—The Examples of Howard, Sharpe, Clarkson, and Lancaster.—A mixture of virtuous and vicious Characters in the World.—The Practice of Virtue, even as it regards this Life, to be preferred.—But there is a God: Man is accountable and immortal, and should act with constant reference to these great Truths.—Concluding Exhortation 78

VI.

The Moral, no less than the Physical World, subject to convulsions and changes.—The present an age of Political Revolutions.—Our Country involved in the contentions of Nations.—Importance of the Era in which we live.—The hopes of Society in the rising Generation.—Knowledge is Power.—The Savage and the civilized Man compared.—The dominion of Mind, as exhibited in the general and statesman—in the example of ancient Athens.—Encouragements to Perseverance in the pursuit of Intellectual Superiority.—Examples of Homer and Demosthenes.—Power beneficent only when associated with Goodness.—Human Endowments should be consecrated to Religious and Moral ends.—Nature of Civil Government, and duty of Obedience to it.—Exhortation to de-

fend the free Institutions of our Country.—Whatever Trials befall the Christian here, his Reward is sure hereafter
Page 97

VII.

Love of Distinction.—Honour and Religion, though distinct, are allied to each other.—Modern definition of the Law of Honour.—Fallacies of this Definition exposed.—A sense of Honour in different degrees operative on all Minds except the most debased.—The offices of this Feeling and of Conscience contrasted.—Purpose for which the Sense of Honour was implanted in the human breast.—Its Perversion an abuse.—Dignity of Man, and the lofty distinction conferred on him by his Maker.—His Fall and Recovery.—His Rank, Capacities, Parentage, and Destination, all call upon him to persevere in a steady Course of honourable Action, in his Amusements, his Pleasures, and his Occupations.—Dignity of the good Man in his last moments.—All false and deceptive appearances will be exposed in a future state; and those only who are truly and sincerely good will be accounted worthy of acceptance and honour 111

VIII.

Public Opinion as opposed to the Moral Law.—Games of Chance.—Objectionable because they unprofitably consume Time.—Because they lead to a misapplication of Property.—Because they impart no Expansion or Vigour to the Mind.—Because their Influence on the Affections and Passions is deleterious.—Dreadful Effect of Gaming on Morals and on the Sympathies of our Nature.—It leads to Debauchery, to Avarice, to Intemperance.—The finished Gambler has no Heart.—Example of Madame du Deffand.—Brutalized and hopeless State of the Gambler and Drunkard.—Warning to Youth to avoid the Temptations which lead to these soul-destroying Vices 128

IX.

Skeptical Notions in regard to the Providence of God, and his retributive Justice.—The condition of the Virtuous and Vicious in this World affords no argument against the position that God will reward the one and punish the other.—A future State of Existence is certain, and must be taken into account in judging of the Character and Designs of God.—The inward Peace enjoyed by the Virtuous, and the Trouble and Remorse experienced by the Vicious, indications of God's Moral Government.—The Trials of the Righteous intended to exalt and purify their Character.—Consolations of the Righteous in the view of Death, and the Happiness that awaits them in a future State of Being . . . . . . Page 147

X.

Instability of all earthly Things.—Motives to early Piety.—Filial Love and Gratitude.—Parental Affection.—Anxiety of Parents to promote the Happiness of their Children.—Christian Parents.—Instructions of Solomon.—Early Piety interesting in itself.—Leads to Happiness.—Joy of Christian Parents in pious Children, in Life and in Death.—Example of a pious Child.—The Good on Earth and the Angels in Heaven rejoice over Souls converted from Sin to Righteousness.—Union of Parents and Children in Heaven . . . 159

XI.

Effects of the Apostacy.—Man vainly seeks for Happiness in Riches—in Power—in Wisdom.—Man's boasted Wisdom considered—in the Philosophy of Mind—in the Philosophy of Matter.—Chymistry.—The Microscope.—Astronomy.—The Telescope.—The Fixed Stars.—True Wisdom consists in the Knowledge of God.—Pagan and Christian Theology, in their Character and Effects, compared.—The Bible the source of the most precious Knowledge.—To be truly Wise is to understand the great Truths which it reveals, and comply with its Requirements 179

XII.

Absolute Independence predicable only of God.—The Relations between Parents and Children.—A foolish Son a Grief to his Father.—Sin the greatest of all Folly.—The Sinner's Character and Course described.—The Effects of Sin.—Children growing up in Sin.—The Prodigal Son.—The Anguish occasioned to Parents by dissolute Children.—Their Affliction in leaving such Children behind them.—Their Hopelessness in the Death of such Children.—David and Absalom.—The Petition of Dives.—Future State of the Wicked.—Close of the Argument 206

XIII.

All wish to Die with the Assurance of Happiness hereafter.—As Youth is the most important, it is also the most dangerous Period of Life.—Religion only can guard against the Temptations incident to this Period.—The Example of Josiah.—All Men mean to repent of their Sins.—Danger of delaying Repentance—from the uncertainty of Life and of the continued possession of Reason—from the hardening effects of Perseverance in Sin—from being left to a Reprobate Mind . . . . Page 226

XIV.

Character and Design of the Bible Society.—Christian Communities do not sufficiently appreciate their indebtedness to the Bible.—Nearly all that is pure in Morals or kindly in Feeling derived from it.—In the first Ages of the World, God's Communications to Man were direct, and were perpetuated and extended by Tradition.—The early Longevity of Mankind favourable to this.—The Traditions and Institutions of heathen Nations coincide with and confirm the sacred Records of the Jews.—Divine Revelation and the Speculations of human Reason, as exhibited in their different Effects.—Dreadful Moral Corruption of the heathen World.—Influence of Christianity in ameliorating the Condition and Morals of Mankind.—Unspeakable importance of Divine Revelation in regard to a future State.—The duty of Christians to extend it to all Nations 240

XV.

Difference in the Intellectual and Moral Condition of Individuals and Nations.—Ignorance and Knowledge the principal Causes of this Difference.—Advantages of Associated Efforts in promoting Science.—Intelligence and Happiness capable of being vastly extended.—First crude Discoveries in Science contrasted with the Progress since made.—Present State and future Prospects of Scientific Research.—Chymistry.—Astronomy.—Mineralogy and Botany.—Meteorology.—Electricity.—Medicine.—Political Science.—Popular Governments.—The United States.—Anomaly of domestic Slavery, in its Origin, &c., considered.—Ameliorations in our Institutions and Laws in regard to Debtors—to Criminals.—Religious Freedom.—Multiplicity of Religious Sects not incompatible with Christian Union.—Science and Religion reciprocally aid each other, and should never be disunited . 275

ADDRESSES.

I.

DELIVERED MAY 1, 1805.

[Sanguine Anticipations of the Young.—Education should be the Business of Life.—Duty of controlling and subjugating the Passions.—Of cultivating and cherishing the Sympathies of our Nature.—Of practising Justice, and adhering scrupulously to Truth.—Religion inseparable from our Nature.—Christianity: its Character, Effects, Objects, Encouragements, and Rewards.]

Young gentlemen, this day closes your collegiate life. You have continued the term and completed the course of studies prescribed in this institution. You have received its honours, and are now to go forth adventurers—unsuspecting, perhaps, and certainly inexperienced—into a fascinating but illusive world: a world where honour flaunts in fictitious trappings; where wealth displays imposing charms, and pleasure spreads her impoisoned banquets. And that, too, at a period when the passions are most ungovernable, when the fancy is most vivid, when the blood flows rapidly through the veins, and the pulse of life beats high. Already does the opening scene brighten as you approach it; and happiness, smiling but deceitful, passes before your eyes and beckons you to her embrace.

Called to address you at this affecting crisis, and

for the last time, had I, like the patriarch of the East, a blessing at my disposal, how gladly should I bestow it. But I have not; and can therefore only add to the solicitude which I feel, my counsel and my prayers.

Permit me to advise you, then, young gentlemen, when you leave this seminary, and even after you shall have chosen a profession and entered on the business of life, still to consider yourselves only learners. Your acquirements here, though respectable, are the rudiments merely of an education which must be hereafter pursued and completed. In the acquisition of knowledge you are never to be stationary, but always progressive. Nature has nowhere said to man, pressing forward in the career of intellectual glory, "Hitherto shalt thou come, but no farther." Under God, therefore, it depends upon yourselves to say how great, how wise, how useful you will be. Men of moderate talents, by a course of patient application, have often risen to the highest eminence, and, standing far above where the momentary sallies of uncultivated genius ever reach, have plucked from the lofty cliff the deathless laurel. Indeed, to the stature of the mind no boundary is set. Your bodies, originally from the earth, soon reach their greatest elevation, and bend downward again towards that earth out of which they were taken. But the inner man, that sublime, that rational, that immortal inhabitant which pervades your bosoms, if sedulously fostered, will expand and elevate itself, till, touching the earth, it can look above the clouds and reach beyond the stars.

Go, then, and, emulous to excel in whatever is splendid, magnanimous, and great, with Newton, span the heavens, and number and measure the orbs which decorate them; with Locke, analyze the human mind; with Boyle, examine the regions of organic nature: in one word, go, and with the great, the wise, and the good of all nations and all ages, ponder the mysteries of Infinite Wisdom, and trace the Everlasting in his word and in his works. A wide and unbounded prospect spreads itself before you, in every point of which Divinity shines conspicuous; and on whichever side you turn your enraptured eyes, surrounded with uncreated majesty, and seen in the light of his own glory, God appears. He leads the way before you, and sheds radiance on his path, that you may follow him.

Control and subjugate your passions.—Originally order pervaded human nature. The bosom of man was calm, his countenance serene. Reason sat enthroned in his heart, and to her control the passions were subjected. But the days of innocence are past, and with them has also passed the reign of reason. Phrensy ensues. He who was once calm and rational is now blind and impetuous. A resistless influence impels him. Consequences are disregarded, and, madly pressing forward to the object of desire, he exclaims, " My honour, my property, my pleasure;" but is never heard to say, " My religion, my duty, my salvation."*

While reason maintained her empire, the passions were a genial flame, imparting warmth to the sys-

* See Saurin on the Passions.

tem, and gently accelerating the circulation of the blood. But, that empire subverted, they kindle into a Vesuvius, burning to its centre, and pouring out on every side its desolating lava. The passions, said an inspired apostle, war against the soul; and the same apostle who said this commands you to overcome them.

Cultivate and cherish the sympathies of your nature.—These, though blighted by the apostacy, still retain the tints of faded loveliness; and when sanctified in the heart and unfolded in the life even of fallen man, they possess a resistless charm, and furnish some faint idea of what he must have been in a state of innocence.

For the exercise of these sympathies in all the paths of life, you will meet with pitiable objects, who will present their miseries to your eye, and address the moving eloquence of sorrow to your heart. Always listen to this eloquence; always pity this misery, and, if possible, relieve it. Yes, young gentlemen, whatever seas you may navigate, or to whatever part of the habitable world you may travel, carry with you your humanity. Even there divide your morsel with the destitute; advocate the cause of the oppressed; to the fatherless be a father, and cover the shivering limbs of the naked with your mantle. Even there sooth the disconsolate, sympathize with the mourner, brighten the countenance bedimmed with sorrow, and, like the God of mercy, shed happiness around you, and banish misery before you.

In all your intercourse with mankind, rigidly

practise justice and scrupulously adhere to truth: other duties vary with varying circumstances. What would be liberality in one man would be parsimony in another: what would be valour on one occasion would be temerity on another; but truth and justice are immutable and eternal principles—always sacred and always applicable. In no circumstances, however urgent, no crisis, however awful, can there be an aberration from the one, or a dereliction of the other, without sin. With respect to everything else, be accommodating; but here, be unyielding and invincible. Rather carry your integrity to the dungeon or the scaffold than receive in exchange for it liberty and life. Should you ever be called upon to make your election between these extremes, do not hesitate. It is better prematurely to be sent to heaven in honour, than, having lingered on the earth, at last to sink to hell in infamy. In every situation, a dishonest man is detestable, and a liar is still more so.

I have often, young gentlemen, recommended to you a sacred adherence to truth. I would on this occasion repeat the recommendation, that I may fix it the more indelibly on your hearts. Believe me when I tell you, that on this article you can never be too scrupulous.

Truth is one of the fairest attributes of the Deity. It is the boundary which separates vice from virtue; the line which divides heaven from hell. It is the chain which binds the man of integrity to the throne of God; and, like the God to whose throne it binds him, till this chain is dissolved his word may be relied on. Suspended on this, your property, your reputation, your life are safe. But against the malice of a liar there is no security. He can be bound by nothing. His soul is already repulsed to an immeasurable distance from that Divinity, a sense of whose presence is the security of virtue. He has sundered the last of those moral ligaments which bind a mortal to his duty. And, having done so through the extended region of fraud and falsehood, without a bond to check or a limit to confine him, he ranges, the dreaded enemy of innocence—whose lips pollute even truth itself as it passes through them, and whose breath blasts, and soils, and poisons as it touches.

Finally, cherish and practise religion.—Man has been called, in distinction from the inferior orders of creation, a religious being, and justly so called. For, though his hopes and fears may be repressed, and the moral feelings of his heart stifled for a season, nature, like a torrent which has been obstructed, will break forth and sweep away those frail barriers which skepticism may have erected to divert its course.

There is something so repulsive in naked infidelity, that the mind approaches it with reluctance, shrinks back from it with horror, and is never settled till it rests on positive religion.

I am aware that that spirit of devotion, that sense of guilt and dread of punishment, which pervade the human mind, have been attributed to the force of habit or the influence of superstition. Let the appeal be made to human nature. To the position of irreligionists on this article, human nature itself furnishes the most satisfactory refutation. Religion is a first principle of man. It shoots up from the very seat of life; it cleaves to the human constitution by a thousand ligaments; it entwines around human nature, and sends to the very bottom of the heart its penetrating tendrils. It cannot, therefore, be exterminated. The experiment has again and again been tried, and the result has always proved worthy of the rash attempt.

Young as you are, you have witnessed, with a view to this extermination, the most desperate efforts. But just now a formidable host of infuriate infidels were assembled. You heard them openly abjure their God. You saw them wreaking their vengeance on religion. For a season they triumphed. Before them every sacred institution disappeared, every consecrated monument fell to dust. The fervours of nature were extinguished, and the lip of devotion palsied by their approach. With one hand they seized the thunders of the heavens, and with the other smote His throne who inhabits them. It seemed to crumble at the stroke. Mounting these fancied ruins, Blasphemy waved its terrific sceptre, and, impiously looking up to those eternal heights where the Deity resides, exclaimed, " Victory !"

Where now are those dreaded enemies of our religion? They have vanished from the sight. They were, but are seen no more. Nor have the consequences of their exertions been more abiding. A great nation, indeed, delivered from the restraints of moral obligation, and enfranchised with all the liberties of infidelity, were proclaimed free. But have they continued so? No: their minds presently recoiled from the dismal waste which skepticism had opened before them, and the cheerless darkness it had spread around them. They suddenly arrested their steps; they retraced, in sadness and sorrow, the paths which they had trodden; they consecrated again the temples they had defiled; they rebuilt the altars they had demolished; they sighed for the return of that religion they had banished, and spontaneously promised submission to its reign.

What are we to infer from this? That religion is congenial to human nature; that it is inseparable from it. A nation may be seduced into skepticism, but it cannot be continued in it. Why, I would ask, has religion existed in the world in ages which are past? why does it exist now? why will it exist in ages to come? Is it because kings have ordained and priests defended it? No: but because God formed man to be religious. Its great and eternal principles are inscribed on his heart; they are inscribed in characters which are indelible; nor can the violence of infidelity blot them out. Obscured indeed they may be by the influence of sin, and remain not legible during the rage of passion. But a calm ensues: the calm of reason or the night of adversity, from the midst of whose darkness a light proceeds, which renders the original inscription visible. Man now turns his eye inward upon himself. He reads "Responsibility;" and, as he reads, he feels a sense of sin and dread of punishment. He now pays, from necessity, homage to religion—a homage which cannot be withheld : it is the homage of his nature. We have now traced the effect to its cause, and referred this abiding trait in the human character to its principle.

The question is not, then, whether you will embrace religion—religion you must embrace—but whether you will embrace revealed religion, or that of erring and blind philosophy. And, with respect to this question, can you hesitate ?

The former has infinitely more to recommend it than the latter. It originated in heaven. It is founded, not on conjecture, but on fact. Divinity manifested itself in the person, and shone in the life of its Author. True, he appeared in great humility; but though the humility in which he appeared had been greater than it was, either the sublimity of his doctrines or the splendour of his actions had been sufficient to evince his Messiahship, and prove that he was the Saviour of the world. He spoke as man never spoke! Whence did he derive wisdom so transcendant? From reason? No: reason could not give it, for it had it not to give. What reason could never teach, the gospel teaches—that in the vast and perfect government of the universe, vicarious sufferings can be accepted; and that the dread Sovereign who administers that government is gracious as well as just. Nor does it rest in declaration merely. It exhibits before our eyes the altar and the victim—the Lamb of God, which taketh away the sins of the world.

The introduction of Christianity was called the coming of the kingdom of Heaven. No terms could have been more appropriate; for through it man shared the mercy, and from it caught the spirit of the heavens. The moral gloom which shrouded the nations receded before it. The temples of superstition and of cruelty, consecrated by its entrance, became the asylums of the wretched, and resounded with their anthems of grace.

Most benign has been the influence of Christianity; and were it cordially received and universally submitted to, war would cease, injustice be banished, and primeval happiness revisit the earth. Every inhabitant, pleased with his situation, resigned to his lot, and full of the hopes of heaven, would pass agreeably through life, and meet death without a sigh.

Is the morality of the gospel pre-eminently excellent? So is its object pre-eminently glorious. Philosophy confines its views to this world principally. It endeavours to satisfy man with the grovelling joys of earth, till he returns to that dust out of which he was taken. Christianity takes a nobler flight. Her course is directed towards immortality. Thither she conducts her votary, and never forsakes him till, having introduced him into the society of angels, she fixes his eternal residence among the spirits of the just.

Philosophy can only heave a sigh, a longing sigh, after immortality. Eternity is to her an unknown vast, over which she soars on conjecture's trembling wing. Above, beneath, around, is an unfathomable void; and doubt, uncertainty, or despair is the result of all her inquiries.

Christianity, on the other hand, having furnished all necessary information concerning life, with firm and undaunted step crosses death's narrow isthmus, and boldly launches forth into that dread futurity which borders on it. Her path is marked with glory. The once dark, dreary region brightens as she approaches it, and benignly smiles as she passes over it. Faith follows where she advances; till, reaching the summit of everlasting hills, an unknown scene, in endless varieties of loveliness and beauty, presents itself, over which the ravished eye wanders, without a cloud to dim or a limit to obstruct its sight. In the midst of this scene, rendered luminous by the glory which covers it, the city, the palace, the throne of God appears. Trees of life surround it; rivers of salvation issue from beneath it. Before it, angels touch their harps of living melody, and saints, in sweet response, breathe forth their grateful songs. The redeemed of the Lord who remain upon the earth, catch the distant sound and feel a sudden rapture. 'Tis the voice of departed friendship—friendship, the loss of which they mourn upon the earth, but which they are now assured will be restored in the heavens—from whence a voice is heard to say, " Fear ye not, death cannot injure you; the grave cannot confine you; through its chill mansion, Grace will conduct you up to glory. We wait your arrival: haste, therefore, come away." All this Christianity will do for you. It will do more than this: it consecrates the sepulchre, into which your bodies, already touched by death, will presently descend. There, mouldered into dust, your flesh shall rest in hope. Nor will the season of its humiliation last for ever. Christianity, faithful to her trust, appears for its redemption. She approaches, and stands before the tomb: she stretches out her sceptre and smites the sepulchre; its moss-grown covering rends asunder; she cries to the silent inhabitants within it; her energizing voice echoes along the cold, damp vaults of death, renovating skin and bones, and dust and putrefaction. Corruption puts on incorruption, and mortal immortality. Her former habitation, thus refined and sublimated by the resurrection, the exulting soul re-enters, and thenceforth the measure of her joy is full.

Here thought and language fail me. Inspiration itself describes the glories of futurity by declaring them indescribable. Eye hath not seen, ear hath not heard, neither hath it entered into the heart of man to conceive the things which are prepared for the people of God. What ideas are these? How must the soul exult at the prospect, and swell with the amazing conception!

As Christianity exhibits the most enrapturing motives to the practice of virtue, so it urges the most tremendous considerations to deter from vice. She declares, solemnly and irrevocably declares, "That the wages of sin are death." And, to enforce her declaration, points to the concluding scene of nature—when, amid a departing heaven and a dissolving world, the Son of Man shall descend, with the voice of the archangel and the trump of God, to be glorified in his saints and take vengeance on his enemies!

Such is the gospel: and here I rest my observations. At this affecting crisis, my beloved pupils, this gospel I deliver you. It is the most invaluable gift; and I solemnly adjure you to preserve it inviolate for ever. To whatever part of God's creation you may wander, carry this with you. Consult it in prosperity; resort to it in trouble; shield yourselves with it in danger, and rest your fainting head on it in death.

Do this: and, though the world be convulsed around you, the elements dissolve, and the heavens depart, still your happiness is secure. But should you ever, in an hour of rashness, be tempted to cast it from you, remember that with it you cast away salvation. 'Tis the last hope of sinful, dying man. This gone, all is lost! Immortality is lost, and lost also is the soul, which might otherwise have inherited and enjoyed it. Under these impressions, go forth to the world: and may God go with you.

Committing you to his care, and with a heart full of parental solicitude for your welfare, I bid you an affectionate and final FAREWELL.

II.

DELIVERED JULY 30, 1806.

[Nature of Man threefold: Sensitive, Intellectual, and Moral.—Pleasures of Sense: Lawful and Innocent in themselves, and Forbidden and Pernicious only when sinfully and excessively indulged.—Intellectual Pleasures: their elevated, refined, and durable Character.—Man's Moral Nature, and the Responsibilities derived from it.—Virtue alone leads to Happiness.—The duty of judging charitably of others: of avoiding Slander.—Claims of Parents upon their Children.]

Young gentlemen, most affecting to a parent is the moment when his children, commencing masters of their fortune, leave their paternal home and enter on the world. The disasters which may dissipate their property, the temptations which may corrupt their virtue, and the maladies which may assail their persons, present themselves in clusters to his eye, and crowd upon his mind. Were it possible, gladly would he accompany, counsel, and direct them on their way. But it is not possible. He can, therefore, only vent his full heart in benedictions, and, looking up to God, commit the inexperienced adventurers to his care.

Parting with a class endeared to me by a course of the most filial and affectionate conduct, my situation and my feelings resemble those of a parent parting with his children.

Dear pupils, thus far your instructers have accompanied and directed you in your studies and pursuits. But the time of separation has arrived:

we have reached the point where our ways divide. Before we part, indulge a word of counsel, the last to be communicated by him who now addresses you.

The end that each of you has in view is happiness. To be informed beforehand of the course that will conduct to it, must be infinitely important: because, should you mistake the means, with however much ardour and constancy you may pursue the end, your efforts will be vain, and your future experience prove but the sad disappointment of your present hopes. How, then, may success be ensured? what manner of life will conduct to happiness? To answer this interrogation, the character of man must be developed, his constitution analyzed, his capacities of enjoyment ascertained, and the correspondencies between those capacities and their respective objects unfolded.

What, then, is man? Man is a being in whom are mysteriously combined *a sensitive, an intellectual, and a moral nature:* each of which should be kept in view in the present inquiry, and the comparative claims of each considered in making a decision.

You have been told by an author, more esteemed for the benevolence of his heart than the profoundness of his doctrines, " *that human happiness does not consist in the pleasures of sense,* in whatever variety or profusion they may be enjoyed." It is true that human happiness does not consist exclusively or principally in these. The senses, however, are a real source of enjoyment; nor would I wish you either to despise or undervalue them.

The God of nature has not thought it derogatory to his wisdom, his goodness, or his sanctity, to bestow on you this class of enjoyments; and surely it cannot be derogatory to yours to receive them at his hand.

No inconsiderable part of the happiness allotted to man is conveyed through the medium of the senses, at least in the present world, and, perhaps, in the world to come. For the bodies we inhabit, the sleep of death being ended, will be rescued from the tomb; and it is not easy to perceive why they should be rescued, if their recovery is to have no influence on the pleasures and pains of eternity; to add nothing to the amount of endless misery or immortal bliss.

True, they deposite in the grave (I speak of the redeemed) all their present grossness, pollution, and corruptibility: for they are to be raised from thence *spiritual bodies*. But whether this transformation, this refinement, this sublimation, which the renovated body undergoes, puts an eternal end to its influence on the happiness of the exulting soul, which at the resurrection enters it, or whether this mysterious change do not rather exalt its powers, and render them capable of communicating a happiness more refined and sublimated, is an article on which, though revelation were silent, it should seem that reason could scarcely entertain a doubt.

I know that there are men, and good men too, who calumniate, indiscriminately, all the pleasures of sense. I say calumniate, for the language they utter is neither the language of reason nor revelation. The finger of God is too manifest in the sensitive part of human nature to admit a doubt concerning the innocence of those enjoyments which spring from it. Christianity, instead of abjuring, approbates the pleasures of sense. She claims them as her own, and bids the possessor indulge them to the glory of the God who gave them. And the author of Christianity, that great exemplar of righteousness and model of perfection, *came eating and drinking*. Again and again he graced the festive board with his divine presence: he delivered his celestial doctrines amid the circles of social friendship, and the *first* of that splendid series of miracles which signalized his life was performed at a *marriage supper*.

But, though the pleasures of sense constitute a part, and an innocent part, it is but a very humble part of human felicity. While they are restrained within the limits, and conformed in all respects to the decorum of gospel morality, they are perfectly admissible. But if this decorum be violated, if these limits be transgressed, order is subverted, and guilt, as well as misery, ensues.

On this article nature herself coincides with religion, and fixes at the same point her sacred and unalterable boundary. She has stamped on the very frame of man her *veto* against excess; and the apathy, the languor, the pains and disgusts consequent upon it, are her awful and monitory voice, which says distinctly to the devotee of passion, "Rash mortal, forbear: thou wast formed for temperance, for chastity; these be the law of thy nature. Hitherto thou mayest come, but no farther; and here must all thy appetites be stayed."

Attend to the voice of nature: obey her mandate. Consider, even in the heat of youthful blood, consider thy frame, "*how fearfully, how wonderfully made;*" how delicate its texture, how various, how complicated, how frail its organs; how capable of affording thee an exquisite and abiding happiness, and, at the same time, how liable, by one rash act of intemperate indulgence, to be utterly deranged and destroyed for ever.

And let me forewarn you that the region of innocent indulgence and guilty pleasure border on each other; a single step only separates them. If you do not regulate your pleasures by principles fixed and settled; if you do not keep in your eye a boundary that you will never pass; if you do not impose previous restraints, but leave your hearts to direct you amid the glee of convivial mirth and the blandishments of youthful pleasure, it requires no prophetic eye to foresee, that, impelled by the gusts of passion, " conscience will swing from its moorings," and that your probity, your virtue, your innocence will be irrevocably shipwrecked.

The intellectual nature of man.—And here the design of the Creator is more than intimated. The posture of man is erect, and his countenance, irradiated by an expressive intelligence, is directed towards the heavens. If he possesses some faculties in common with animals, he possesses others distinct from theirs: faculties as much superior to those of sense, as the stars which decorate the firmament of God are higher and more resplendent than the worthless pebble that sparkles amid the dust and rubbish on his footstool: faculties which no indulgence surfeits, no exercise impairs, or time destroys: often sustaining the infirmities of age; often beaming with intellectual radiance through the palsied organs of a dying body, and sometimes even gilding the evening of animal existence with the anticipated splendours of immortal life.

The appetites of the body are soon cloyed, and the richest banquets of sense disgust. But the appetites of the mind, if I may speak so, are never satisfied. In all the variety, in all the plenitude, in all the luxury of mental enjoyment, the most favoured individual was never surfeited, or once heard to say, "It is enough." The more of these delicate, these pure, these sublime, I had almost said holy pleasures, an individual enjoys, the more he is capable of enjoying, and the more he is solicitous to enjoy. It is the intellectual eye that is never satisfied with seeing, the intellectual ear that is never satisfied with hearing.

The powers in question are not more superior to those of sense than the provision for them is more abundant. Beauty, grandeur, novelty—all the fine arts—music, painting, sculpture, architecture, gardening, considered scientifically, are so many sources of mental enjoyment. But why do I mention these particulars? All the region of nature—earth with its varieties—heaven with its sublimities—the entire universe, is spread out before the intellectual observer.

Nor the visible creation alone. To principalities and powers; to thrones, dominions, and all the nameless orders which constitute the interminable line of heavenly excellence, man is introduced: orders for ever advancing in wisdom, and brightening in the splendours of intellectual glory, at the head of which appears the Eternal Being, who alone changes not, because infinite perfection cannot change. The pleasure which springs from the knowledge and contemplation of these objects, this universe of good, is so ineffable, so transcendent, that the wretch who does not prefer it to the mere indulgence of sense, though free of other crimes, evinces a depravity which merits eternal reprobation.

His moral nature.—Man was made to be religious, to acknowledge and reverence God, and to be conformed in his moral conduct to the law of God. You have only to consult your hearts to be convinced of this. The proof is there inscribed in characters which are indelible.

When even the child looks abroad into the works of the Creator, he naturally refers the objects which surround him to an adequate first cause, and asks, "Where is God their maker." If sudden danger threatens him, his eye is directed to the heavens for relief. If unexpected happiness overtakes him, his heart breaks forth in grateful acknowledgments to an unseen benefactor. Even the untutored savage surveys the wilderness of nature—the extended earth, the distant heavens—with religious awe, and pays to their creator an instinctive homage.

Devotion is a law of human nature; and you can with no more consistency deny its existence, than you can deny the existence of the laws by which heaven and earth are governed. You may as well deny that there is a principle in your bodies that binds them to the earth, as that there is a principle in your souls which elevates them to the heavens.

Nor is the reality of the moral sense more questionable. Self-complacency springs from the performance of duty; shame and regret from the commission of sin. Skepticism may endeavour to persuade you to the contrary, but it never can. It has indeed weakened the faith and clouded the hopes of thousands, but it never gave a single individual a settled, firm, and abiding belief that there is no God, no futurity, or that man is not accountable. There have been serious and awful moments in the lives of the boldest champions of infidelity when they have discovered symptoms of dereliction: moments when the struggles of nature could not be repressed, and when the voice of nature has been heard to break forth. The punishment of Cain, given up to the tortures of a guilty mind, was greater than he could bear; and the spectre of John the Baptist haunted the bedchamber of Herod long after the tomb had become to that martyr a bed of repose. Who was it, think you, that anticipated the prophet in interpreting the handwriting of Belshazzar, and smote the sacrilegious wretch with trembling? Why did Galerius relent on his death-bed? And what made Caligula afraid when it thundered? It was conscience: who, startled by danger from her slumbers, shook her terrific sceptre, and uttered her monitory voice.

Nor is it material to inquire why man is thus formed. It is a fact that he is so formed; nor is it possible for him to be happy in a course of conduct which does violence to his nature. From the penalties of the mind you can no more escape than from the appetites of the body. You may avoid the malediction of an earthly tribunal. You may avoid, says the irreligionist, the malediction of God: but yourselves—the retribution of justice within your own bosoms—how is this to be avoided? Conscience, like that Divinity of which it is a symbol, with respect to you, is omnipresent. Though you ascend to heaven—though you make your bed in hell—though you take the wings of the morning, and dwell in the uttermost parts of the earth, this avenger of sin will accompany you: watching with an eye from which no darkness can conceal, and chastising with a thong that no fortitude can endure. *The spirit of man will sustain his infirmity, but a wounded spirit who can bear?*

Such briefly is man: in providing for whose happiness his entire constitution must be consulted, each distinct capacity of enjoyment must be furnished with appropriate objects, and a due proportion between them all must be preserved.

Be this your care. Despise not corporal pleasures, neither exalt them too highly. Hold them subordinate to intellectual enjoyments, and these subordinate to moral. Your intellectual and moral nature is what allies you to angels and assimilates you to God. Age will presently rob you of all the delights of sense; but of intellectual and moral delights neither age nor death can rob you. To the votary of science and religion, the last cup of heavenly consolation is not poured out till his eye is closing on the world, and his flesh descending into the grave in hope.

A life of virtue and happiness, then, exactly coincide. To practise the one is to secure the other. The God of virtue formed every faculty of pleasure, and has made them all subservient to duty. There are those, I am sensible, who represent religion shrouded in gloom and covered with scowls; but the attitude, the drapery, the features are unlike the divine original, and betray the pencil of an enemy. There never was, nor ever will be, one source of happiness which religion does not authorize.

Some, indeed, speak of all the pleasures of sense as pleasures of sin. But such language is at once an outrage to common sense and an indignity to God. Sin never gave the faculties of sense, and let not sin claim the bliss that springs from them. There is not a being in the universe that owes to sin a single enjoyment. The immortal God is the author of them all. He made you what you are; and if, in the abuse of the faculties he has bestowed, a single delight remain, it is owing to his clemency.

Which of the faculties is it, I would ask, that sin improves? Is it the eye? Is it the ear? Is it the palate? Does sin add any new faculties? No; she only palsies the energies, perverts the use, and poisons the pleasures of those which before existed: these are her baneful and damning work—under whose influence, delights, once desired, disgust the thoughts and pall upon the senses. My God! if you are beguiled by an idea of the pleasures of sin, look once upon the emaciated body, the pallid countenance, the bloated features, and the mutilated face of the loathsome and worn-out sensualist! Look again! And can you believe the place of his resort is the habitation of pleasures? No: 'tis the *temple* of pollution, of disease, of death; there *sin, accursed sorceress*, mingles her cup and infuses her poison. Mark the place, avoid it, turn from it, and flee away.

After this, will you believe that virtue is your enemy? that religion requires sacrifices? If so, in the name of God, what are they? I know of none, unless of disease, of pain, of infamy.

True, you may not riot at the banquets of Bacchus; but you may participate in temperance at the table of convivial mirth, and, exhilarated, rise from thence to give God thanks. You may not steal at midnight to the infamous pleasures of the brothel; but you may cherish at your homes the refined, the hallowed pleasures of connubial friendship. You may not, indeed, so much as lay your head upon the lap of Delilah; but you may live joyfully with the wife whom you love all the days of your pilgrimage, for it is the portion which God gives you under the sun.

As we have said, a life of virtue and a life of happiness coincide; and he who seeks the latter in opposition to the former, counteracts the laws of nature; contradicts the experience of ages; and, to succeed, must transcend not himself only, but his Maker also, and become more potent than *omnipotence* himself. The body can subsist in health without aliment as easily as the soul without virtue : nor is poison more fatal to the one than the venom of sin to the other. This is a matter of experience, of fact ; and whoever asserts to the contrary, belies his heart, and contradicts the testimony of a world.

I have detained you so long on the means of happiness, that time would fail me were I to enter in detail on the conduct of life. The great principles of morality and piety are involved in the argument we have been pursuing. An incidental thought or two, suggested by the times in which we live, is all that will be attempted.

Permit me, then, particularly to enjoin you to conduct honourably and charitably towards those who are opposed to you in their opinions. Diversity of sentiment is inevitable in a state of things like the present. The dispensation of time is an obscure dispensation, and, till the light of eternity shall break upon the mind, it is not to be expected that erring mortals will see eye to eye. While groping in this world, and following the guidance of that erring reason which is scarcely sufficient to direct us through it, it must be folly to suppose ourselves always in the right, and more than folly to reprobate those whom we consider in the wrong.

Society, on which you are about to enter, is already divided into various sects in religion, and agitated by contending parties in politics. Between these hold the balance with an equal hand, and let merit, and not prejudice or interest, turn the beam.

To judge correctly, you must take a comprehensive view of the whole field of controversy; and, having honestly formed your judgment, give full credit to the merit of those who differ from you, and be sparing of the censure which you conceive to be their due.

Beware of judging bodies of men in the gross, as though each individual were chargeable with the vices of the whole. There is no body of men among whom you may not find something to admire and much to blame. Be careful to separate, therefore, the gold from the dross, and to distinguish the precious from the vile.

If there can be anything that can disgrace civilized society, it is a spirit of indiscriminate and wanton slander; a spirit, the vilest with which any nation can be cursed. And yet this spirit exists. It exists among us. It pervades the whole extent of a country once proudly pre-eminent for every social virtue. It insinuates itself into the cottage of the peasant; it enters, I had almost said resides, in the mansion of the great. It is cherished by every party; it moves in every circle. It hovers round the sacred altar of mercy; it approaches the awful seat of justice. In one word, it surrounds us on every side, and on every side it breathes forth its pestilential vapour, blasting talents and virtue, and reducing, like the grave, whose pestiferous influence it imitates, the great, and the good, and the ignoble, and the vile, to the same humiliating level.

Permit me to indulge the hope, young gentlemen, that you will never enlist under the banner of this foe to human happiness, nor prostitute your talents, or even lend your names, to this work of intellectual massacre.

Having taken so much pains and expended so much treasure in preparing for future usefulness, will you consent to become mere scavengers in society, and spend your lives in collecting and retailing filth? Remember that the course of the eagle is directed towards the heavens, and that it is the serpent that winds along the fens, creeps upon his belly, and licks the dust.

Whatever party you may join, or in whatever rivalships you may engage, let your warfare be that of honourable policy, and not the smutty contest which succeeds by blackening private character. Convinced of the sacredness of reputation, never permit yourselves to sport with the virtues, or even lightly attack the vices of men in power. If they pass a certain boundary, indeed sufferance would be pusillanimity, and silence treason. But the public good, and not private interest or private resentment, must fix that boundary.

There is a homage due to the sanctity of office, whoever fills it: an homage which every man owes, and which every good man will feel himself bound to pay, after the sublime example of him who, though a Jew and residing at Jerusalem, rendered honour and paid tribute to Cæsar at Rome.

I cannot sum up all that I would wish to say to you on practical duty better than by placing the entire character of Jesus Christ before you as a perfect model, in the imitation of which will alike consist your happiness and glory. On every important question, ask what would have been his opinion, what his conduct; and let the answer regulate your own.

Methinks your parents, some of whom I see in this assembly, add their sanction to the counsel I am now delivering. Parents whom I cannot but commend particularly to your ingenuousness, and from their kindness and solicitude derive an argument to enforce all that I have said. You will never know, till the bitterness of filial ingratitude shall teach you, the extent of the duty that you owe them. On you their affections have been placed: on you their treasures expended. With what tenderness they ministered to your wants in helpless infancy; with what patience they bore with your indiscretions in wayward childhood; and with what solicitude they watched your steps in erring youth. No care has been too severe; no self-denials too painful; no sacrifices too great, which would contribute to your felicity. To your welfare the meridian of life has been constantly devoted, and even its cheerless evening is rendered supportable by the prospect of leaving you the heirs of their fame and of their fortune. For all this affection and kindness, the only reward they expect, the only requital they ask, is, that, when you enter on the world, you will act worthy of yourselves, and not dishonour them.

And shall this requital be denied them? Will you, by your follies, disturb even the tranquillity of age; rob declining life of its few remaining pleasures, and, snatching away from the palsied hand of your aged parents the last cup of earthly consolation, bring their gray hairs with anticipated sorrow to the grave?

It was a noble spectacle, amid the flames that were consuming Troy, and while the multitude were intent only on rescuing their paltry treasures, to see the dutiful Æneas bearing on his shoulders the venerable Anchises, his aged father, to a place of safety. But ah! how rare such examples of filial piety! My God! the blood freezes in the veins at the thought of the ingratitude of children. Spirits of my sainted parents, could I recall the hours when it was in my power to honour you, how different should be my conduct! Ah! were not the dead unmindful of the reverence the living pay them, I would disturb the silence of your tombs with nightly orisons, and bedew the urn which contains your ashes with perpetual tears!

It is within your power to prevent the bitterness of such regrets. But I must arrest the current of my feelings. Your future usefulness, your eternal salvation, constitute a motive so vast, so solemn, that, were I to yield to its overwhelming influence, I should protract the hour of separation, and fill up with counsel and admonition the declining day.

I shall address you no more. I shall meet with you no more, till, having passed the solemnities of death, I meet you in eternity. So spend the intervening period, I adjure you, that that meeting may be joyous; and the immortality which shall follow it splendid as the grace of that God is free, to whom, surrendering my charge, I now commit you. Leaving with you this counsel, I bid you an affectionate and final FAREWELL.

III.

DELIVERED JULY 29, 1807.

[The young require to be specially cautioned against the predominant Vices of the Day.—Spirit of mutual Injury, Recrimination, and Revenge characteristic of the Times.—Definition of Revenge, and its wicked and odious Character described.— Private Revenge forbidden by the Divine Law, and Vengeance declared to belong to God alone.—Under what circumstances, and how far we may resist Personal Injuries.— False and True Honour.—The practice of Duelling: its Sinfulness and awful Consequences.—Christian Treatment of Enemies.—An arrogant, ambitious, and revengeful Disposition in the last degree hateful in a Christian minister.—The Character of the Saviour, his Precepts and perfect Example teach us how we should at all times act under Injuries.]

YOUNG gentlemen, a seminary is a world in miniature. The resemblances are strong and numerous: none of which, however, strike the mind more forcibly than that succession of actors, who, tripping over the stage, sustain the parts of the passing drama. As generation follows generation, so class follows class; and the gladsome smile of social intercourse soon gives place to the solemn gloom of final separation. On these occasions, custom authorizes an address to the young adventurers, and nature sanctions what custom authorizes. Anxious for your future welfare, your instructers, who have hitherto guarded your virtue and watched for your happiness, seize on the parting interview, and, by the solemn circumstances which crowd upon the mind, urge their last counsel.

It is not possible, in the few moments allotted to this address, to develop, or even hint at all those doctrines of faith which demand your attention; nor should I feel as if I had discharged the sacred duty which I owed you, had I left these to a hasty discussion in this place and on this occasion. To furnish you with a complete summary of practical duty is also impossible. A glance only at a topic or two is all that will be attempted. The real friend adapts his admonitions to the dangers which threaten, and shapes his cautions to the spirit of the times: *the spirit of the times is a spirit of mutual injury, recrimination, and revenge.* In such an age, to hope to pass through life unassailed is vain. The only question is, therefore, how are you to sustain the assault; how treat the assailant?

Were the *world* to utter its voice in this place, it would tell you to be ever vigilant to discover causes of offence; quick in repelling, and inexorable in revenging to the uttermost the slightest attack upon your person or your honour. The *gospel*, however, adopts a different counsel, and, in the bland accents of its Author, inculcates forbearance and forgiveness.

The crimes and miseries resulting from revenge have been witnessed in every country and regretted in every age. Philosophy, in attempting to regulate, hath increased the evil. Christianity alone directs her weapons at its root, and aims at preventing the effects by exterminating the principle.

Revenge has been defined, *the inflicting of pain upon the person who has injured or offended us, far-*

ther than the *just ends of punishment or reparation require.* "There can be no difficulty in knowing when we occasion pain to another, nor much in distinguishing whether we do so with a view only to the ends of punishment or from revenge; for in the one case we proceed with reluctance, in the other with pleasure."

Most, if not all the human passions, have their use in the economy of life; and, when sanctified by grace, conduce no less to virtue than to happiness. But how can a passion which has misery as its object be useful—how agreeable to the Deity? Where could have been its sphere of action in the primeval state—or towards whom could it have been directed, while mutual love predominated in the breast of man? To these interrogations it is not easy to give a satisfactory answer. Is revenge, then, a new principle resulting from the apostacy? I know that the apostacy touched the vital principle of man with death; that it corrupted and perverted those faculties and powers which before existed; but I do not know that it created new ones. And when man shall be restored to that perfection from which he hath fallen, the restoration will consist, not in the annihilation of any of his faculties, but in the recovery of his entire nature from sin to holiness; so that he who before hated will now love his Maker *with all his heart, soul, mind, and strength, and his neighbour as himself.*.

May it, then, not be supposed, that the principle in question is not a new one; but the ruins of a once holy principle implanted in the breasts of moral agents, predisposing them to acquiesce in distributive justice, and to say, in view of the executed penalties of the fearful law of God, *true and righteous are thy judgments?* and which principle, now perverted and depraved, prompts the proud possessor not to acquiesce in, but to seize on the administration of Jehovah : to utter his maledictions, and hurl his thunders on every being who has done, or is supposed to have done him an injury.

Though there cannot be an intentional injury without sin, and though pain is, and for ever will be, the just desert of the sinner, it is not the province of any created being to ascertain the degree of pain due for any offence, or to inflict the same when ascertained. This is an act of distributive penal justice, which belongs to God, and to him exclusively. *Vengeance is mine, saith the Lord.*

So minute are the causes which operate on human minds, so imperceptible are the shades of moral turpitude, that the Omniscient Being alone is competent to distributive justice. In civil governments, even penal codes are not founded on distributive, but general justice ; nor do these aim at the apportionment of penalties to personal demerit, but at the prevention of crimes or the reformation of offenders—a thing totally different in its nature from the assignment of a certain degree of suffering to a certain degree of criminality. Hence the difficulty of detecting, and the necessity of preventing certain offences, and not the malignity of each particular case, determine human legislators in the severity of their penalties.

But, if civil governments, authorized by Divine appointment, are not to execute vengeance on offenders, much less are individuals to do this. It is, therefore, no apology for, or, rather, justification of, an act of vengeance, that the person who is the object of it is guilty: nor does it alter the case that that guilt has been incurred by an injury done to you. He may deserve to be chastised for his temerity, but you are not constituted either the judge or the executor of that chastisement.

Not that I would inculcate that pain may never be inflicted on the individual who has done you wrong. It sometimes may and ought to be inflicted. But the motive to this infliction of pain, and the measure of pain to be inflicted, are to be looked for in the good it will produce, and not in the misery due to the offender. There are cases of personal injury where the will of the great Lawgiver is expressed. In every other instance your own good, the good of the offender, or the public good, can alone constitute a justifiable motive for punishing, or fix the measure of the punishment. And where neither of these ends can be answered, no matter of what crime an individual may have been guilty—no matter what punishment he deserves from God, his Maker and his Master, he deserves none from you. *Avenge not yourselves, but rather give place unto wrath.* These are the words of an apostle. *But I say unto you that you resist not evil: but whosoever shall smite thee on thy right cheek, turn to him the other also. And whosoever will take away thy coat, let him have thy cloak also.*

These are the words of Christ. They are, however, not to be interpreted literally, but proverbially: inculcating habitual forbearance, and the overcoming of evil with good.

Express declarations of Scripture give you a right, in extreme cases, to defend yourselves, even at the expense of the life of the assailant. Here the motive is self-defence, and the force made use of ought to be proportioned to the danger, and not to exceed it. In such cases, where human laws cannot operate for your protection, or repair the evil to which forbearance might subject you, the Divine law interposes, and constitutes you the executor of its justice; and where the alarm does not produce a state of mind incompatible with moral agency, your act on the invader of your rights may be considered as an official one. But these acts are essentially different from those revenges which are every day taking place, where the injury done *to* the aggressor neither prevents nor repairs the injury done *by* him. Besides, those acts are in direct violation of civil government, which make the laws umpire in cases of controversy, and leaves not the injured individual to be judge in his own cause.

Far be it from me to wish to extinguish in your bosoms the genuine principles of honour. These spring up from the very seat of virtue; and where these are not, greatness disappears—probity, integrity, and valour are no more. Rather let me inculcate high notions of personal character; let me foster a lofty sense of individual dignity, and adjure you scrupulously to avoid whatever would tend to stain the one or degrade the other; but let me tell you that is but a sorry honour which requires to be established by a challenge or vindicated by a shot.

Personal bravery is commendable. You live not for yourselves, but for your friends, your country, your God. In a good cause you ought not to regard even life itself. On great occasions, and when the voice of public justice calls you, face danger, tread with undaunted step the field of death, and covet the place of desolation. But in your own individual cause; in the little pitiful neglects and insults which may be offered you, be too great to feel them, too magnanimous to resent them.

Shall you, then, desert your honour? No: defend it—scrupulously defend it. How? By a good life; by a uniform course of probity, integrity, and valour. Whenever you are accused, you will either be guilty or not. If guilty, an exchange of shots cannot expiate that guilt: if you are not guilty, the liar's tongue cannot make you so.

What a humiliating spectacle do those appellants, in cases of personal controversy, to the chancery of firearms, furnish to the world!

But to this degrading farce there is appended a solemn after scene, which stifles irony, and from which appalled humanity turns away with horror. Suddenly the scene changes into the tragic pomp of death. The mania of passion subsides. The *etiquette* of honour is laid aside; the stream of life, flowing out from the wounded heart, quenches the fire of vengeance, and swallows up the injuries which produced a catastrophe so awful. Conscience

E

awakes; the fictitious drapery which custom had flung around the rash adventurer falls off; the fell assassin stands, naked and aghast, over the expiring victim of his anger; a witness of that blood, which, issuing forth, attaches to his person the stain of murder, and lifts from the steeped earth its accusing voice to the *God of life.* With the emotions of Cain imbrued in his brother's blood, he goes back into the world from the field of death. There his eye meets the frantic stare of the wife whom his wrath hath made a widow. The plaints of her hapless children, whom he has doomed to perpetual orphanage, sigh upon the breeze and linger on his ear: while a distracted father shakes his gray locks, and utters from his quivering lips his deep-toned execration on the wretch who has felled at a blow his hopes, and consigned to the grave his son!

From these sad objects he tears himself; but, as if the tomb refused to repose the dust consigned to it by violence, the form of his fallen adversary pursues him. He hears, amid the silence of the midnight hour, a groan—and sees blood still issuing from the wound which in his wrath he opened.

And for what is this rash act indulged, which drags in its train such accumulated horrors? For an unguarded word—a turn of wit—the omission of a nod—or, perhaps, the fighting of a spaniel. Great God! and is this the boasted magnanimity of duellists? Sooner may my joints indurate in their sockets, or mine arm fall severed from my shoulder-blade, than be raised in such an action.

But, aside from powder and bullets, and all that

nameless machinery of justice which constitutes the tribunal of honour (a tribunal before which, I pray God, you may never disgrace yourselves by appearing), it remains a question how you are to meet those disingenuous attacks to which you will inevitably be exposed?

The law of retaliation is *an eye for an eye, and a tooth for a tooth.* Sheltering themselves under the rigour of this law, men of implacable temper indulge resentment; and when a malicious slanderer spits forth the venom of *his* heart, they spit forth the venom of *theirs* in return. *But I say unto you, resist not evil, but overcome evil with good.* Must you, then, always restrain your pen, and, passive to injury, seal your lips in silence? No: there may be cases in which the cause of truth requires not only the avowal of your sentiments, but also a firm and manly vindication of them. When this is the fact, to shrink from the ordeal of scrutiny were pusillanimity—were treason. When this is the fact, be regardless of personal consequences, encounter reproach, and become a voluntary martyr to righteousness. But, even in the act of martyrdom, watch your deceitful hearts, that righteousness, not *self*, be your motive.

There may, too, be cases in which a reply to disingenuous insinuations or open slanders may be requisite as a vindication of yourselves. These cases, however, are fewer, much fewer than you imagine; and prudence, not passion, will point them out. You may never reply for the sake of goading your adversary, however much you may have him in your power; and seldom, very seldom, will it be wise to reply as a personal defence.

Scandal, left to itself, usually loses its power to injure. Suspicion will not easily attach to the character of a good man while he acts consistently, and remains in the dignified posture of self-approving silence. He who pursues the path of duty, nor swerves from his purpose, however attacked, carries his vindication with him; and usually proceeds more successfully, and always more nobly, than he who, halting, stoops to indulge the littleness of anger, and either growls at the tiger, or barks back at the whelps and "whiffets" that follow, and yell and yelp along his path.

Where the public have no interest in being deceived—where their passions and prejudices are not embarked, slander seldom needs any other refutation than that furnished in the spirit of its author. But will the public always be impartial? Can their candour always be relied on? No: party-spirit, political prejudice, "sectarian zeal," and self-righteous bigotry, often blind the eyes of men to justice, and stop their ears to truth. But when this is the case—when prejudice, and bigotry, and passion are called into action, a wise man will hardly expect, by apology, by argument, by explanation, to stop their progress. Expect to stop their progress by apology, by argument, by explanation! You might as well expect to tame the lightnings; to confine the tempest, or lash the maddened ocean to submission. No: rather stand in silent confidence; let the storm pass by, and wait the returning calm of reason.

Moreover, our enemies, uncandid as they may be, often declare the truth of us—and truth which our friends would be likely to conceal. Their statements, however disingenuous, may therefore be improved to our advantage if we have magnanimity to examine them impartially, and humility to correct the errors which occasioned, or, at least, countenanced what we may deem invective. But the moment we put ourselves on the defensive—the moment we become apologists for our faults—that moment we become blinded and wedded to them.

Nor is this all. We cannot enter the lists of invidious controversy without placing our peace of mind in jeopardy. Revenge, even in a war of words, cannot be indulged with impunity. A spark of it is never smitten from the flinty heart without kindling the fire of *hell*, which it is in vain to hope will remain unextinguished in the bosom without consuming it. The boiling fury of resentment scalds the heart from which it is poured out. When an enemy imparts to you his gall, when he provokes you to recriminate, then it is that he may claim *victory*; for he has torn away your shield, and your happiness lies naked to his scorpion sting. What, then, shall you do? Retire into the sanctuary of your own integrity; and while the enemy of your peace struts, and roars, and swells, and foams around you, remote in your feelings from the tumult he occasions, enjoy the holy calm of forgiving mercy: recollecting that *he who is slow to anger is better than the mighty; and he that ruleth his spirit than he that taketh a city*

You will not construe this advice into an encouragement to that haughty, self-confident demeanour, which indicates insensibility to praise, and contempt for the opinions and censures of the world. It is in virtue's self, and not the affectation of virtue, that true greatness lies. I never see a man tranquil under injuries, and candid and ingenuous towards enemies, but his character rises in my estimation, and I pay to him a voluntary homage. Nor do I ever see one vindictive, railing at his enemies, crying down their talents, affecting to despise their opinions, and to regard their censures only as the idle wind, but, in the act of doing this, his character suffers degradation. This is the language of wounded pride, intended, indeed, to conceal, but which, in fact, discovers most effectually the chagrin which is felt and the vexation which is suffered. In questions that affect yourselves or that affect your enemies, as on every other occasion, be candid.

If you have taken a wrong position, abandon it: if you have committed an error, correct it; but if your conscience is satisfied with the part you have acted or the duty you have performed, tranquil and self-possessed, abide the issue. If an enemy revile you, revile not in return: if that enemy have talents, honour them; and if he merits respect, render it unto him. Favour his interests, deal gently with his failings, shield his fame. Do even more than this. If he be in affliction, sympathize with him; if he be poor, feed him; if naked, clothe him, *and let his loins be warmed with the fleeces of your flock;* and as for the injury you may have suffered, nobly forgive it, and pray God that it may be forgiven. By so doing you will heap coals of fire upon his head: coals not to consume, but to melt him into righteousness. This, *this*, if I may speak so, is the most effectual and the only laudable revenge.

Particularly, should any of you enter the sacred ministry, let me enjoin on you this conduct.

Never do haughty egotism, captious animadversion, and acrimonious rebuke appear so unsightly as in the minister charged from the meek and lowly Jesus with an embassy of peace. And yet, alas! unsightly as these appear, we are sometimes compelled, with regret and sorrow, to behold them.

A particular profession or pursuit does not alter the nature of the human passions, but only gives to them a different direction. The wrath of Paul was as deadly as that of Herod. The one assassinated out of complaisance to a giddy girl, the other persecuted for conscience' sake. This circumstance, however, made no difference to the wretched victims whom his malignant zeal pursued to death.

Under the cover of religion, men perhaps more frequently indulge the bitterness of passion without compunction than in any other situation. The wretch who wantonly, and without some "*salvo* to his conscience," attacks private character, feels self-condemned. But the sour, sanctimonious, grace-hardened bigot embarks all his pride, gratifies all his revenge, and empties his corroded bosom of its gall, and, having done so, smooths over the distorted features of a countenance on which sits the smile of Judas, and says, and half believes, that *he has done God service.*

The proud, ambitious, arrogant clergyman takes his stand in the church with the same views that the proud, arrogant, and ambitious statesman takes his in the world.

Is self-aggrandizement the motive of the latter? so it is of the former. And this is to be sought in pursuits and studies which ought, above all others, to sweeten the temper and humble the pride of man. But these studies and pursuits, where grace is not interposed, do not alter human nature. The arch casuist soon, indeed, acquires a zeal for religion, but it is cruel: he learns to contend for the faith, but he contends with acrimony; and even the *cross*, the sacred symbol of his Saviour's sufferings, is borne about with him as an ostentatious emblem of his own humility. His own creed is the standard of doctrine, his own church is the exclusive asylum of faith. He fancies that he possesses, *solus in solo*, all the orthodoxy, all the erudition, all the taste of the kingdom; and swaggering, like Jupiter on the top of Olympus, he seats himself as sole umpire in all matters of faith, of fact, of science. If any one dares to pass the boundary he has fixed, or to adopt a mode of expression he has not authorized, he brands him with the appellation of *heretic*, and instantly hurls at his devoted head a thunderbolt.

If an individual stands in his way, and particularly if that individual possesses an influence which he envies, or fills a place which he covets, he marks him as his victim. The sacrifice, however, must be orthodoxly performed, and attended with all the external forms of sanctity. To prepare the way for this, disingenuous insinuations are thrown out against the hated object ; his sentiments are misstated, his language is perverted, and his performances are dissected and combined anew, and held up in opposition to sound doctrine, in order to awaken jealousies, to weaken the confidence, and steal away the affection of his Christian friends.

In the mean time, and the more effectually to conceal the ultimate design, the sacred names of friendship, of sincerity, of candour, are flung around the devoted individual, like the garlands with which the pagans covered the victim they had selected for the altar. Profession swells on profession: a sense of duty, a love of truth, and even thy glory, God of mercy, is declared by the insatiate executioner to govern him, while he feels at the moment the malice of *hell* rankling in his bosom, and dips his pen in the venom of the *damned*. The assault, indeed, is conducted under the banner of Jesus Christ. But it is immaterial whether it be the banner of Jesus or Mohammed. A proud, haughty, persecuting spirit, wherever and in whomsoever found, would transform the mild accents of heavenly grace to execrations, and steep as soon the Evangelists as the Alcoran in blood. To the victim who is sacrificed to pride or arrogance, it matters not whether the ceremony be performed on the scaffold or at the altar.

You may imagine that there is no occasion for cautioning those entering the sacred ministry against such a temper in themselves, or to instruct them how to meet it in others. But if you so imagine, it is because you know little of yourselves or of others. There is among Christians, and even among Christian ministers (alas! that it should be so), a rebuke that blasts and a zeal that consumes. Do you not remember who they were that preferred the sanguinary request even to Jesus Christ in person, whether they should not command fire to come down from heaven, and consume a whole village of Samaritans, because they had treated them less urbanely than they expected? And do you not also remember the mild, the heavenly, the endearing, and yet pointed rebuke he gave them—rejecting their proposal, and disclaiming the spirit which produced it? Do you not remember the anathemas which have been uttered, and the gibbets which have been erected, by ecclesiastical authority? Ah! had the spirit of the world never pervaded the sacerdotal order, the saints would not so often have been compelled to famish in dungeons or wander in exile.

Human nature is the same now as formerly; and happy will you be should you never, even within the pale of the Christian church, experience the bitterness of the wrath of man. Happy will you be should you receive no wound in the house of your own and your Saviour's friends—should you always find in them the same meek, humble, unassuming goodness—the same sincerity of friendship, the same celestial charity and gentleness of rebuke which appeared in him. But should it be otherwise; should you, where you least expect it, meet with envy, with treachery, with invective, be neither surprised nor disturbed at it.

In the church as in the world, you will form your

own character; nor can your enemies prevent it. Their calumny will injure you less than you imagine. The theological calumniator, however muffled up in the habiliments of piety, and notwithstanding all the parade he may make of candour, impartiality, and a sense of duty, will be much more successful in deceiving himself than in deceiving the world. No matter how loudly he vociferates the glory of God, while his movements evince that he is seeking exclusively his own glory. However disguised, the real temper of his heart will discover itself; his insidious calumny will be referred to the proper motive, and his wounded pride will be seen scowling vengeance from behind the tattered mantle of hypocrisy which is interposed to cover it. Community will not be brow-beaten into a surrendry of their independence to the insolent pretensions of any individual; and the self-puffing censor, who aims at being universal umpire, will have the mortification to see that public, on whom he looks down with supercilious contempt, instead of placing implicit confidence in his decrees, examining and deciding for themselves. He will have the mortification to see the very individuals whom he has denounced and marked for the grave, still living unhurt in the midst of execrations, which produce no effect except to burn and blister the lips that utter them; and though it were more in character for such an intellectual Goliah to curse his opponents in the name of *Dagon* than in that of Jesus, yet, should he adopt the latter (making the gospel the vehicle of scandal, and seasoning the doctrines of grace with malice), still remember *that you have not so learned Christ;* who forbids you *to give place to the devil,* and commands you, *putting away lying, to speak every man truth with his neighbour.* Let not the subtility of an adversary beguile you into the spirit of the world, nor the rudeness of his attack provoke you to use in your defence the weapons of the world. These ill befit a Christian : these are not his armory. It was Abishai, not David, who proposed to go over and take off the head of Shimei that cursed him.

It is not the prostration of an enemy, but the forgiveness of him, that evinces a Divine filiation, and conducts to the noblest victory : not perhaps the noblest in the estimation of partial friends, who, irritated by insult, wish to see you *thrash* an adversary : not in the estimation of men of honour, who account it magnanimous to avenge an injury. But are these the real judges of true greatness ? or are you influenced by the multitude ? Whom, then, call you the multitude? The pigmies on this little planet who surround you, or the principalities, and powers, and thrones, and dominions, and all those orders of perfect beings who throng the heavens, and fill the house of God's almightiness? Behold the thousands of thousands who minister unto him, and the ten thousand times ten thousand who stand before him ! In the estimation of these just appraisers of things, which, think you, is deemed more godlike, to forgive an injury or to avenge it? Seeing, therefore, you are compassed about by so great a cloud of witnesses, lay aside all malice, and that wrath that will so easily beset you ; and on this article as every other, look with steady eye to Jesus Christ, the author and finisher of your faith. Had he—pardon, exalted Mediator, pattern of perfection, this derogating supposition, made with reverential awe, and to exalt thy clemency—had he engaged in a single duel, or partook in one revengeful contest—but he did not. Whatever is endearing in goodness or touching in mercy, collected into one assemblage, forms his character; a character on which arrogance has not cast a shade or envy fixed a stain: a character splendid with virtues, which render poverty venerable and humility august. That great Exemplar of righteousness, the purity of whose life baffled the scrutiny of malice, and compelled that bloodstained wretch, who had often sported with the rights of innocence, to exclaim, "I find no fault in the man," how did *he* meet injuries, and what was *his* demeanour towards his enemies?

Mark his entrance into Jerusalem, that city blackened by crime and steeped in the blood of martyrs. From the Mount of Olives it opened to his view; at which sad sight he wept—wept, not over friends, but enemies; enemies who had rejected, vilified, persecuted him; and who were still waiting, with fiendlike impatience, to wreak their vengeance on his person, and quench their malice in his blood. Nor is this a solitary instance of benignity. Trace his paths from Bethlehem to Calvary, and you will find him everywhere meek, humble, long-suffering. Surrounded by adversaries, and called to meet calumny and persecution, he supported his matchless clemency to the end; and left the world good above conception, great beyond comparison.

From the toils and trials of a distressing but perfect life, follow this illustrious personage to the place of death. Approach his cross, and fix your attention on the prodigies which signalize his sufferings, and stamp divinity on his martyrdom! Think not that I allude to the terrific drapery which in that dread hour was flung around the great theatre of nature. No: 'tis not the darkened sun, the bursting tombs, the quaking mountains, or the trembling world that I allude to! These indeed are prodigies; but these vanish before the still greater prodigies of meekness, humility, and sin-forgiving goodness displayed in the dying Saviour. When I behold him, amid the last agonies of dissolving nature, raising his dying eyes to heaven, and, forgetful of himself, interceding with the God of mercy with his last breath, and from his very cross, in behalf of those wretches whose insatiable malice had fixed him there—then it is that the evidence of his claims rises to demonstration, and I feel the resistless force of that impassioned exclamation, which burst from the lips of infidelity itself, "If Socrates died as a philosopher, Jesus Christ died as a God!"

And shall a worm covered with crimes, and living on sufferance in that same world where the agonizing Saviour uttered his dying supplication, and left his dying example for imitation—shall such a worm, tumid with resentment, lift his proud crest to his fellow-worm, and, incapable of mercy, talk of retribution? No: blessed Jesus, thy death is an antidote to vengeance. At the foot of thy cross I meet my enemies, I forget their injuries, I bury my revenge, and learn to forgive those who have done me wrong, as I also hope to be forgiven of thee.

Almighty God, give us grace to do this, and to thy name shall be the glory.

IV.

DELIVERED JULY 26, 1809.

[Two opposite Systems offered to our acceptance, the one founded on *Human Reason*, the other on *Divine Revelation*.—Man, by his own wisdom, never has, nor ever can have, a true and proper conception of God.—Contradictory, false, and unworthy notions entertained by the wisest of the ancients in regard to the nature and attributes of the Supreme Being, their confused and erroneous ideas as to Virtue and Vice, and the gross immorality of their Lives.—The appearance of Christianity in the World dispelled the darkness and delusion that had before universally prevailed, and brought in a new era of Light, and Hope, and of pure and perfect Morals.—The simplicity and purity of the Christian System soon corrupted by being incorporated with the errors of ancient Philosophy.—Modern Infidelity, and the pernicious and absurd Doctrines on which it is founded.—Skeptical System of Hume (see Note).—Infidelity and Christianity, in their Character, Moral Effects, and ultimate Results, contrasted.—The Christian alone can have hope in Death, and assurance of a blessed Immortality.

YOUNG gentlemen, this day *we* resign our charge, and *you* become the masters of your fortune. For the future, two opposite systems will offer you their guidance and proffer you their rewards. On the one hand, *human reason ;* on the other, *Divine revelation.* Which shall be the object of your choice? Consider well the prerogatives of each, and then determine.

Man is a created being, and therefore dependant Neither self-government nor self-guidance befits him. Unreserved submission to the will of his Creator is, and must for ever be, the law of his nature. The first instance of departure from this law was the speculation indulged by the misguided parent of our race upon the tree of knowledge. You recollect the fatal incident. You have tasted, and still taste, the bitter consequences. One rash conclusion, drawn in opposition to the revealed will of God, was the inceptive step to apostacy, and issued in the destruction of a world. Six thousand years have elapsed since this catastrophe, during which, in every nation, reason has asserted its claims and opened its schools, but nowhere has it done anything to recover its fallen glory. Not a beam of light has it shed on that moral darkness which enshrouds the world. The nations whom faith guides not, still grope benighted; and all the efforts of their sages only prove *that this world by wisdom knows not God*.

And how should this world by wisdom know him? To deduce the character and design of a workman from his workmanship, the entire fabric which he has constructed must be understood. But of all that Omnipotence hath done, we have seen a small part only; and that part we comprehend not, or, at most, but imperfectly comprehend. How preposterous for a being who yesterday emerged from the dust, and to-morrow will return to dust again, to pretend, *by searching to find out God, or by researching to find out the Almighty to perfection*. What homage he requires of us; whether he is propitious or inexorable to sinners; or, if propitious, in what way? These are questions that philosophy agitates only to darken. It mocks with delusive and conjectural answers the interrogatories of the dying sinner, and the foundation which it lays to

F

sustain his immortal hopes is as faithless and insufficient as hay, wood, and stubble would be for the base of a pyramid. The more ingenuous of the pagans acknowledge their weakness and deplore their ignorance. At Athens, the seat of science, there stood an altar inscribed, confessedly, *to the unknown God;* and even that prince of philosophers, Socrates himself, wavered and hesitated at the moment of his death. Others indeed there have been, less humble than Socrates, who have dared to pronounce upon the character of God and the chief good of man. But the systems which imbody their dogmas are now known only as monuments of human weakness or of human wickedness.

Do you wish for proof of this?—the schools of philosophy will furnish it.

That the world arose from chance, and that the providence of God does not extend to it; that sensual pleasure constitutes the supreme good, and that virtue for its own sake is unworthy of esteem or choice, were doctrines of the Epicureans.

That it is impossible to arrive at truth; that the existence of God is doubtful; that the immortality of the soul is doubtful; that whether virtue is preferable to vice is doubtful, were doctrines of the Academics.

Aristotle taught, that God, though happy in himself, was regardless of the happiness and indifferent to the virtue of man. The Stoics, that God was under the control of fate. The Persian philosophers, that there was not one God, but two—

coequal, coeternal, and with opposite characters and interests.

It was not illustrious virtues, but egregious crimes, that signalized the gods and goddesses of Greece and Rome. Hence that degeneracy of manners which became so universal. A father, without reproach, might adopt or abandon his infant child. The massacre of slaves formed a customary part of the funeral solemnity. For having asserted the rights and defended the liberties of their country, prisoners of war were crucified. Unnatural lust was sanctioned by high authority, and even public brothels were consecrated as an act of religious worship.

This degeneracy was the natural result of their philosophy. Zeno had taught them that all crimes were equal. Cleanthes, that children might devour their parents; and Diogenes, that parents might devour their children. Plato, that lewdness was justifiable; and even Cicero, that it was only a venial fault. The lives of the philosophers corresponded with their doctrines; nor were their examples less infamous than their dogmas. If Plutarch can be believed, both Socrates and Plato were intemperate and incontinent. Nor was the character of Seneca less execrable, if Dion Cassius can be believed. Xenophon was a sodomite. Aristippus kept a seraglio, and Zeno murdered himself. Such was the wisdom of philosophy; such were the examples it furnished; such the morals it inculcated.

In the midst of this night of pagan darkness the Sun of righteousness burst upon the world. As from a long and deathlike slumber, the nations awoke to behold its splendours. A new era commenced. The unlettered apostle delivered his artless narrative, and the omnipotence of truth was felt. Kingdom followed kingdom in making their submissions, till at length the new religion was established throughout the Roman empire.

Christianity was now in prosperity. Philosophy therefore courted her alliance. It was granted. But did either faith or morals gain by the concession? No: on the contrary, morals were subverted and faith bewildered by those mystic mazes through which the Gnostic teachers led their hearers. The gospel, thus adulterated by those unhallowed ingredients which philosophy mixed with it, lost its characteristic influence. The simplicity of truth disappeared; the fervour of piety disappeared; a spirit of dogmatizing ensued, and the minds of men were gradually prepared, by perplexing and contradictory theories, for that profound indifference to truth, that absolute lethargy of mind, which characterized the dark ages.

When, however, the Peripatetic philosophy was superseded by the Cartesian, this unnatural alliance was dissolved. Then reason, abjuring that faith which it had courted and corrupted, under the name of *infidelity* commenced a new era.

To detail the systems of Herbert, Hobbes, Shaftesbury, Wollaston, Tindal, Chubb, and Bolingbroke, would be as tedious as unedifying: suffice it to say, that the reign of reason was the jubilee of sinners. Every important duty was weakened;

every detestable crime was palliated by some one or other of these new apostles. Each contested the palm of having contributed most towards subverting the morals and unsettling the opinions of mankind. Amid this galaxy of malignant stars, Hume arose, in whose sickly light all things appeared dim and doubtful. Real life vanished; the material universe vanished; the souls of men vanished; and spectres only flitted through the brain. To whom the award was due it was no longer doubtful. Even his competitors stood amazed at the bolder march of his genius, who, by one mighty effort, subverted both his own and all other systems, and reached at once the point of universal skepticism.*

* What illumination was shed on the science of unbelief by this great master of negations, can be known only by the perusal of his writings. To those who have not access to those writings, the following summary (the fidelity of which, Bishop Horn says, was never, so far as he could find, questioned) may serve as a specimen.

OF THE SOUL.

That the soul of man is not the same this moment that it was the last; that we know not what it is; that it is not one thing, but many things; and that it is nothing at all. That in this soul is the agency of all the causes that operate throughout the sensible creation; and yet, that in this soul there is neither power nor agency, nor any idea of either.

That matter and motion may often be regarded as the cause of thought.

OF THE UNIVERSE.

That the external world does not exist, or that its existence may reasonably be doubted.

That the universe exists in the mind, and that mind does not exist.

That the universe is nothing but a heap of perceptions without a substance.

That though a man could bring himself to believe, yea, and have reason to believe, that everything in the universe proceeds

Philosophy had to make but a single advance more to reach its *ultimatum*. That advance it has from some cause, yet it would be unreasonable for him to believe that the universe itself proceeds from some cause.

OF HUMAN KNOWLEDGE.

That the perfection of human knowledge is to doubt.

That we ought to doubt of everything, yea, of our doubts tnemselves; and, therefore, the utmost that philosophy can do is to give a doubtful solution of doubtful doubts.

That the human understanding, acting alone, does entirely subvert itself, and prove by argument that by argument no thing can be proved.

That man, in all his perceptions, actions, and volitions, is a mere passive machine, and has no separate existence of his own, being entirely made up of other things, of the existence of which he is by no means certain ; and yet the nature of all things depends so much upon man, that two and two could not produce four, nor fire produce heat, nor the sun light, without an act of the human understanding.

OF GOD.

That it is unreasonable to believe God to be infinitely wise and good while there is any evil or disorder in the universe.

That we have no good reason to think the universe proceeds from a cause.

That, as the existence of the external world is questionable, we are at a loss to find arguments by which we may prove the existence of the Supreme Being, or any of his attributes.

That when we speak of power as an attribute of any being, God himself not excepted, we use words without meaning.

That we can form no idea of power, nor any being endued with power, much less one endued with supreme power; and that we can never have reason to believe that any object, or quality of any object exists, of which we cannot form an idea.

OF THE MORALITY OF HUMAN ACTIONS.

That every human action is necessary, and could not have been different from what it is.

That moral, intellectual, and corporeal virtues are nearly of the same kind. In other words, that to want honesty, tc want understanding, and to want a leg, are equally the objects of moral disapprobation.

That adultery must be practised if man would acquire all the advantages of life ; that, if generally practised, it would in time since made, passing by an easy and natural transition from wavering skepticism to confirmed atheism. A great nation, energized by the doctrines of its sapient declaimers against God and nature, has arisen in its strength, and shaken off the restraints of moral obligation, as the toiled lion shakes from his mane the dewdrops of the morning. By a solemn decree, Jehovah has been banished from his empire and his throne; the universe absolved from its allegiance; the earth converted into one vast common, and the men and women who inhabit it turned out like cattle to herd together. By a solemn decree, too, the soul has been deprived of immortality; and, lest the sepulchre should permit the bodies it imprisons to escape, death has been declared by law to be *everlasting sleep.*

But let us turn from this lunacy of the schools, these ravings of distempered minds. Thanks to our God, we are not under the necessity of following such guides. He who formerly sent his prophets to enlighten mankind, has in these last ages spoken to the world by his Son. How know we this? By evidence the most indubitable. In him the prophecies were fulfilled; by him the gift of healing was dispensed; unheard-of miracles sealed his commission, and the doctrines he delivered evinced that he was sent of God.

cease to be scandalous; and that, if practised secretly and frequently, it would by degrees come to be thought no crime at all.

Lastly, as the soul of man, according to Mr. Hume, becomes every moment a different being, the consequence must be, that the crimes committed by him at one time are not imputable to him at another.

It is as characteristic of revelation to exalt, as it is of philosophy to degrade human nature. The unity and perfection of God support, and are supported in, every part of this heaven-descended system. In the light of His uncreated glory whom the Scriptures reveal, contemplate the obscene and cruel rabble of pagan divinities. Beside the Christian, offering the homage of his heart to the author of his being, behold the Greek, celebrating with songs the lascivious Pan, or the Roman, inebriated at the orgies of the drunken Bacchus. But if the pagan appears degraded in the presence of the Christian, much more does the skeptic and the atheist appear so. To the one it is God who rides upon the storm and directs the tempest. To the other, the tumult of the elements is the confusion of chance. Rich in prospect, the one looks up to immortality, and fastens his hope to the rock of ages. The being of the other hangs on nothing, and he has nothing in expectancy but to drop from life into eternal non-existence.

It was not reason, but revelation, that brought futurity to light; that discovered an atonement; that proved sin pardonable, and God, against whom it is committed, propitious.

The Bible is as pure in its morals as it is spiritual in its worship or rich in its hopes. By its sanctifying influence thousands have been subdued to holiness and raised to happiness. Not like the bewildering theories of the schools, it speaks to the conscience, and its influence is seen in the life of man. Were its rules of action observed, war would cease; injustice would cease; and the earth would become an asylum of righteousness. Of Christian nations, in the strict and proper acceptation of the term, we cannot speak; because in this sense there are no Christian nations. Here and there only an individual is found whose character is formed on the model, and whose conduct is regulated by the maxims of Christianity. Small as this number is, they everywhere counteract the dominion of sin, and exert on every community in which they reside a redeeming influence. These unassuming, and often obscure individuals, sprinkled like salt among the nations, impart a tincture of godliness, which, though it heals not, preserves the common mass from putrefaction. Hence, wherever the gospel is preached, the standard of morals is raised, and public opinion banishes those gross and brutal crimes which were unblushingly committed in pagan countries. At home and abroad alike we see this position verified. No massacre of slaves signalizes the death of our patriots; no theatre exhibits for the amusement of our populace the horrid spectacle of lacerated combatants; no impure temples invite our youths to lascivious banquets; nor in any part of Christendom does there stand an altar for human sacrifice.

But if mankind in general are indebted to Christianity for the amelioration of their condition, much more are the poor and the friendless indebted to it for this. Of these the Christian lawgiver has taken especial cognizance; for these he has made especial provision. To those whom philosophy disregarded is the gospel preached. More than this: in that gospel their rights are guarded, and relief is provided for their miseries by that celestial charity which it inculcates. How must the heart susceptible of pity vibrate at the rehearsal of those words of Jesus Christ, uttered during his humiliation, and which he will repeat when he shall appear in his triumph: "Come, ye blessed of my father, inherit the kingdom prepared for you from the foundation of the world. For I was an hungered, and ye gave me meat; I was thirsty, and ye gave me drink; I was a stranger, and ye took me in; naked, and ye clothed me; I was sick, and ye visited me; I was in prison, and ye came unto me;" adding, "Inasmuch as ye have done this unto one of the least of these my disciples, ye have done it unto me."

The resurrection of the body is peculiarly a doctrine of revelation. Philosophy shed no light upon the sepulchre. It was not till the star of Judah arose that the grave ceased to be dark and sombrous; and had he, whose goings forth were from Bethlehem, announced this single oracle, "Behold, the hour is coming in which all they that are in their graves shall hear the voice of the Son of God, and come forth; they that have done good to the resurrection of life, and they that have done evil to the resurrection of condemnation," and added no more, his mission had been deserving of that costly exhibition of types which prefigured, and of miracles which confirmed it. How much more so, then, since it has put not only the question of the resurrection of the body, but that of the immortality of the soul also to rest: since it has imbodied the purest system of morals, the sublimest system of doctrines; since it has called into action immortal virtues, and awakened deathless hopes. How much more so, since it has held out to righteousness the strongest of possible motives, and imposed on unrighteousness the strongest possible restraints. To the sinner it is announced, that, however he may escape punishment from man, the Lord our God will not suffer him to escape his righteous judgments: that, when the Son of Man shall come to be glorified in his saints, he will also execute eternal vengeance on his enemies.

In whatever light the claims of these two systems which offer you their guidance are viewed, the odds appears immense.

Reason tells the parent of a family that his children are no better than vermin, and that he is not even bound to rear them. Revelation tells him that they are heaven-descended, and that he must train them up for glory.

Reason tells the child that gray hairs are a reproach; that filial gratitude is not a virtue; and that he is at liberty to abandon his aged parents. Revelation tells him to reverence the hoary head; as he hopes for long life, to honour, in the Lord, those to whom he is indebted for his being; and that the eye that mocketh at his father, and refuseth to obey its mother, the eagle shall pick it out, and the young eagle shall eat it.

Reason tells the sufferer that his pains are imaginary, and, if not imaginary, that they are irremediable, and must therefore be borne in hopeless and sullen silence. Revelation tells him that they are parental chastisements, enduring but for a moment, and that they shall work out for him a far more exceeding and eternal weight of glory.

Reason tells the mourner that his tears are as absurd as useless, for the grave is a place of oblivion, and that the dead have perished for ever. Revelation tells him that they are invisible only, not extinct; and repeats, beside the urn that contains their ashes, "*This corruption shall put on incorruption, and this mortal immortality.*"

But it is at the bed of sickness and in the hour of dissolution that the superior claims of revelation are most apparent. Here reason is dumb, or only speaks to aggravate the miseries, and render still more horrible the horrors of the death-scene. No relief is given to soften the grim visage of *the king* of terrors. As *nearer* he approaches, how the night darkens! how the grave deepens! Trembling on its verge, the affrighted soul asks what the nature of death is. And the grave—what are its dominions? The treacherous guide answers, "Both are unknown : that darkness no eye penetrates ; that profound no line measures. It is conjectured to be the entrance to eternal and oblivious sleep ; the precipice down which existence tumbles. Beyond that gulf which has swallowed up the dead and is swallowing up the living, neither foresight nor calculation reaches. What follows is unknowable ; ask not concerning it ; thus far philosophy has guided you ; but without a guide, and blindfold, you must take the last decisive leap—perchance to hell, perchance to non-existence!" How the scene brightens when revelation is appealed to! As the ark of the testimony is opened, a voice is heard to say, "*I am the resurrection and the life; he that believeth in me, though he were dead, yet shall he live again.*" It is the voice of the angel of the covenant. His bow of promise is seen arching the sky, and reaching down even to the sepulchre, whose dark caverns by its radiance are illuminated. Behind those mists of Hades, so impenetrable to the eye of reason, eternal mansions rise in prospect. Already the agony of death is passed. To the redeemed sinner there is but one pang more. Shouting victory, he endures that pang; and, while he is enduring it, the last cloud vanishes from the firmament, and the heavens become bright and serene for ever.

Young gentlemen, I shall not longer detain you. In a more exalted sense than could be said of Cato at Utica,

"Your life, your death, your bane and antidote,
Are both before you."

You must choose between them, and that choice will decide your destiny. May Almighty God direct you in it, and to his name shall be the glory.

V.

DELIVERED JULY 24, 1811

[Painful feelings of Teachers in parting from their Pupils.—Responsibility of Teachers.—Constant succession of Actors on the stage of Life.—Motives held out to the Young to act their part well.—Discouragements to an honourable Ambition removed.—The examples of Howard, Sharpe, Clarkson, and Lancaster.—A mixture of virtuous and vicious Characters in the World.—The practice of Virtue, even as it regards this Life, to be preferred.—But there is a God: Man is accountable and immortal, and should act with constant reference to these great Truths.—Concluding Exhortation.]

Young gentlemen, another collegiate anniversary has arrived. Again we are called to reciprocate our commingled joys and sorrows. Parting addresses occupy us; parting sympathies afflict us; and the sundering ties of duty and of friendship admonish us that another year has been measured by the rapid flow of time: that resistless torrent, which is ingulfing in its course the members of human society, and sweeping away the monuments of human glory.

To *us*, your instructers, this is a moment of the deepest as well as of the tenderest interest. Here we stand like the sorrow-stricken parent at the threshold of his door, whither he has accompanied his adventurous sons, leaving their parental home to return no more. My God! what a trust, what responsibility is this! to be the appointed guardians of the public hopes and the public safety; to feed and direct those streams which, as they flow, must either desolate or fertilize our country, and the churches of our God; to train and send abroad an annual corps of actors destined to corrupt or to reform life's ever-varying drama, and prove the future benefactors or the future scourge of mankind.

To you, our pupils, this is a moment of no common interest. That world on which you are entering, like this retreat of science you are leaving, changes with rapid succession its inhabitants. As you approach it, indeed, every place of honour, of confidence, of profit, appear preoccupied: there seems to be no room for action. The thought oppresses you, and you feel, perhaps, a kind of melancholy presage of that penury and obscurity which, from the present state of things, you must be doomed to suffer. Believe me, it is a deceptive view that you are taking. If all those places of honour, of profit, of confidence, are not already vacant, it is precisely the same to you as if they were so. Death and age are vacating, and will vacate them in time for you to occupy. Soon the laurels of yonder hero will have withered; those venerable senators will be incapable of legislating; those erudite judges of presiding; the tongue of that resistless advocate will falter as he pleads; the persuasive accents of yonder pulpit orator will die away and be heard no more; and all that intelligence and virtue, that active and successful talent which adorns the age, will disappear, and its honoured possessors, conducted in succession to their graves, will moulder amid sepulchral ashes, forgotten, or remembered only by the monuments of glory they shall have during their transitory life erected.

As you advance, the stage will clear before you; and the honours, the responsibilities, the treasures, and the destinies of mankind will be committed to the rising generation, of which you form a part; and at the head of which you may, and ought to hold a conspicuous rank. They who now award to you these collegiate honours—he who now addresses to you this collegiate charge—this board of trust—that board of regency, will soon give place: and this seat of science—what am I saying? every seat of science, every temple of law, of justice, and of grace, will be placed under your care and guardianship. To you, under God, the state, the church, the world, must look for whatever of good it hopes for, or of evil it dreads.

Entering on such a theatre under such circumstances, can you disappoint the high hopes of those parents who will leave you the inheritors of their fortunes and the guardians of their fame? Can you disregard the reasonable claims of that future public, that will soon be anxious to employ you in its service and to crown you with its honours? *Entering on such a theatre in such circumstances*, are you willing to disgrace yourselves by meanness or to destroy yourselves by wickedness? Are you willing to forego the glory to which God calls you, and to prostitute the talents God has given you? To employ your intellectual vigour in maturing and evolving plans of lust and treachery; to become the companions of the vile, the panders of the profligate, the ministers of evil, and coadjutors of Satan; in distracting human society, in disturbing human peace, and in counteracting the benevolent purposes of Deity? Your hearts revolt from the idea; you shudder at the thought. Such, however, is truly the sinner's employment, such his character, and such surely will be yours if you attach yourselves to his society and accompany him in his career; your influence will become malignant, your example infectious, and your names descend to posterity black with infamy. Sin diseases the body: it degrades the mind, and damns alike the reputation and the soul. In the records of human glory which are kept in heaven, there is not inscribed one profligate, unreclaimed, unrepentant sinner's name.

You will not make the profligate's wretched choice, his desperate sacrifice. Your past conduct, your present resolutions, are pledges that you will not: God grant you may not; but it is not enough that you will not do this.

Again I ask, therefore, whether, entering *on such a theatre under such circumstances*—a theatre where there is so much good to be accomplished and so much glory to be won—whether the mere negative praise of living harmless and inoffensive is all you aspire to? Are you willing, after all the pains which have been taken with you, after all the treasures that have been expended on you, after all the prayers that have been offered up for you—are you willing to become, not to say injurious, but useless to society? Are you willing merely to grovel through life; to creep away from this seminary like unfledged reptiles from their cells, and, buried in obscurity, pass your future years in inglorious sloth, till finally,

G

mere excrescences, you perish unnoticed, unremembered, and unlamented? willing to perish from that world in which you received your being, without having wiped away a tear, without having mitigated a sorrow, without having imparted a pulse of joy, or left one monument on earth, or sent one messenger to heaven, to testify that you have not lived literally *in vain?* Can the vivacious, the buoyant, the bold, the daring spirit of ingenuous youth be satisfied by the prospect of such a destiny?

But what can a youthful adventurer, a mere individual, hope to accomplish for the benefit of virtue or the world? What! Almost anything he wills to undertake and dares to persevere in. This world is made up of individuals. All the fame that has been acquired, all the infamy that has been merited, all the plans of happiness or misery that have been formed, all the enterprises of loyalty or of treason that have been executed, have owed their existence to the wisdom or folly, to the courage or temerity of individuals—mere youthful adventurers as you are; and, though only individuals, each of you possesses a capacity for doing either good or evil, which human foresight cannot measure nor human power limit. Your immediate exertions may benefit or injure some; your example may reach others; those whom your example reaches may communicate their feelings to individuals more remote, by whom those feelings may be again communicated to those who will recommunicate them: all of whom may transmit the influence which commenced with you to a succeeding generation, which in its turn may transmit it to the next, to be again transmitted. Thus the impulse given either to virtue or to vice by a single individual may be immeasurably extended, even to distant nations, and communicated through succeeding ages to the remotest generations.

Voltaire, Rousseau, and their infidel coadjutors collected their materials, and laid a train which produced that fatal explosion which shook the civilized world to its centre. Governments were dismembered; monarchies were overthrown; institutions were swept away; society was flung into confusion; human life was endangered: years have elapsed; the face of Europe is yet covered with wrecks and desolations; and how long before the world will recover from the disastrous shock their conspiracy occasioned, God only knows. Yet Voltaire, Rousseau, and their infidel coadjutors were individuals.

Did not Cyrus sway the opinions, awe the fears, and direct the energies of the world at Babylon? Did not Cæsar do this at Rome, and Constantine at Byzantium? And yet Cyrus, Cæsar, and Constantine were individuals. But they were fortunate; they lived at critical conjunctures, and in fields of blood gathered immortality. And is it at critical conjunctures, and in fields of blood only, that immortality can be gathered? Where then is *Howard*, that saint of illustrious memory, who traversed his native country, exploring the jail and the prison-ship, taking the dimensions of that misery which these caverns of vice, of disease, and of death had so long concealed? whose heroic deeds of charity the dungeons alike of Europe and of Asia witnessed; and whose bones now consecrate the confines of distant Tartary, where he fell a martyr to his zeal—when, like an angel of peace, he was engaged in conveying through the cold, damp, pestilential cells of Russian Crimea the lamp of hope and the cup of consolation to the incarcerated slave, who languished unknown, unpitied, and forgotten there.

Where is *Grenville Sharpe,* the negro's advocate, whose disinterested efforts, whose seraphic eloquence, extorted from a court tinctured with the remains of feudal tyranny that memorable decision of Lord Mansfield, which placed an eternal shield between the oppressor and the oppressed; which raised a legal barrier around the very person of the enslaved African, and rendered liberty thereafter inseparable from the soil of the seagirt isles of Britain? It was this splendid triumph of reason over passion, of justice over prejudice, that called from the Irish orator that burst of ingenuous feeling at the trial of Rowan, when he said, "I speak in the spirit of the British law, which proclaims even to the stranger and the sojourner, the moment he sets his foot on British earth, that the ground on which he treads is holy. No matter in what language his doom may have been pronounced: no matter what complexion incompatible with freedom an Indian or an African sun may have burned upon him: no matter in what disastrous battle his liberty may have been cloven down: no matter with what solemnities he may have been devoted upon the altar of slavery, the first moment he touches the sacred soil of Britain, the altar and the god sink together in the dust; his soul walks abroad in her own majesty; his body swells beyond the measure of his chains, that burst from around him, and he stands redeemed, emancipated, disenthralled, by the irresistible genius of *universal emancipation.*"

Where is *Clarkson*, who has been so triumphantly successful in wiping away the reproach of slavery from one quarter of the globe, and in restoring to the rights of fraternity more than twenty millions of the human family: that man who, after so many years of reproach and contumely—after sufferings and perseverance which astonish as much as they instruct us, succeeded in turning the current of national feeling, in awaking the sense of national justice, and, finally, in obtaining from the Parliament of England that glorious act, *the abolition of the slave-trade?* an act to which the royal signature was affixed at noonday, and just as the sun reached the meridian: a time fitly chosen for the consummation of so splendid a transaction—a transaction which reflects more honour on the king, the Parliament, the people, than any other recorded in the annals of history. Where is this man, whose fame I had rather inherit than that of Cæsar? for it will be more deathless, as it is already more sacred. And should Africa ever arise from her present degradation—and rise she will, if there be any truth in God—what a perpetual flow of heartfelt eulogy will, to a thousand generations, commemorate the virtues, the sufferings, and the triumph of the ingenuous, the disinterested, the endeared, the immortal Clarkson—

the negro's friend, the black man's hope, the despised African's benefactor!

Where is *Lancaster*, who has introduced and is introducing a new era in the history of letters, and rendering the houses of education, like the temples of grace, accessible to the poor? owing to whose exertions and enterprises thousands of children, picked from the dirt and collected from the streets, are this day enjoying the inestimable benefits of education, and forming regular habits of industry and virtue, who must otherwise have been doomed, by the penury of their condition, to perpetual ignorance, and probably to perpetual misery.

Ah! had this man lived but two thousand years ago—to say nothing of the effect which might have been produced on morals and happiness generally by the wide diffusion of knowledge and the regular formation of habits—to say nothing of that vulgarity which would have been diminished, or of that dignity which might have been imparted to the character of the species—could this man have lived two thousand years ago, and all the rude materials in society have undergone only that slight polishing which, under his fostering care, they are now likely to undergo, how many mines of beauty and riches would have appeared! How many gems, made visible by their glittering, would have been collected from among the rubbish! Or, to speak without a figure, had this man lived two thousand years ago, how much talent might have been discovered for the church, for the state, for the world, among those untutored millions who have floated unknown and unnoticed down the tide of time? Had this man lived two thousand years ago, how many Demosthenes might have lightened and thundered? How many Homers soared and sung? How many Newtons roused into action, to develop the laws of matter? How many Lockes to explore the regions of mind? How many Mansfields to exalt the bench? How many Erskines to adorn the bar? And perhaps some other Washington, whose memory has now perished in obscurity, might have been forced from the factory or the plough to decide the fate of battle and sustain the weight of empire.

And yet Howard, Sharpe, Clarkson, and Lancaster, were individuals; and individuals, too, gifted by no extraordinary talents, favoured by no peculiar theatre of action. They were only common men, brought up in the midst of common life. No princely fortunes had descended to them; no paternal influence had devolved on them; no aspiring rivals provoked their emulation; no great emergencies roused their exertions. They produced, if I may so speak, the incidents which adorn their history, and created for themselves a theatre of action. Animated by the purest virtue, and bent on being useful, they seized on the miseries of life as the world presented them; and by deeds of charity and valour performed in relieving those miseries, they converted the very abodes of ignorance and wo into a theatre of glory.

And, young gentlemen, after all that has been done by these patrons of virtue, these benefactors of mankind, remains there no prejudice to correct;

no ignorance to instruct; no vice to reclaim; no misery to alleviate? Look around you: still there is room for youthful enterprise, for manly exertion. Go, then, into the world: cherish the spirit, imitate the example, and emulate the glory of these illustrious worthies. Let no disasters shake your fortitude; let no impediments interrupt your career. Come what will, of this be assured, that in every enterprise of good God will be on your side; and that, should you even fail, failure will be glorious: nor will it ever be said in heaven of the man who has sincerely laboured on the earth to glorify his God or benefit his country, *that he has lived in vain.*

Whatever profession you may select, enter it with zeal, with ardour, with elevated and expanded views, with noble and disinterested motives, as becomes a youth of liberal education, an enlightened adventurer, bent on glory, and setting out in a career of immortality. Always be alive to the promotion of virtue, to the suppression of vice, to the relief of misery. Always be projecting and maturing new plans of public and glorious enterprise: nor feel as if anything had been done while anything of good remains to be accomplished.

It is a false as well as a degrading doctrine, that you were made for individual benefit, and live only for yourselves. This is true of no one. Much less is it true of *you*, whom God has selected from the multitude, and distinguished by better means and greater opportunities. And why has he done this? From individual partiality? No. Doubtless not. But that he may qualify a chosen number to fill a higher station ; to move in a more extended sphere, and practise a sublimer charity. He has done this that you may become the guides of the ignorant, the benefactors of the wretched, the patrons of the multitude ; that you may protect the more effectually the poor that cry; the fatherless, and him that hath none to help him ; that you may be eyes to the blind, feet to the lame ; that the defenceless may be shielded by your influence, the profligate awed by your integrity, and the country saved by your virtue and your valour.

But, when all the world are mean and mercenary, is it to be expected that you will be dignified and disinterested? It is false. All the world are not mean and mercenary. If it were so, the stream of life would have corrupted as it flowed, and the race become extinct.

It is conceded, because it cannot be denied, that mean and mercenary motives prevail ; that a crowd of guilty actors have converted the drama of life into one vast exhibition of fraud and falsehood, of deceit and treachery, of avarice and revelry : among whom personal interest predominates, and individual emolument forms the bond of criminal alliance. But at the same time it is contended that there exists a countervailing influence ; that a counter scene is continually carried forward, in which actions of a different type are unfolded : actions which tend to relieve the picture of human guilt, and soften the intenseness of human misery. In the worst of times and in the most depraved of countries, there are always scattered some individuals of a benign

H

and virtuous character, whose benevolent exertions are limited by no boundaries of territory, shades of complexion, or ties of blood; who, with a perseverance that never relaxes and a vigilance that never slumbers, are pursuing, not their own, but the public welfare; whose hours of relaxation and of business are alike occupied with plans of utility or of reform; and the grand and predominant object of whose exertions and whose prayers is the happiness of the human family.

If you knew the world better than you do, you would know that it comprises a great variety of character: "that none are absolutely perfect; that those who approach towards perfection are few; that the bulk of mankind are very imperfect, and that many, but not the majority, are exceedingly profligate, deceitful, and wicked."

But, though the world were universally as mean and mercenary as the objection states, it would not alter the counsel we are giving you. In such a world it would behoove you, the alumni of this seat of science, to be nobly singular. From such society I would separate; against such principles I would protest. However the multitude might live, for my single self I would act uprightly; I would frown on vice, I would favour virtue—favour whatever would elevate, would exalt, would adorn character, and alleviate the miseries of my species, or contribute to render the world I inhabited, like the heavens to which I looked, a place of innocence and felicity. Though all mankind were profligate I would, by a uniform course of probity and integrity, show in what school I had been nurtured and to what faith I belonged.

And I would do this, because I would rather stand alone, or be pointed at among only those ten righteous men who would have saved Sodom, than swell the number of my companions by all the vagabond profligates that could be raked from the sewers of earth or collected from the caverns of hell.

Even though there were no God, no immortality—no accountability, I would do this. Vice in itself is mean, degrading, detestable: virtue commendable, exalted, ennobling. Though I were to exist no longer than those ephemera that sport in the beams of the summer's morn, during that short hour I would rather soar with the eagle, and leave the record of my flight and of my fall among the stars, than to creep the gutter with the reptile, and bed my memory and my body together in the dunghill. However short my part, I would act it well, that I might surrender my existence without disgrace and without compunction.

But you are not called to do this. The profane may sneer and the impious scoff; but, after all, THERE IS A GOD—MAN IS ACCOUNTABLE—MAN IS IMMORTAL; and the knowledge of this stamps value on existence, and renders human action grand and awful. These truths announced, this world rises in importance. Its transitory scenes assume a more fearful aspect and awaken a more solemn interest. No portion of existence claims such regard or involves such hazard: for it is here, upon this little ball, and during this momentary life, that *eternity* is staked; that hell is merited, or heaven won.

This is not conjectural, nor is it merely probable, but certain—infallibly certain. A revelation proceeding from God, sealed by a thousand martyrdoms; confirmed by a thousand prophecies; demonstrated by a thousand miracles, has put human speculation at rest for ever, and settled, imperatively settled, the question of man's eternal destiny. Yes, you are now, young gentlemen, forming your characters and pronouncing your doom for a duration that has no measure, because it has no end!

The tenure of your being, the hazards of this state of trial, are as incompatible with indolence and ease as with prodigality and pleasure. You were not made to repose on a bed of sloth. You were not sent into the world to lounge and loiter, but to act and to suffer. You are called to brave the storm and struggle against the tempest, as you press forward with never-fainting and never-failing steps in the path of duty: a path which, you are told beforehand, leads not the downward course, but crosses rugged and lofty mountains: mountains which the patriarchs, and prophets, and righteous men have crossed before you, the impress of whose feet is left upon the flinty road they trod, and whose acclivities are smoothed as well as stained by the blood and tears they shed as they passed over them. Beyond these mountains lies the heaven that terminated their sufferings and crowned their joys. There is Abraham; there is Moses; there is Paul; together with all those sainted spirits which in successive ages have adorned, preserved, and blessed the earth.

Having chosen those men to be your future companions; having dared to encounter the trials they encountered; having commenced the journey they have completed, and pressing forward towards the heaven they so triumphantly have entered, you will not, I trust, fear the sinner's frowns nor feel his tauntings.

He will talk to you, indeed, of a laxer discipline; of a less rigorous course, and of more immediate as well as of more licentious pleasures. You will tell him, in reply, *That you have been nurtured in the school of virtue; that you have been baptized in the name of Christ; and, as becomes his followers, are bent on immortality,* a pursuit incompatible alike with inglorious ease and brutal pleasure.

He will smile—he will sneer—perhaps attempt to pity you for naming Christ and thinking of immortality. And again he will talk of ease, of pleasure, of freedom from hope and fear, as he holds forth to you the skeptic's cup, mingled with more than Circean poison, which degrades the wretch who drinks of it in his own estimation from the standing of a man, and sends him, transformed into a mere animal, to root and wallow with the swine; to caper and grin with the monkey; to crouch and growl with the tiger; to mew and purr with the kitten, or fawn and yelp with the spaniel, during a momentary degraded life, and then consigns him to putrefy and rot, together with all this fraternity of brutes, in the kennel—their common sepulchre.

You will reply to him again as you have already replied to him; and oh! with what triumphant superiority, in point of dignity and destination, will you reply to him: "*That you have been nurtured in the school of virtue; that you have been baptized in the name of Christ; and that, as becomes his followers, you are bent on immortality.*" You will tell him that his hopes may be correspondent to his life; that to him such pursuits, and pleasures, and prospects may be in character, but that they are not so to you: that you have no ambition to live brutes, barely that you may have the boasted privilege of dying so; that you claim no kindred to, that you aspire to no affiance with the bristled offspring of the sty, nor wish to be indoctrinated in that sublime philosophy which is to teach you to believe that the race of men were made to manure the soil, and that they only go at death to increase the general aggregate of carcasses and carrion! In one word, you will tell him that YOU ARE CHRISTIANS; and that, as such, the all-perfect God, the rewarder and the reward of virtue, calls you to a different course, and has promised you a different destiny. Sinners indeed you are, and as such, by the law of nature, stand condemned: not so by the law of grace, which provides, through the merits of a Saviour, for your recovery of the character and restoration to the felicity of those who have never sinned.

And now, young gentleman, we separate. In a few years, perhaps—within a century at most—we shall all meet again. Where? Beyond the grave, and on the borders of eternity. Life is only a narrow *isthmus;* an isthmus already washed and wasted by the flow of time. The earth on which we tread is undermined or undermining : near the margin—perhaps upon the very brink—we tremble. No matter though it be so. It is not the length, but the manner in which the journey is performed, that secures the plaudit. While it lasts, therefore, and till the earth sinks under us, we will acquit ourselves like men, and contend valiantly for the cities of our brethren and the honour of our God.

You will live and act when he who now addresses you will neither be known nor numbered among the living. Soon the cold clod will press upon this bosom : this voice, silent in death, will no longer warn the sinner nor sooth the sufferer ; nor will this arm, stiffened and nerveless in the grave, ever again be raised to wipe away the tears of orphanage or to distribute the alms of charity. To you we commend these objects—anxious for those who will live after us. With you, beloved pupils, we leave this memorial ; and we charge you, by the love of virtue, by the hope of immortality, to see that the poor has bread, the mourner consolation, the friendless friends, the oppressed advocates, the Saviour of sinners disciples, and the God of heaven worshippers, so long as you remain on earth. And should we, your instructers—ah triumphant hope !—be so happy as to enter those mansions which grace has prepared for the redeemed of all nations, see you that the spirits of the dying, as they ascend to join us, bring with them tidings of your faith, and patience, and labours of love. Let us hear by every sainted messenger, by every returning angel, of something you have done, or are doing, or are projecting to do for Christ—for virtue—for the happiness and honour of the world you live in. Let it be told in heaven that another Howard, or Sharp, or Brainard, or Schwartz has appeared on the earth to enlighten human ignorance ; to mitigate human suffering, and to exemplify and perpetuate the knowledge and the love of our Lord and Saviour. God Almighty grant that our hopes may not be disappointed, and to his name shall be the glory.

VI.

DELIVERED JULY 22, 1812.

[The Moral, no less than the Physical World, subject to convulsions and changes.—The present an age of Political Revolutions.—Our Country involved in the contentions of Nations.—Importance of the Era in which we live.—The hopes of Society in the rising Generation.—Knowledge is Power.—The Savage and the civilized Man compared.—The dominion of Mind, as exhibited in the general and statesman—in the example of ancient Athens.—Encouragements to Perseverance in the pursuit of intellectual Superiority.—Examples of Homer and Demosthenes.—Power beneficent only when associated with Goodness.—Human Endowments should be consecrated to Religious and Moral ends.—Nature of Civil Government, and duty of Obedience to it.—Exhortation to defend the free Institutions of our Country.—Whatever Trials befall the Christian here, his Reward is sure hereafter.]

YOUNG gentlemen, the admission of a class to collegiate honours always excites solicitude; particularly so at seasons of doubtful and momentous incident. The course of nature itself is not uniform. At intervals, and after a time of tranquillity, a season of disaster and convulsion ensues. The balance of the elements seems to be destroyed; rivers change their beds; seas their basins; mountains are removed; valleys are filled up, and the solid world is shaken. Again the balance of the elements is restored; the conflict subsides; the regions of matter are tranquillized; and order in a new form takes place.

The course of the physical, in these respects, is emblematical of the course of the intellectual and moral world; at least of that part of it with which we are conversant. In civil society, after a season of tranquillity, a season of convulsion usually, perhaps necessarily, ensues. Suddenly, institutions are changed; the opinions of men are changed; their habits and manners are changed. Attempts of bold and daring enterprise are hazarded; and they succeed. More is undertaken—more is accomplished in a few years, and by a single set of actors, than was accomplished, or could have been accomplished by preceding generations, and during successive ages. Again tranquillity ensues; things settle down in a new form, and society enjoys the blessings which have been conferred, or suffers the injuries which have been inflicted by the change.

It is our lot to live at a time peculiarly disastrous. Change has followed change in continuity. The course of things has been as unaccountable as alarming. Foresight has proved blind; calculation has been baffled; and sages and statesmen have gazed in consternation at a series of events so improbable in their nature, so rapid in their succession, as to appear in retrospect more like the illusions of fancy than the actual phenomena of real life. Half the civilized world has suddenly been revolutionized. Institutions the most solid in their materials, as well as the most firm in their contexture, have been swept away. Fabrics which human skill had been for ages rearing up and consolidating, have been demolished; and from their ruins, as from another chaos, a new order of things has arisen.

Hitherto we have contemplated these changes as spectators merely. Awed indeed we have been by their magnitude, amazed at their celerity. The scene of suffering which has been disclosed has interested our feelings: we have sympathized with the sufferers. We have sighed for the restoration of peace, and the return of repose to the world. We have done this, however, rather out of charity to others than apprehension for ourselves. The ark of our safety, we imagined, was anchored too firmly, and in a harbour too remote to be driven from its moorings by any rude blast or swelling surge. The scene of devastation has, however, been perpetually extending; wider and wider the destructive vortex has spread itself; realm after realm has been dragged into its rapid and hitherto fatal whirl. The current at length has reached us; our bark begins to be carried forward by the stream, whether to be moored again in safety, or to be wrecked and lost for ever, God only knows. Our character, perhaps our existence as a nation, is staked upon the issue of that contest in which we are about engaging. We shall not be hereafter what heretofore we have been. Either we shall rise united under that heavy pressure which will soon be felt, or we shall sink beneath it, divided, humbled, and disgraced. War is an experiment on our form of government which has not yet been tried. A momentous experiment, involving alternatives for which no human being can be responsible, and to the issue of which wise men will look forward not without awe and trembling. Perhaps—but I will not agitate this question, nor indulge that anxious train of thought which occupies my mind and presses on my heart.

At such a time, every new actor that steps upon the stage is an object of more than ordinary interest: for at such a time the facilities of doing either good or evil are increased. Life itself becomes of additional importance; it becomes more rich in incident; and, if years were measured by political events, it would become longer in duration.

Attached to the institutions of our country, and sensible that its dearest interests will soon be committed to those who will survive us, we feel anxious concerning the part which they hereafter are to act. Hence, as we welcome them into life, we charge them to become the guardians of the public weal; to preserve what is good, to remedy what is defective, and remove what is evil from our civil, our literary, and our religious institutions.

It is not to the risen, but to the rising generation that we look for great and beneficial changes. The maturity of manhood is too inflexible to admit of being recast in a new and a nobler mould. But if the whole of that group of beings denominated the rising generation be important, how important, then, must be that portion of this group which, in distinction from the residue, has been privileged by a public and liberal education. Every post of duty is indeed a post of honour. We revere industry and integrity; and we ought to revere them at the plough and in the workshop.. Still, however, when these virtues are combined with polished manners and liberal science, they shine with brighter lustre and command profounder reverence. No determinate number of perfectly untutored beings, so far as human society is concerned, can be put in competition with a youth of splendid and cultivated talents. The reason is obvious. The ability of such a youth to exalt or to depress, to reclaim or to corrupt community, is greater, and will be of longer continuance than that of any determinate number of his illiterate contemporaries. The latter, limited in their sphere of action to the place where they reside and to the time in which they live, soon sink into the grave, when, ordinarily, their deeds of virtue or of villany are forgotten. The former acts in a higher style and on a broader scale. Nations feel the influence of his genius while living, nor does death itself take aught from the effect of his precepts or example.

Not that in point of physical strength, youth of erudition acquire any superiority over the rudest children of nature. The contrary is the fact. In muscular exertion, in acts of agility, in the chase, at the tournament, and the cæstus, you will be their inferiors. Not so in point of moral influence. Education qualifies for doing either greater good or greater evil. It is this, young gentlemen, that gives to your existence so much importance, and excites in your behalf so deep an interest.

It is an old proverb, *That wealth is power*. The same may be said, and more emphatically, with respect to knowledge. Look into the world, and contemplate the native savage, surrounded by forests, and in jeopardy from beasts of prey, binding his bark sandals to his feet, and flying from the tiger, or vainly attempting to pierce the fawn with his pointless arrow. How wild and awful the state of nature! How pitiable and impotent this state of man! Contemplate now the citizen. Walled cities are at once his accommodation and defence. By him the forest has been felled, the acclivities of the mountains depressed, the deep morass filled up: by him ferocious animals have been destroyed, the noxious productions of the earth have been subdued, and monuments of art erected. Amazing change! All surrounding nature bespeaks his sovereignty and contributes to his comfort. Whence this prodigious difference in condition? What circumstance has contributed so much to exalt one portion of the species? By what magic has a being of so little physical strength been enabled to acquire a dominion so vast, and establish a government so absolute? The answer is manifest. By knowledge he has done this.

Man possesses less muscle than many, but more intelligence than any other terrestrial inhabitant. He alone has skill to analyze and combine anew the rude materials which surround him; to dig from the mine its precious metals, and mould from the ores his weapons of conquest and defence. Those mechanical powers which he has discovered and learned to apply, remedy the effects of his natural imbecility. Thus enlightened by science and fortified by art, he is enabled to control and tame the most ferocious animals, to raise and remove the heaviest masses, and to direct to the accomplishment of his purposes the very elements of nature itself.

As knowledge extends the dominion of man over matter, so also does it over mind. What an immense advantage does he possess who not only understands the machinery of language, but also the influence of motive: who comprehends the economy of the passions; to whom the principles of action are familiar, and the avenues of the heart open: who knows how to remove prejudice, to conciliate affection, and to excite attention: who can at pleasure sooth or rouse, inflame or allay, restrain or hurry on to action: what an immense advantage does such a man possess over him who can only stammer out his ill-timed, ill-digested, and incoherent sentiments in a manner so rude and repulsive as to disparage the cause he advocates, and defeat the attainment of the object for which he has lent his talents.

Nor less the advantage of science in every other department of life. It is Minerva who gathers even for Mars his laurel, and wins for Bellona her fields. How august a spectacle of power does an intelligent and intrepid general exhibit at the head of a numerous and well-appointed army, himself the bond of union and the centre of influence; wielding this tremendous force, and directing it when to act and where to strike, with as much certainty and as terrible effect as if the whole were animated by a single soul.

A spectacle scarcely less august is exhibited by the sagacious statesman, who, from the retirement of his closet, diffuses a secret influence, tincturing the opinions of courtiers, guiding the decision of princes, embroiling or reconciling different and distant nations, and producing through a thousand intermediate agents, and in regions, perhaps, which he has never seen, the most surprising changes, the most improbable events.

It was science, displayed in her literature and her arts, that made Athens what she was and still is—the admiration of the world. The record of her triumphs and of her overthrow has been preserved in the midst of the unwritten ruins of a thousand barbarous states. Ages of succeeding darkness have not obscured her glory; the ravages of time have not obliterated her monuments. The history of Athens is still read, and it is dear: dear, too, are the memorials of her greatness, and dear is the spot where Athens stood.

By a tincture only of science, Russia, amid her snow-covered forests, has recently assumed a loftier attitude, and taken a higher stand among the nations. Indeed, knowledge furnishes the facilities and the instruments of operating as certainly, as efficaciously, and more extensively upon the mind than the mechanical powers do upon matter. And the man of erudition, aided by these facilities, surpasses in intellectual potency—in a capacity of action and of influence, the unlettered boor, as much as the scientific artificer, aided by machinery, surpasses the wild man of the woods, who can only apply to the impediments in his path the mere strength of his native muscles.

Archimedes affirmed that he could lift the earth could he but find a place to rest his lever on. What Archimedes found not in the regions of matter, some intellectual geometrician may yet find in the regions of mind; and, finding, exhibit the amazing spectacle of a single individual, but a few years old and a few feet high, concentrating the influence, swaying the opinions, and wielding in his hand the nations of the world.

Towards the attainment of mental superiority, during your collegiate course you have made some advance. Other and still greater advances remain hereafter to be made. You may now be youth of promise; but you must long and diligently trim the midnight lamp before you will arrive to the stature of intellectual manhood.

Preparing for professional duties; shortly to mingle among the busy actors on yonder interesting theatre; destined to take sides on those questions which now agitate or which will hereafter agitate community, and on the decision of which the happiness or the misery of unborn millions hangs suspended; can any sacrifices be deemed great, or any discipline severe, which will enable you hereafter to act a more conspicuous part, or exert a more controlling influence?

Perseverantia vincit omnia. Do you not remember what obstacles obstructed Homer's path to glory? The Grecian orator, too, had to struggle against the influence of constitution. By perseverance, however, he surmounted the most discouraging impediments, and supplied by art the defects of nature. His lungs he expanded by climbing the steep and rugged mountains; by speaking with pebbles in his mouth he corrected his stammering; and his voice he strengthened by haranguing on the surge-beaten shore to the winds and the waves. Let his successful efforts encourage yours; let no ordinary obstacles dishearten you; let no ordinary attainments satisfy you. Remember always, as we have said, that knowledge is power: but remember also, that no degree of power—no, not even power almighty, is in itself an object of complacency. We tremble before the Deity when we hear him utter his voice in thunder; when we behold him riding on the storm, and mark his terrific course amid the tempest. But it is his goodness that endears him to us. We love to contemplate him in the robe of mercy—to trace his footsteps when relieving misery or communicating happiness. As goodness is essential to the glory of God, so it is to the glory of his creatures. In him wisdom, truth, and justice are combined with power. And, because they are so, the interests of the universe are secure. But, without these essential attributes, almighty power would only be an instrument of evil, and its possessor an object of detestation.

Nor less truly an object of detestation is a finite being possessing power apart from goodness. Every unprincipled youth, therefore, that goes forth crowned from our seats of science, is, and ought to be viewed as an assassin doubly armed and let loose upon the world. No matter whether he mingles poison as a druggist, utters falsehood as an advocate, preaches heresy as a minister, practises treachery as a statesman, or sheds blood as a soldier; everywhere alike, he will strengthen the hands of sinners, increase the amount of guilt, and add to the mass of misery. Lucifer may originally have been as sagacious and as potent as Gabriel; and, had his submission been as profound and his morality as blameless, he might still have enjoyed a fame as fair and as deathless. Oh! that the failure and the fall of angels were duly considered and attended to by men.

It is the fear of God and the faith of Jesus only that can consecrate your talents—consecrate your influence, and make you to your friends, to your country, and to the universe, instruments of good. Far be it from me to pronounce any benediction on endowments not devoted to the Almighty. There may be cunning, there may be temerity; but greatness and glory there cannot be where religion is not. The sinner's splendour is as transient and as ominous as the meteor's glare. It is only the path of the righteous which, like the morning light, brightens continually to the perfect day.

You will enter on life at a critical conjuncture. Your country stands in need of all the talent and all the influence you can carry with you to her assistance. May I not hope, that, when you shall be numbered among her patriots and statesmen, your prudence will be as exemplary as your zeal? Though you should differ in political opinions, be one in affection, one in the pursuit of glory, and one in the love of your country. Do nothing, say nothing, to produce unnecessary rigour on the one part, or lawless resistance on the other. Beware how you contribute to awaken the whirlwind of passion, or to invite to this sacred land the reign of anarchy

Whatever irritations may be felt, whatever questions may be agitated, and however you yourselves may be divided, be it your part to calm, to sooth, to allay, to check the deed of violence; to charm down the spirit of party; to strengthen the bonds of social intercourse; and to prove by your own amiable deportment—by your own affectionate intercourse, that it is possible for brethren to differ and *be brethren still.* Differ indeed you may, and avow that difference. Freedom of speech is your birthright. The deed which conveys it was written in the blood of your fathers; it was sealed beside their sepulchres, and let no man take it from you. But remember that the deed which conveys, defines also, and limits this freedom. And remember, too, that the line which divides between liberty and licentiousness is *but a line,* and that it is easily transgressed. The assassin's dagger is not more fatal to the peace of community than the liar's tongue. Nor does the sacred charter of the freeman's privileges furnish to the one, any more than to the other, an asylum.

It is your happiness to live under a government of laws. Nor, were it demonstrated that those laws were impolitic, or even oppressive, would it justify resistance. There is a redeeming principle in the Constitution itself. That instrument provides a legitimate remedy for grievances; and, unless on great emergencies, the only rightful one. Under a compact like ours, the majority must govern; the minority must submit, and they ought to submit; not by constraint merely, but for conscience'-sake.

The powers that be are ordained of God; and, while they execute the purpose for which they were ordained, *to resist them is to resist the ordinance of God.*

You remember that Jesus Christ paid tribute even unto Cæsar, than whom there has not lived a more execrable tyrant. You remember, too, that his immediate followers, as became the disciples of such a master, everywhere bowed to the supremacy of the Roman laws. It is a fact that will for ever redound to the honour of the Christian church and of its divine founder, that its members, though everywhere oppressed and persecuted for three successive centuries, were nowhere implicated in those commotions which agitated the provinces, nor were they even accessory to those treasons which, during that period, so often stained the capital with blood.

In the worst of times, and however you may differ with respect to men and measures, still cling to the Constitution; CLING TO THE INTEGRITY OF THE UNION; cling to the institutions of your country. These, under God, are your political ARK of safety; the ark that contains the cradle of liberty in which you were rocked; that preserves the vase of Christianity in which you were baptized; and that defends the sacred urn where the ashes of your patriot fathers moulder. Cling, therefore, to this ark, and defend it while a drop of blood is propelled from your heart, or a shred of muscle quivers on your bones. Triumph as the friends of liberty, of order, of religion, or fall as martyrs.

I now bid you adieu. What scenes await you,

your friends, and your beloved country, I know not; and you know not. But this we know, that the Lord God omnipotent reigneth. And, because He reigneth, though the sea roar, and the waves thereof be lifted up, Mount Zion will not be removed.

This world is the region of sin; and for the reason that it is the region of sin, it is also the region of disaster. But though *here* the tumult of battle rage, and the garments of innocence be rolled in blood, *yonder* in heaven is a secure abode. There lay up your treasure, thither direct your hopes. This done, face danger, and defy the menaces of death. Unsuccessful indeed you may be. Your fame may be blasted, your property may be plundered, and your bodies doomed to exile or to execution; but your souls, as they mount from the stake or from the scaffold, looking down from the scene of utter desolation, may exclaim in triumph, "Our eternal interests are secure; amid this wreck we have lost nothing." May Almighty God preserve you from evil, or enable you to meet it as triumphantly as the saints met martyrdom, and to his name shall be the glory.

VII.

DELIVERED JULY 28, 1813.

[Love of Distinction.—Honour and Religion, though distinct, are allied to each other.—Modern definition of the Law of Honour.—Fallacies of this Definition exposed.—A sense of Honour in different degrees operative on all Minds except the most debased.—The offices of this Feeling and of Conscience contrasted.—Purpose for which the Sense of Honour was implanted in the human breast.—Its Perversion an abuse.—Dignity of Man, and the lofty distinction conferred on him by his Maker.—His Fall and Recovery.—His Rank, Capacities, Parentage, and Destination, all call upon him to persevere in a steady Course of honourable Action, in his Amusements, his Pleasures, and his Occupations.—Dignity of the good Man in his last moments.—All false and deceptive appearances will be exposed in a future state; and those only who are truly and sincerely good will be accounted worthy of acceptance and honour.]

YOUNG gentlemen, your term of pupilage is almost closed. The last scene is acting in which you will take a part on the collegiate theatre. Testimonials of approbation have been delivered, badges of distinction conferred. The tokens of respect from your *Alma Mater*, with which you will return to your friends and your home, presuppose attainments of no mean value, and are calculated to inspire you with lofty ideas of personal consequence. Man loves distinction, and he ought to love it. That God had originally created him but little lower than the angels, and crowned him with majesty and honour, was among the considerations that touched the heart of David with gratitude, and filled his lips with praise.

Let it be remembered, however, that the majesty and honour with which man was originally crowned, differ essentially from that spurious majesty, that affectation of honour, in which he too often now appears. And let it also be remembered, that vice itself is never so dangerous as when it appears in the habiliments of virtue. In nothing is the truth of these positions more manifest than in that self-complacency with which little men practise those guilty meannesses which fashion sanctions and folly celebrates.

Honour and religion are indeed distinct; but, though distinct, they are allied; and there can be no high attainments in the one without corresponding attainments in the other. There is nothing, for instance, estimable or elevating in a mere act of suffering; in the dislocation of joints, or even in the consuming of the body by fire. But there is a majesty that strikes, a grandeur that overwhelms in the constancy of the martyr who endures both without a murmur for God's and for righteousness' sake.

We do often, indeed, render honour to whom it is not due; but we do this because we are governed, and are obliged to be governed, in our appraisement of merit by external appearances. When, however, any action is pronounced honourable, some internal motive is supposed to have induced to its performance, which, if it had truly induced to its performance, would have rendered such action in reality what it is now, perhaps, in appearance only. This is a delicate point, and one on which you are liable to be misguided. I have therefore chosen it for discussion.

The law of honour has been defined to be *a system of rules, constructed by people of fashion, and calculated to facilitate their intercourse with one another; and for no other purpose.*

To this definition two objections may be made. It does not discriminate between the object of *this* law and that of *other* laws; and it limits to people of fashion a law which is as extensive as the human race.

Is it peculiar to the law of honour to facilitate intercourse among those who are subject to it? Does not the civil law also aim at this? And is not this an object at which the divine law aims, and which it moreover effectually accomplishes? Again: is the law of honour recognised by fashionable people only? Or who are meant by fashionable people? Those so denominated in one country would be denominated the reverse in another. And, even in the same country, the term comprehends no precise and definite portion of community. The highest are fashionable only by comparison: the intermediate ranks, by a like comparison, are fashionable. The series descends from grade to grade, and terminates only with that ignoble herd, in comparison with whom there are none more ignoble. Who, then, are those fashionable people by whom the law of honour has been constructed? Are they those only who occupy the first rank? The terms of this law are familiar to, and its sanctions are acknowledged by people of every description. Neither husbandmen nor mechanics are destitute of rules for facilitating intercourse; nor among them can such rules be violated without dishonour. Remaining traces of the influence of this law are sometimes found among ruffians and banditti: hence we hear, and the terms are not without significancy, of honour among thieves.

The fact is, I believe, that the law of honour is common to man, because the sense of honour on which it is founded is common: a law which had existence previous to any association of fashionable people, and would have continued to exist though no such association had ever taken place.

By adverting to such a system of rules as the definition under discussion supposes, an individual might become acquainted with the legalized etiquette of fashionable life. By experience he might farther learn, that the observance of certain rules facilitated intercourse; but nature alone could teach him understandingly to say, this action is honourable, that dishonourable; because nature alone could give him that inward feeling from which the very idea of honour is derived.

This inward feeling or sense of honour is allied to, if it be not a constituent part of, the moral sense. It exists, perhaps originally, in different degrees in different individuals. Its sensibility may be increased by culture or diminished by neglect. Its influence may be blended with other influences; its decisions may be biased by custom, by education, by prevalent modes of thinking and acting; it may discover itself in different ways among different individuals and in different classes of community; but among all who have not ceased to be men and be come brutes, some indications of its existence, some traces of its influence remain.

It is by this sense of honour that we ascertain what pleasures, what pursuits, and what demeanour accord with our nature and rank. Its province is to distinguish between dignity and meanness, as that of the moral is to decide between innocence and guilty; and its penalty is *shame*, as that of the moral sense is *remorse*. It would exist if there were no fashionable society, nor even society of any sort. The wanderer in his solitude, and communing only with his heart, would recognise its influence, and, guided by inward feeling, discriminate between actions, high and low, dignified and mean. And, without this feeling, he could not, even in society, make such discrimination. Experience would teach to distinguish what was useful from what was injurious; conscience to distinguish what was virtuous from what was vicious; but to distinguish what was honourable from what was dishonourable, could only be taught by a sense of honour.

This ennobling principle was implanted to prevent the degradation of the species, and to secure on the part of man a demeanour suited to his nature and station, who, being the offspring of God, once wore a crown of righteousness, and was invested with regal honours. This high purpose, it is admitted, in the present state of things, is very imperfectly attained. The apostacy has diffused its mortal taint through the entire nature of man, and neither honour nor conscience any longer performs with due effect its sacred office. And yet, degraded as human nature is, it would be still more degraded—vice would appear in new and more debasing forms if all sense of honour were suspended. Like native modesty against lust, honour, so far as its influence goes, is a barrier in the heart against meanness. Like all those moral tendencies usually comprehended under the idea of conscience, its influence is feeble, and may be counteracted; its decisions are erring, and may be swayed by passion or prejudice; and its sensibility, always defective, may, by criminal indulgence, be greatly blunted, if not utterly destroyed.

Envy, malice, pride, and lust are ever struggling for dominion in the breast of man. And, where grace is not concerned, they have dominion. To the prevalence and potency of these abominable passions it is owing that, in fashionable circles, so many virtues are disregarded; so many vices are practised, although no sanction is afforded to profligacy by honour or its laws; the unbiased decisions of which are for ever in favour of whatever is dignified and ennobling, as those of conscience are in favour of whatever is virtuous and holy; and it is not till their joint influence has been resisted—has been stifled and overcome, that the degraded debauchee can, without shame and without compunction, enjoy his degradation.

The result to which this inquiry would conduct us, but which we have not now time to pursue, may be thus summed up. The law of honour has its foundation in an original sense of honour: this sense is common to all men; it is capable of being either improved or corrupted: its province is to distinguish between dignity and meanness; and its final design is the elevation of the human race.

I am aware, young gentlemen, that in these degenerate times terms of honour are insensibly changing their significance, and becoming terms of opprobrium. And it is fit that it should be so. Since the contemptible vapouring of principals and seconds in their humiliating rencounters are conveyed exclusively through the medium of these once reputable and sacred terms, it is befitting that the terms themselves should lose their sacredness; and that the expression, "a man of honour," should be understood to mean, what, in fact, in the modern use of it, it does often mean, an empty, arrogant, and supercilious coxcomb.

But, because words are misused, do not suppose that they never were significant, or that the things to which they were once rightfully applied no longer have existence. To you, not as *people of fashion*, but as intellectual, moral beings, belong the sense and the law of honour.

Man is ennobled by his descent, by his faculties, and by his destination. A vast chasm intervenes between him and the highest link in the chain of mere animal existence. His port, his attitude, the texture of his frame, the grace and expression of his countenance, bespeak a heavenly parentage, an origin divine. The reptile creeps, the brute bends downward to the earth. Man walks erect; his elevated brow meets the sunbeam as it falls by day;

and by night, the immeasurable firmament presents its resplendent garniture to his heaven-directed eye.

> "Two of far nobler shape, erect and tall,
> Godlike erect, with native honour clad,
> In naked majesty, seem'd lords of all."

No wonder that the primeval state of man excited in the poet such ideas. The grandeur of his body strikes not, however, so forcibly as the grandeur of his mind. How august a spectacle is a being so limited in his corporeal dimensions, and yet so vast in his intellectual resources. Reason, memory, fancy, and imagination are eminently his: no space limits his researches, no time bounds his excursive sallies; in a certain sense, he pervades the past, the present, and the future. His soul, indestructible in its nature, and capable of endless improvement, is but the miniature of what it shall hereafter be. Immortality—immortal progression! what more could Adam covet! what more can Gabriel boast of!

Like a palace for its monarch, this world was reared up that it might become the residence of man. Already were the land and water divided; already was the earth covered with herbage, and the fruit-tree with fruit; already had the stars been set to rule the night, and the sun to rule the day, when man, the last and the noblest of terrestrial beings, was, from his native dust, ushered into life. Fresh in the robe of innocence, and bearing on his heart his Maker's image, he was solemnly inducted into the legal office, and constituted sovereign of the world. "And have dominion," said the Almighty, addressing himself to our first parents, "And have dominion over the fish of the sea, and over the fowl of the air, and over every living thing that moveth upon the earth." It was on the review of this inauguration that David broke forth in that strain of admiration to which we have already alluded. "When I consider thy heavens, the work of thy fingers; the moon and the stars which thou hast ordained; what is man that thou art mindful of him, and the son of man that thou visitest him? For thou hast made him a little lower than the angels, and hast crowned him with glory and honour; thou madest him to have dominion over the works of thy hands; thou hast put all things under his feet."

What a lofty distinction to belong to such a race— to be descended from such a parentage—to be destined to such a career of progressive and interminable glory! With what profound reverence ought you to recognise the Author of your being! with what a burst of filial gratitude ought you to approach His throne, who has bestowed on you such a profusion of honours, and made you the heirs of such exuberant felicity!

Say not that the loss of primeval honour, the change of original destination which the apostacy occasioned, has absolved you from claims which would otherwise press upon you. The apostacy cancels no debt of gratitude, it severs no tie of duty. And, were it otherwise, such plea to man, under the present dispensation, were unavailable. All that was lost by the apostacy of Adam has been recovered, and recovered with boundless increase, by the mediation of Christ. To be restored to the Divine image, to be reinstated in the Divine favour, to be translated to the heavens, and to be numbered among the sons of God—this honour have all His saints.

"If the surrendry of my honour," said an illustrious captive, "be the condition of my liberty, give me back my chains and reconduct me to my dungeon. I can brave torture, I can meet death, but I cannot do an act that will disgrace one in whose veins circulates the blood of a royal ancestry." Oh! that souls in captivity to sin° would consecrate this sentiment, and act with like becoming dignity.

Let the animal browse, let the reptile grovel, let the serpent creep upon his belly and lick the dust; but let not man, heaven-descended, heaven-instructed, heaven-redeemed man, degrade himself.

Your rank, your capacities, your parentage, and your destination, alike bind you to a uniform course of honourable pursuit, of dignified exertion. In your *amusements*, in your *pleasures*, in your *occupations*, on your deaths, be sensible of this.

In your amusements.—Man was made for serious occupation, but not for such occupation perpetually. As the bow, unstrung, recovers its elasticity, so the mind acquires fresh vigour from sleep, "kind nature's sweet restorer." Nor from sleep alone. During his wakeful hours, severe pursuits must sometimes be suspended; but suspended only that, after a short interval, they may be the more successfully resumed. Such temporary suspension, either of labour or study, implies no waste of time, involves no degradation of character.

Newton was still the philosopher when engaged in blowing air bubbles; Socrates still the moralist when joining in the gambols of the Athenian children. How does the gravity of pagan philosophers reprove the levity of many a frivolous pretender to character in Christendom. Those active, real sages trifled but to live: these idle, spurious Christians only live to trifle.

> "On all-important time, through every age,
> Though much and warm the wise have urged, the man
> Is yet unborn who duly weighs an hour.
> 'I've lost a day,' the prince who nobly cried
> Had been an emperor without his crown;
> He spake as if deputed by mankind.
> So should all speak; so reason speaks in all."

In your pleasures.—The organic pleasures are usually overrated by youth, and often by age. And yet these pleasures are destitute of dignity. It is admitted that man must eat and drink to live. So also must the ox and the oyster. The viands of the table, in point of elevation, are on a level with the fodder of the stall. And the guests that partake of the one, so far as the gratification of animal appetite is concerned, are no more on an equality than the herd that devours the other. Nor can any pre-eminence be claimed for the former, unless it be on the ground of a less voracious appetite, or a more temperate indulgence of it. Not so with the pleasures of the eye and of the ear: not so with intellectual pleasures. These are dignified as well as exquisite. Honour, no less than enjoyment, springs from a participation in them. You have tasted of those pleasures, but you have not exhausted them. The clas-

K

sic fountain is still open. The streams of Grecian and Roman eloquence and poesy, commingling with those no less pure, of more modern origin, still flow within your reach. The Academy invites you to its groves, the Lyceum to its intellectual banquets. These are pleasures that become a scholar, that become a man, and that are not incompatible with the temperance and sanctitude of a Christian man. But the pleasures of the debauchee—from these, honour, conscience, every ennobling feeling, no less than reason, revolt; and no man ever for the first time seated himself at the gaming-table, joined the loud laugh at the horserace, took the inebriating cup at the dram-shop, or crossed the polluted threshold of the brothel, without feeling that his honour had received a stain, and that his character suffered degradation.

In your pursuits.—Useless, or even trivial pursuits illy befit the majesty of the human soul. Still less do these mischiefs and meannesses befit it, to which genius even is sometimes liable. But, though genius is sometimes guilty of acts of this sort, such acts are by no means indications of genius. There is a trickishness, a dexterity in low and little arts, that characterizes the monkey rather than the man. Shallow minds, like shallow waters, often, perhaps usually, babble loudest.

Being young is no apology for being frivolous. Frivolity suits no state unless it be a state of idiocy. True, you are just entering on life. The life, however, on which you are entering is life without end. These are the inceptive steps in the career of immortality. Not even death interrupts the continuous flow of being. Thus situated, are you willing to forfeit your title to character on earth, and make God, the just appraiser of honour in heaven, the witness of your low actions?

The sublime in morals is exhibited only in great and useful pursuits; and he only is an honourable man who acts worthy of himself, and worthy of the approbation of God, his Maker and his Master; who attends to every duty in its season; who fills with dignity his appropriate station, and directs the whole vigour of his mind to the diffusion of knowledge, the promotion of virtue, and the accomplishment of good; who can make sacrifices; who can confront danger; who can resist temptation; who can surmount obstacles; and who, trampling alike on the world and on the tomb, pursues with undeviating step his march to glory.

In your death.—There is at least one great occasion in the life of every man; there is one decisive act that tries the spirit, and puts the destinies of the soul at issue. Neither the skeptic's wavering confidence nor the duellist's blind temerity befits this dread solemnity. The wretch that thrusts himself into his Maker's presence, and the wretch who, being called for, dares, without preparation and without concern, to enter it, deserves alike our reprobation. The one resembles the maniac who leaps the precipice; the other, the sot who staggers off it, regardless of its height, and unmindful of the shock that awaits his fall. From such spectacles of self-destruction, the mind turns away with mingled emotions of pity, disgust, and horror. How unlike the good man's death. Here there is real majesty. Nothing below exceeds, nothing equals it. To see a human being crowded to the verge of life, and standing on that line that connects and divides eternity and time, excites a solemn interest. But oh! what words can express the grandeur of the death-scene, when the individual about to make the dread experiment, sensible of his condition, and with heaven and hell, judgment and eternity full in view, is calm, collected, confident; and, relying on the merits of his Saviour and the faithfulness of his God, is eager to depart! Perhaps the sainted Stephen here occurs to mind: Stephen, with heaven beaming from his countenance, as, sinking under the pressure of his enemies, he raises his dying eyes to glory, and says, "Lord Jesus, receive my spirit." Perhaps the Israelitish prophet, as, dropping his consecrated mantle on his pupil, he mounts the whirlwind from the banks of Jordan; or perhaps Saul of Tarsus, exclaiming, in prospect of the fires of martyrdom, "I am ready to be offered up; I have fought the good fight; I have kept the faith; and there is henceforth laid up for me a crown of righteousness, which the righteous Lord will deliver unto me; and not to me only, but to all those that love his appearing."

> "How our hearts burn within us at the scene!
> Whence this brave bound o'er limits set to man?
> His God supports him in his final hour.
> His final hour brings glory to his God.
> We gaze, we weep mix'd tears of grief and joy;
> Amazement strikes; devotion burns to flame;
> Christians admire, and infidels believe."

I repeat, young gentlemen, in concluding this address, a remark which was made at its commencement. *Though honour and religion are distinct, they are allied, and there can be no high attainments in the one without corresponding attainments in the other.* Strictly speaking, there is not in the universe, nor is it possible that there ever should be, such a being as an honourable sinner. A sinner may indeed, and often does, perform actions which seem to indicate lofty and honourable sentiments. A factitious splendour is thus flung around his person, which may, till death, emblazon his character. The light of eternity, however, will dissipate that splendour. Then the mean and mercenary motives which governed him will appear; and, appearing, will betray to the just appraisers of merit in heaven a very wretch, in the person of one whom the blinded inhabitants of earth delighted to honour. In that light the duellist, now pitied for his sensibility or celebrated for his courage, will be seen to have been either a trembling coward, who wanted nerve to endure a sneer, or a malicious murderer, who, could he have as certainly escaped the gallows, would have employed, not the soldier's, but the assassin's weapon in his work of death. In that light many a sainted patriot will be discovered to have been only a wily traitor; and in many a titled conqueror there will be recognised only the grim and ferocious visage of a human butcher.

It is not the outward action, but the inward motive, that will in heaven secure the plaudit. To you all the path of honour is open, because the path of duty is so. Those titles and distinctions which little minds look up to and covet are merely adventitious. Neither the bishop's lawn nor the judge's ermine confers any real dignity. He only on the bench who imitates the justice of that awful Being who is himself a terror to the wicked; he only at the altar who imitates the clemency of that merciful Being who is the consolation of the righteous; he only in the field who has drawn his sword from principle, and from principle risks his life in defence of the people and the cities of his God, will, in the consummation of all things, be accounted an honourable man. Let the ferocious savage present his crimsoned tomahawk as he mutters his orisons to the demons of destruction, and boast of the sculls he has severed and the scalps he has strung; but let not the Christian victor count on glory achieved by cruelty. The God of Christians smiles not at carnage, delights not in blood. Nor is glory to be gathered only on the public theatre or in the tented field. You may lead an obscure life, and yet an honourable one. There is in the cottage, no less than in the palace, a majesty in virtue. In presiding over the devotions of the parental board; in the morning prayer, in the evening anthem; in those acts of supplication and praise by which the soul mounts upward to the throne, and enters the presence of the God of heaven, there is an honour inferior in degree, but not in nature, to that which principalities and powers enjoy. If the favour of princes confer distinction on those around their persons, what must be the distinction of that contrite man in whom the spirit dwells, and whom the Father delights to honour!

That it sanctifies the soul, that it brings peace to the conscience, these are, indeed, the grand prerogatives of our religion; but they are not its only prerogatives. The gospel of grace is rich in honour as well as rich in consolation. Its high purpose is to recover the sinner from his apostacy, and to signalize him hereafter among the sons of God. But, in attaining this purpose, and as incidental to it, it does signalize him here among the children of men. There is no illumination so divine as the illumination of the spirit; there are no virtues so divine as the graces of the spirit; nor is there any march so truly glorious as the march through faith and patience to immortality.

Go, young gentlemen; aim at being great only by being good; and hope to be good only by confiding in that glorious Redeemer, through whose merits alone it is possible that a sinner should become so.

God grant you this grace, and to his name shall be the glory.

VIII.

DELIVERED JULY 27, 1814.

[Public Opinion as opposed to the Moral Law.—Games of Chance.—Objectionable because they unprofitably consume Time.—Because they lead to a misapplication of Property.—Because they impart no Expansion or Vigour to the Mind.—Because their Influence on the Affections and Passions is deleterious.—Dreadful Effect of Gaming on Morals and on the Sympathies of our Nature.—It leads to Debauchery, to Avarice, to Intemperance.—The finished Gambler has no Heart.—Example of Madame du Deffand.—Brutalized and hopeless State of the Gambler and Drunkard.—Warning to Youth to avoid the Temptations which lead to these soul-destroying Vices.]

Young gentlemen, man is susceptible of moral no less than of intellectual improvement. These are the two grand objects of collegiate education. Hence its importance, not only to the individual, but to community itself.

No matter what the printed code of civil law may be in any country—no matter what the printed code of canon law may be, to an immense majority, public opinion constitutes a standard of paramount authority. But public opinion itself is directed and settled among the many by the few, who, either by merit or by management, have acquired an ascendancy, and become the acknowledged arbiters of faith and of practice. Some of the points where the moral law and public opinion are at issue, have on similar occasions been discussed; there are still other points which demand discussion.

A good man regulates even his amusements, no less than his serious occupations, by the maxims of morality. *Be ye perfect as I am perfect*, is the unqualified mandate of the Christian lawgiver; and till we are perfect as He is perfect, we never attain that sublime distinction, to which, as candidates for heaven, we should for ever be aspiring.

About to bid adieu to this seat of science, permit me to admonish you, that it will be your part not to receive a tone from, but to give a tone to public feeling; not to learn those lessons of morality which the world will inculcate, but to inculcate on the world those lessons which you have elsewhere learned.

We have a collegiate law which prohibits cardplaying, and the other fashionable games related to it. In future life, let this law be adopted as one of those inviolable rules of action which, being irrevocably settled, are not to be transgressed. Why? Because the transgression of it in you, whatever it may be in others, will be improper. Do not mistake my meaning; I am not about to insist on any argument drawn from the supposed sacredness of *games of chance*.

But, if these games are not objectionable as games of chance, why are they objectionable?

To this question I will attempt an answer. Before I commence, however, I would premise, that nothing is more foreign from my design than to hold up to universal obloquy all those who occasionally indulge in any of these games. That candour, which on all occasions I would wish to exercise

L

as well as inculcate, obliges me to concede, that there may be found, among the groups at the chess-board or the card-table, individuals of very respectable character; in other particulars, of irreproachable morals, and even, perhaps, of exemplary piety. But they are individuals, notwithstanding, whom I believe to be in error. Individuals whom public opinion has misguided, and who, like that apostle who thought he did God service, have this apology, they sin ignorantly. Their situation, in a moral point of view, is similar to his, who, in a country where slavery is common, inconsiderately holds a fellow-creature in bondage. Were that practice the subject of discussion—far from comprehending in the same sweeping sentence of reprobation the humane master who treats with paternal indulgence the blacks he inherited from his father, without even suspecting that they are not as rightfully his property as the sheep and oxen which he also inherited—far from comprehending this man in the same sweeping sentence of reprobation with the unfeeling wretch who, in despite of conscience, of reason, and of law, still drives that trade, which he knows to be a felony, and deliberately amasses a fortune by the sale of human blood—far from comprehending this man in the same sentence, I could, on the contrary, admit that he might be a philanthropist, and even, in the strictest sense of the word, a Christian. But, having made this admission, were I called to speak in his presence of slavery, I would speak of it as a man and a Christian ought to speak of it, with utter detestation; and in the same manner I mean to speak of gaming. No matter how many fashionable people may be implicated, no matter how many of my own personal friends may be implicated, I have a duty to perform, and I shall neither be allured nor awed from the performance of it. The question now returns, WHY ARE THESE GAMES OBJECTIONABLE?

They are objectionable *because they unprofitably consume time, which to every man is precious: because they lead to a misapplication of property, for which every man is accountable: because they impart no expansion or vigour to the mind; and because their influence on the affections, and passions, and heart, is deleterious.*

1st. *Because they unprofitably consume time, which to every man is precious.* Had I your future lives at my disposal, I would not wish to impose on you any unreasonable austerity. There must be seasons of relaxation as well as seasons of exertion. Rest necessarily follows action, and is in its turn conducive to it. It is conceded that a student needs recreation of mind; but the card-table does not furnish him with it. He needs exercise of body; neither does it furnish him with that. With what, then, that is worth having, does it furnish him? With nothing. From hours thus spent there is no result beneficial to himself or to any other human being. The time elapsed is wasted. To all the useful purposes of life, of death, or of existence after death, it is as though it had never been.

But who, during a trial so momentous and so transitory, has vacant hours at his disposal? Has the young man preparing for action? Has the old man sinking down to death? Has the father, charged with the education of his sons? Has the mother, intrusted with the instruction of her daughters? Ah! could I address these eternal idlers with the same freedom that I address myself to you, I would ask them whether so many hours were given to play because there no longer remained to them any duties to be performed? I would ask them, are the hungry fed? Are the naked clothed? Are the sick visited? Is the mourner consoled? Is the orphan provided for? Are all the offices of friendship and of charity executed? Are all the demands of the closet and of the altar cancelled? All, all cancelled! And yet, as successive days glide away, does there remain in each such a dismal void to be filled with the frivolous, not to say guilty, amusements of the card-table? Perhaps it is so. But, oh God! thou knowest it was not thus with those saints of old whom thou hast held up to us as examples. Their time was wholly occupied. With labours of love each day was filled up. Nor were their evenings devoted to play: nay, nor even their nights to repose. Often, for the performance of omitted duties, hours were borrowed from the season of rest which the shortness of the season of action had denied.

2d. *Because they lead to a misapplication of property.* Games of hazard, particularly where cards are concerned, tend imperceptibly to gambling.

Play at first is resorted to as a pastime, and the gamester becomes an idler only. This is the inceptive step. But mere play has not enough of interest in it to excite continued attention, even in the most frivolous minds. To supply this defect, the passion of avarice is addressed by the intervention of a trifling stake. This is the second step. The third is deep and presumptuous gambling; here, all that the adventurer can command is hazarded, and *gain*, not amusement, becomes the powerful motive that inspires him. These are the stages of play at cards: that delusive and treacherous science which has beggared so many families, made so many youth profligates, and blasted for ever so many parents' hopes.

But is a stake at play wrong in principle? It is so. Nor is the nature of the transaction changed by any increase or diminution of amount. Not that it is a crime to hazard, but to hazard wrongfully; to hazard where no law authorizes it; where neither individual prudence, nor any principle of public policy requires it. Property is a trust, and the holder is responsible for its use. He may employ it in trade; he may give it away in charity, but he may not wantonly squander it: he may not even lightly hazard the loss of it for no useful purpose, where there is no probability that the transaction will, on the whole, be beneficial, either to the parties or the community.

But I may not pass thus lightly over this subject. The nature of gambling, considered as an occupation, and the relative situation of gamblers, ought to be attended to. The issue which the parties join, the rivalship in which they engage, neither directly nor indirectly promote any interest of community. They have no relation to agriculture, none to commerce, none to manufactures. They furnish no bread to the poor, hold out no motive to industry, apply no stimulus to enterprise. Gaming is an employment *sui generis*. The talent it occupies is so much deducted from that intelligence which superintends the concerns of the world; the capital it employs is so much withdrawn from the stock required for the commerce of the world. Let the stake be gained or lost, as it will, society gains nothing. The managers of this ill-appropriated fund are not identified in their pursuits with any of those classes whose ingenuity or whose labours benefit society; nor by any of those rapid changes through which their treasure passes is there anything produced by which community is indemnified.

The situation of gamblers with respect to each other is as singular and unnatural as their situation with respect to the rest of mankind. Here, again, the order of nature is reversed, the constitution of God is subverted, and an association is formed, not for mutual benefit, but for acknowledged mutual injury. Precisely as much as the one gains, the other loses. No equivalent is given, none is received. The property indeed changes hands, but its quality is not improved, its amount is not augmented.

In the mean time, the one who loses is a profligate, who throws away, without any requital, the property he possesses. The one who gains is a ruffian, who pounces like a vulture on property which he possesses not, and which he has acquired no right to possess; while both are useless members of society — mere excrescences on the body politic. Worse than this, they are a nuisance; like leeches on the body of some mighty and vigorous animal, which, though they suck their aliment from its blood, contribute nothing to its nourishment. No matter how numerous these vagabonds (for I will not call them by a more reputable name) may be in any community; no matter how long they may live, or how assiduously they may prosecute their vocation. No monument of good, the product of that vocation, will remain behind them. They will be remembered only by the waste they have commited or the injury they have done; while, with respect to all the useful purposes of being, it will be as if they had never been.

And is there no guilt in such an application of property as this? Did Almighty God place mankind here for an occupation so mean? Did he bestow on them treasures for an end so ignoble? If Jesus Christ condemned to outer darkness that unprofitable servant who, having wrapped his talent in a napkin only, buried it in the earth, what think you will be his sentence on the profligate, who, having staked and lost his all, goes from the gaming-table, a self-created pauper, to the judgment-seat. Nor will the Judge less scrupulously require an account of the cents you have for amusement put down at piquet, than he would had you played away at brag the entire amount of the shekel of the sanctuary.

But you do not mean to gamble nor to advocate it. I know you do not. But I also know, if you play at all, you will ultimately do both. It is but a line that separates between innocence and sin. Whoever fearlessly approaches this line will soon have crossed it. To keep at a distance, therefore, is the part of wisdom. No man ever made up his mind to consign to perdition his soul at once. No man ever entered the known avenues which conduct to such an end with a firm and undaunted step. The brink of ruin is approached with caution, and by imperceptible degrees; and the wretch who now stands fearlessly scoffing there, but yesterday had shrunk back from the awful cliff with trembling. Do you wish for illustration? The profligate's unwritten history will furnish it. How inoffensive its commencement, how sudden and how frightful its catastrophe! Let us review his life. He commences with play; but it is only for amusement. Next he hazards a trifle to give interest, and is surprised when he finds himself a gainer by the hazard. He then ventures, not without misgivings, on a deeper stake. That stake he loses. The loss and the guilt oppress him. He drinks to revive his spirits. His spirits revived, he stakes to retrieve his fortune. Again he is unsuccessful, and again his spirits flag, and again the inebriating cup revives them. Ere he is aware of it, he has become a drunkard; he has also become a bankrupt. Resource fails him. His fortune is gone; his character is gone; his tenderness of conscience is gone. God has withdrawn his spirit from him. The demon of despair takes possession of his bosom; reason deserts him. He becomes a maniac; the pistol or the poniard closes the scene; and with a shriek he plunges, unwept and forgotten, into—hell.

But there are other lights in which this subject should be viewed. The proper aliment of the body is ascertained by its effects. Whatever is nutritious is selected; whatever is poisonous, avoided. Let a man of common prudence perceive the deleterious effects of any fruit, however fair to the eye, however sweet to the taste; let him perceive these effects in the haggard countenances and swollen limbs of those who have been partaking of it, and, although he may not be able to discover wherein its poisonous nature consists, he admits that it is poisonous, and shrinks from participating in a repast in which some secret venom lurks, that has proved fatal to many, and injurious to most who have hitherto tasted it. Why should not the same circumspection be used with respect to the aliment of the mind? It undoubtedly should. But gaming presents even a stronger case than the one we have supposed; for not only the fact, but the reason of it is obvious; so that we may repeat what has been already said of games of hazard: *they impart little or no expansion or vigour to the mind; and their influence on the affections, and passions, and heart is deleterious.*

When I affirm *that these games impart little or no expansion or vigour to the mind,* I do not mean to be understood that they are or can be performed entirely without intellection. It is conceded that the silliest game requires some understanding, and that to play at it is above the capacity of an oyster, or even of an ox, or of an ape. It is conceded, too, that games of every sort require some study; the most of them, however, require but little; and, after the few first efforts, the intellectual condition of the gamester, so far as his occupation is concerned, is but one degree removed from that of the dray-horse buckled to his harness, and treading over from day to day, and from night to night, the same dull track, as he turns a machine which some mind of a higher order has invented. So very humble is this species of occupation; so very limited the sphere in which it allows the mind to operate, that, if any individual were to remain through the term of his existence mute and motionless—in the winter state of the Norwegian bear—his intellectual career would be about as splendid, and his attainments in knowledge about as great as they would were he to commence play at childhood, and continue on at whist or loo through eternity. For, though the latter state of being presupposes some exercise of the mental facul ties, it is so little, so low, and so uniform, that, if the result be not literally *nothing,* it approaches nearer to it than the result of any other state of being to which an intelligent creature can be doomed short of absolute inanity or death.

How unlike in its effect must be this unmeaning shuffle of cards, this eternal gazing on the party-coloured surface of a few small pieces of pasteboard, where nothing but spades, and hearts, and diamonds, and clubs, over and over again, every hour of the day, every hour of the night, meet the sleepless eye of the vacant beholder: how unlike must be the effect of this pitiful employment, continued for fifty or for seventy years, to that which would have been produced on the same mind in the same period by following the track of Newton to those sublime results, whither he has led the way, in the regions of abstraction; by communing with the soul of Bacon, deducing from individual facts the universal laws of the material universe ; or by mounting with Herschel to the Atheneum of the firmament, and there learning, direct from the volume of the stars, the science of astronomy? How unlike to that which would have been produced in the same period by ranging with Paley through the department of morals ; by soaring with Hervey on the wing of devotion ; or even by tracing the footsteps of Tooke amid the mazes of philology?

Card-playing has not even the merit of the common chit-chat of the tea-table. Here there is some scope for reason, some for the play of fancy, some occasion for mental effort, some tendency to habits of quick association, in attack, in repartee, and in the various turns resorted to for keeping up and enlivening conversation. Much less has it the merit of higher and more rational discourse, of music, of painting, or of reading.

Indeed, if an occupation were demanded for the express purpose of perverting the human intellect; for humbling, and degrading, and narrowing, I had almost said annihilating, the soul of man, one more effectual could not well be devised than the gamester has already devised and resorted to. The father and mother of a family, who, instead of assembling their children in the reading-room or conducting them to the altar, seat them night after night beside themselves at the gaming-table, do, so far as this part of their domestic economy is concerned, contribute not only to quench their piety, but also to extinguish their intellect, and convert them into automatons, living mummies, the mere mechanical members of a domestic gambling-machine, which, though but little soul is necessary, requires a number of human hands to work it; and if, under such a blighting culture, they do not degenerate into a state of mere mechanical existence, and, gradually losing their reason, their taste, and their fancy, become incapable of conversation, the fortunate parents may thank the schoolhouse, the church, the library, the society of friends, or some other and less wretched part of their own defective system for preventing so frightful a consummation.

Such, young gentlemen, are the morbid and degrading effects of play on the human intellect. But intelligence constitutes no inconsiderable part of the glory of man; a glory which, unless eclipsed by crime, increases as intelligence increases. Knowledge is desirable with reference to this world, but principally so with reference to the next. Not that philosophy, or language, or mathematics will certainly be pursued in heaven; but because the pursuit of them on earth gradually communicates that quickness of perception, that acumen, which, as it increases, approximates towards the sublime and sudden intuition of celestial intelligences, and which cannot fail to render more splendid the commencement and the progression of man's interminable career.

But, while gaming leaves the mind to languish, it produces its full effect *on the passions and on the heart*. Here, however, the effect is positively deleterious. None of the sweet and amiable sympathies are called into action at the card-table. No throb of ingenuous and philanthropic feeling is excited by this detestable expedient for killing time, as it is called; and it is rightly so called, for many a murdered hour will witness at the day of judgment against that fashionable idler who divides her time between her toilet and the card-table, no less than against the profligate, hackneyed in the ways of sin, and steeped in all the filth and debauchery connected with gambling. But it is only amid the filth and debauchery connected with gambling that the full effects of card-playing on the passions and on the heart of man are seen.

Here the mutual amity that elsewhere subsists ceases; paternal affection ceases; even that community of feeling which piracy excites, and which binds the very banditti together, has no room to operate; for at this inhospitable board every man's interest clashes with every other man's interest, and every man's hand is literally against every man.

The love of mastery and the love of money are the purest motives of which the gamester is susceptible. And even the love of mastery loses all its nobleness, and degenerates into the love of lucre, which ultimately predominates, and becomes the ruling passion.

Avarice is always base; but the gamester's avarice is doubly so. It is avarice unmixed with any ingredient of magnanimity or mercy. Avarice that wears not even the guise of public spirit; that claims not even the meager praise of hoarding up its own hard earnings. On the contrary, it is an avarice that wholly feeds upon the losses, and only delights itself with the miseries of others; an avarice that eyes with covetous desire whatever is not individually its own; that crouches to throw its clutches over that booty by which its comrades are enriched; an avarice, in short, that stoops to rob a traveller, that sponges a guest, and that would filch the very dust from the pocket of a friend.

But, though avarice predominates, other related passions are called into action. The bosom that was once serene and tranquil becomes habitually perturbed. Envy rankles, jealousy corrodes, anger rages, and hope and fear alternately convulse the system. The mildest disposition grows morose; the sweetest temper becomes fierce and fiery, and all the once amiable features of the heart assume a malignant aspect. Features of the *heart* did I say? Pardon my mistake. The finished gambler has no heart. Though his intellect may not be, though his soul may not be, his heart is quite annihilated.

Thus habitual gambling consummates what habitual play commences. Sometimes its deadening influence prevails even over female virtue, eclipsing all the loveliness and benumbing all the sensibility of woman. In every circle where cards form the bond of union, frivolity and heartlessness become alike characteristics of the mother and the daughter; devotion ceases; domestic care is shaken off, and the dearest friends, even before their burial, are consigned to oblivion.

This is not exaggeration. I appeal to fact. Madame du Deffand was certainly not among the least accomplished or the least interesting females who received and imparted that exquisite tone of feeling that pervaded the most fashionable society of modern Paris. And yet it is recorded of her, in the correspondence of the Baron de Grimm, whose veracity will not be questioned, that, immediately after the death of her old and intimate friend and admirer, M. de Ponte de Vesle, this celebrated lady attended a great supper in the neighbourhood; and as it was known that she made it a point of honour to be accompanied by him, the catastrophe was generally suspected. She mentioned it, however, herself, immediately after entering; adding, that it was lucky he had gone off so early in the evening, as she might otherwise have been prevented from appearing. She then sat down to table, and made a very hearty and merry meal.

Afterward, when Madame de Chatelet died, Madame du Deffand testified her grief for the most intimate of all her female acquaintances by circulating, the very next morning, throughout Paris, the most libellous and venomous attack on her person, her understanding, and her morals.

This utter heartlessness, this entire extinction of native feeling, was not peculiar to Madame du Deffand; it pervaded that accomplished and fashionable circle in which she moved. Hence she herself, in turn, experienced the same kind of sympathy; and her memory was consigned to the same instantaneous oblivion. During her last illness, three of her dearest friends used to come and play cards every night by the side of her couch; and she choosing to die in the middle of a very interesting game, they quietly played it out, and settled their accounts before leaving the apartment.*

I do not say that such are the uniform, but I do say that such are the natural and legitimate effects of gaming on the female character. The love of play is a demon, which only takes possession as it kills the heart. But, if such is the effect of gaming on the one sex, what must be its effect upon the other? Will nature long survive in bosoms invaded not by gaming only, but also by debauchery and drunkenness, those sister furies which hell has let loose, to cut off our young men from without, and our children from the streets? No, it will not. As we have said, the finished gambler has no heart. The club with which he herds would meet though all its members were in mourning. They would meet though their place of rendezvous were the chamber of the dying; they would meet though it were an apartment in the charnel-house. Not even the death of kindred can affect the gambler. He would play upon his brother's coffin; he would play upon his father's sepulchre.

Yonder see that wretch, prematurely old in infirmity as well as sin. He is the father of a family. The mother of his children, lovely in her tears, strives by the tenderest assiduities to restore his

* See Quarterly Review.

health, and with it to restore his temperance, his love of home, and the long-lost charms of domestic life. She pursues him by her kindness and her entreaties to his haunts of vice; she reminds him of his children; she tells him of their virtues, of their sorrows, of their wants, and she adjures him, by the love of them and by the love of God, to repent and to return. Vain attempt! She might as well adjure the whirlwind; she might as well entreat the tiger.

The brute has no feeling left. He turns upon her in the spirit of the demons with which he is possessed. He curses his children and her who bare them; and, as he prosecutes his game, he fills the intervals with imprecations on himself—with imprecations on his Maker—imprecations borrowed from the dialect of devils, and uttered with a tone that befits only the organs of the damned! And yet in this monster there once dwelt the spirit of a man. He had talents, he had honour, he had even faith. He might have adorned the senate, the bar, the altar. But, alas! his was a faith that saveth not. The gaming-table has robbed him of it, and of all things else that is worth possessing. What a frightful change of character! What a tremendous wreck is the soul of man in ruins!

Return, disconsolate mother, to thy dwelling, and be submissive; thou shalt be a widow, and thy children fatherless. Farther effort will be useless: the reformation of thy partner is impossible. God has forsaken him; nor will good angels weep or watch over him any more.

M

Against this fashionable amusement, so subversive of virtue, so productive of guilt, so inseparable from misery, I adjure you to bear, at all times and on all occasions, a decisive testimony. And I do this, not only that you may escape destruction yourselves, but also that you may not be the occasion of others' destruction. What more shall I say? For time would fail me to point out all the dangers that will attend your steps, or to enumerate all the temptations that will assail your virtue. I can only, therefore, in closing this address, repeat to each of you that summary but solemn admonition which the royal preacher once delivered to the youth of Israel: *Rejoice, oh young man, in thy youth, and let thy heart cheer thee in the days of thy youth, and walk in the ways of thine heart, and in the sight of thine eyes; but know thou that for all these things God will bring thee into judgment.*

Creator of our souls, Father of the spirits of all living, grant to our youth wisdom, and to thy name shall be the glory in Christ. AMEN.

IX.

DELIVERED JULY 26, 1815.

Skeptical Notions in regard to the Providence of God, and his retributive Justice.—The condition of the Virtuous and Vicious in this World affords no argument against the position that God will reward the one and punish the other.—A future State of Existence is certain, and must be taken into account in judging of the Character and Designs of God.—The inward Peace enjoyed by the Virtuous, and the Trouble and Remorse experienced by the Vicious, indications of God's Moral Government.—The Trials of the Righteous intended to exalt and purify their Character.—Consolations of the Righteous in the view of Death, and the Happiness that awaits them in a future State of Being.]

YOUNG gentlemen, the God of righteousness is the friend of happiness. Hence man's duty and his interest are inseparable. This has sometimes been doubted, sometimes even explicitly denied. In remote antiquity there lived those who said, "*It is in vain to serve God; and what profit is it that we have kept his ordinances?*"

To adopt this gloomy hypothesis, so fatal to the eternal interests of mankind, was not peculiar to those who lived in remote antiquity. Now, as formerly, there are profane men, who, with respect to all the rewards of virtue, are utter skeptics. Both experience and observation are appealed to; and, as if this transitory life were the whole of man, it is triumphantly asserted, *That the proud are happy; that those who work wickedness are set up, and those who tempt God are delivered.*

Nor is it profane men only who have misconstrued, and who still misconstrue, on this article, the ways of Providence. The saint of Uz, the psalmist of Israel, and even Solomon himself, than whom a wiser prince has not lived, were embarrassed at the seeming prosperity of the wicked.

A bewildering obscurity does indeed hang over this part of the Divine Economy. To a short-sighted and superficial observer, that balance in which the actions of men are weighed seems to be held with an equal hand. To say the least, it is not always and at every stage of being, apparent that God regards the righteous more than the wicked; and because it is not always apparent, men of perverse minds presumptuously infer that he does not.

The Divine care, say they, if indeed there be any Divine care, is extended alike to all. No partiality is discoverable in the distribution of His most public and important gifts. Air, and water, and sunshine are as free as they are abundant. Does food statedly nourish, and sleep refresh the pious? So they do the impious. The flocks of the latter are as vigorous, their pastures are as green, and their husbandry as productive as those of the former. No flower withers as the sinner plucks it; the earth sinks not beneath his unhallowed tread, nor does the sun avert his beams from his heaven-directed eye.

If God be the rewarder of virtue, why do transgressors live? And yet they do live: more than this, they prosper. Those who are hampered by the restraints of duty are overthrown by them; and through crimes and blood they force their way to place and power. His saints cry to him, but he hears them not: they present their claim, but it is disregarded. Rags cover them, and they are fed with the bread of bitterness: a conclusive evidence that there is no God, or that virtue is of little estimation in his sight.

Thus argue the enemies of religion. But let no young adventurer, no aspiring candidate for glory, be misguided by it. All that has been said or that can be said in favour of a theory so humiliating to man, so derogatory to God, is mere sophistry: sophistry disguised, indeed, but gross and palpable.

Because the reward of virtue is not in every instance simultaneous with the act, does it follow that virtue has no reward? Waits not the husbandman for the fruits of his industry until the harvest? And yet who pretends that his care and labour are thrown away? No one. On the contrary, all say, as he goes forth weeping to scatter the precious seed, *Doubtless he will return rejoicing, bearing his sheaves with him.* Can that be true where religion is concerned, that would be false with respect to all things else?

Let the rash theorist remember that he has seen but a very small part of man's existence, and that part, too, which is only inceptive and preparatory. Conclusions drawn from a part to the whole are always defective, and in this instance may prove as fatal as fallacious. Be it remembered that the race must be finished ere the prize is won; that the victory must be achieved before it can be expected that the crown should be placed on the victor's brow.

The unjust steward, as well as the just, retained his talent till the day of reckoning.

It is not the equivocal fact of having been intrusted with a few pieces of money, or with a spot of earth a little larger than others, but the retribution that shall follow the use or abuse of that trust, which will convey to the universe the evidence of God's eternal and impartial justice. To ascertain whether religion be advantageous or not, something more than the fugitive joys and sorrows of this illusive world must be considered. Is what we see the whole of being, or is there an after scene? If so, what is its duration, what its character? And will that which precedes give a complexion to that which follows? These are questions which awaken a solemn interest, and questions, too, which must be answered before it is possible to pronounce, with even a shadow of truth, upon the destiny of man.

True, the ultimate reward of virtue is at present a matter of faith and not of sight; but of faith resting on high and responsible authority. All the phenomena of nature, all the economy of Providence, all the forebodings of the heart of man, intimate, what the Scriptures declare, *That after death comes the judgment.* The impious may sneer, the skeptic may doubt, and guess, and conjecture; but dare even he, in the face of all this evidence, affirm that he *knows* that this is not the case? And if he dare not, then, even the skeptic being judge, the interests of virtue may be secure, and the rapturous anticipations of Saul of Tarsus well founded, who, in the near approach of death, triumphantly exclaimed, *I have fought the good fight!* And should the rapturous anticipation of Saul of Tarsus be well founded, how will stand the account? Ah, hearer! when weighed in the balance of the sanctuary, bonds, and stripes, and imprisonment are only light afflictions, unworthy to be put in competition with that exceeding and eternal weight of glory hereafter to be revealed.

But, eternity apart, it is not true that religion has no reward; and the arrogant assumption that it has not, to whatever period of existence it be limited, or to whatever part of God's creation it be applied, is as false in fact as it is impious in theory. Not that its heaven-approved possessor is uniformly, or even usually signalized by what the sensual call prosperity. And what though he is not? Is he an animal merely, that his health and thrift should be estimated by the limits or the luxuriance of the pasture in which he ranges, or by the quantity of fodder that is thrown before him by his keeper? In testing his well-being, the things that concern the body are of small account. Here, as elsewhere,

"The mind's the measure of the man."

Food and raiment, to an incarnate spirit, are desirable; but they are not the only things that are so. To such a spirit, the precious metals have their value; but there are other gifts within the compass of God's almightiness still more valuable than the precious metals. So David, having made the experiment, decided; so Solomon, having made the experiment, decided. Not all the honours royalty could confer, not all the luxuries that affluence could procure, furnished, in their impartial estimation, so pure or so perfect a pleasure as that which is conveyed to the heart through the consecrated channel of devotion : nor is devotion the only channel of delight, refined and exquisite.

Virtue, in all its acts, carries with it a reward. In the exercise of conscious rectitude, in the performance of charitable offices, in feeding the poor, in ministering to the sick, in consoling the mourner, and in guiding inquiring souls in the way to heaven, there is a blessedness so holy, so divine, that the gross delights of sensuality, and the corrosive joys of avarice and ambition, are in comparison only disguised misery.

There is much illusion in that apparent glory which wealth and honour seem to throw around the sinner. None but a novice will estimate a man's happiness by the extent of his possessions. Solomon is not the only one who has seen *riches kept for the owners thereof to their hurt.* What were crowns and kingdoms worth, to be held by such a tenure? And yet by such a tenure many an envied profligate holds whatever of wealth and honour he possesses. In vain he strives to conceal his misery. He smiles and smiles, but is still accursed.

This is one of the ways in which God, in his inscrutable providence, and notwithstanding appearances to the contrary, distinguishes the righteous from the wicked. To the former, though he give sparingly, he gives in mercy, and it becomes a double blessing. To the latter he gives bountifully; but he gives in wrath, and it proves a curse. Hence the favourites of the world are for ever repining at their lot. And well they may repine at it; for every addition to unsanctified wealth only corrodes the heart with new cares, and agitates the bosom with new desires. This is no exaggeration. I appeal to fact. Long and often has the experiment been tried. Among those prayerless sinners whom so many account happy, wealth has been distributed. But with what effect? Has ambition anywhere been satisfied? Or has avarice ever been heard to say it is enough? No, never. On the contrary, both, hungry as the grave, cry, Give, give. And God does give. But still the cry is repeated, and will continue to be repeated till death stifles it; for it is prompted by an appetite that is never satiated, and by a thirst that is never quenched.

Selfishness may possess the world, but benevolence alone can enjoy it. *Better is a dry morsel with contentment, than a house full of sacrifices with strife.* It is not the flocks that a man numbers, the slaves he commands, or the domains which he calls his own; it is not the palace he inhabits, the crown on his head, or the sceptre in his hand, but the amount of blessedness he derives from them, that is to be taken into the account in determining whether mercy or vengeance be the predominant feature of his lot. The devout eye, in only beholding the fields, and groves, and gardens which display so many beauties around some licentious court or inhospitable mansion, often derives more happiness from the scene than it ever conveys to its graceless and haughty owner.

There is an obscuring and deadening influence in sin. It destroys the sensibility; it perverts the taste; and it sheds over the intellectual and moral eye a sombrous and sickly light, in which heaven, and earth, and nature, and art, appear alike dim and gloryless. No Providence is seen; no parent's love is recognised; no pulse of joy, no throb of gratitude is felt. A dismal *ennui* consumes the solitary hour, and even the social revel is but heartless affectation and mimic mirth. Oh God! it is by prosperity that thou dost inflict upon the wicked thy strange vengeance. Their bane is the mercies which they receive, but acknowledge not; and, not acknowledging them, they cease to be mercies. It was ordained of old that it should be so; and so it is that virtue enjoys more even of this world in rags and cottages, than does vice in robes and courts; and it were better, heaven and hell out of the question, to subsist like Lazarus on crumbs sweetened by submission, than to revel at luxurious banquets with Dives and his faithless guests.

But neither to saints nor sinners is life made up of banquets. This world presents not a uniform, but a mixed scene. Light and shade are blended. And if to all there are some days of sunshine and joy, so to all there are some of darkness and wo. These latter must be subtracted, and the balance of pains and pleasures struck, before we can pronounce with safety on the comparative blessedness of the righteous and the wicked. Though the former were less affluent and honoured, and more despised and trampled on than they are, it would not follow that they are less happy or less favoured of God on that account. Are their afflictions great? So also, and more abundantly, may be their consolations. I am aware that the history of godliness is a history filled with objects of terror; and that many of its scenes are drawn in characters of blood. I am aware that persecution has often prepared her racks and kindled her fires; that men of the purest virtue and of the holiest faith have been seen to pine in dungeons and to wander in exile. But neither dungeons nor exile were to them so great an evil as their persecutors had imagined. Not sighs, but songs, were heard from that prison where Paul and Silas were confined. As joyous as wakeful, at midnight, when deliverance came, it found them praying and singing psalms. Nor were Paul and Silas the only saints that have rejoiced in tribulation. Usually, if not uniformly, the confessor's faith has nobly supported him; nor has the martyr's heart been broken by the stroke that felled his body. And how should the martyr's heart be broken by the stroke that felled his body? The afflictions of the righteous differ essentially in their nature and in their design from those of the wicked, to whom the arm of the Almighty is a scourge, and who, when the world forsakes them, have no deliverer. To the one the cup of sorrow is salutary and mingled with mercy; to the other it is deleterious and overflows with wrath.

The great refiner subjects both the precious metal and the vile to the action of fire, but for very different purposes. It is to purify the one, it is to consume the other; and his purposes are accomplished. The one *is* consumed, the other purified.

Often have the sublimest virtues, the holiest affections been evolved under the influence of sorrow. How much has this globe of earth risen in importance; how much has the race of man been exalted; how much has the universe gained of goodness and glory, by the afflictions through which the saints have been called to pass? Ah! had the trial of virtue been dispensed with, and had there been no such thing in the economy of Providence as tribulation to the righteous, the examples of Abraham, and Moses, and David would have been lost; the examples of the apostles and of the martyrs would have been lost; the field of moral beauty narrowed and sullied, and the record of the tenderest incidents stricken from the history of the world. What good man, what friend of God and of righteousness would have been willing, had the question been submitted to his choice, to purchase temporal ease and affluence by such a sacrifice? No one. It is good for the inhabitants of the earth; it is good for the inhabitants of heaven; it is good for the saints themselves, that they have been afflicted. And we may consecrate, therefore, and apply, without the same incertitude, the words which the exiled Æneas addressed to his desponding followers:

"O passi graviora! dabit Deus his quoque finem.
———— revocate animos, mœstumque timorem
Mittite; forsan et hæc olim meminisse juvabit."

But what crowns the argument, so far as earth and time are concerned, is this: *that virtue, which in affliction enjoys greater consolation, in death suffers less misery.*

Whatever wealth and honour may be worth to the living, they are nothing to the dead, nothing even to the dying! That decisive change sunders all the ties that bind a mortal to the world. The hour of dissolution is emphatically the hour of trial. Then, more than at any other period, the affrighted, agonized victim feels dependance—needs assistance; and if there be anything of power to give this—anything of power to abate the horrors and cheer the darkness of the death-scene, the bestowment of *that*, more than any other token within the gift of Providence, ascertains who they are among the dwellers on the earth whom the God of Heaven delights to favour and to honour. There is *that* which has power to do this. The calm and tranquil, the rapturous and triumphant death of thousands prove it.

The hope of eternal life, the sweet assurance of forgiven sin, the smile of redeeming mercy, the sight of heaven breaking on the soul through the twilight of that long, dismal night, of which death seems but the commencement—there is something so precious, so consoling, so divine in such an exit from the world, that, were it attainable only by a life of perpetual martyrdom, I should still devoutly pray to God, *Let me, even on such terms, die the death of the righteous, and let my last end be like his.* Yes, even on such terms I should account the good man blessed. Yes, even on such terms I should covet the confessor's dungeon, I should covet the martyr's stake

Ah! beloved pupils, we may here, and at the moment of separation, discuss the comparative advantages of vice and virtue; but it is not here that we can feel the full force of that discussion. You will not know how much religion profiteth till you have left this seat of science, till you have visited the abodes of sorrow, till you have stood by the pillow of the dying. What am I saying? You will not know this till you have made the grand decisive experiment yourselves; explored the grave in person, and from the dread solemnities of the judgment-day received instruction. Were the secrets of that great day made manifest—and made manifest they shortly will be—there would exist but one opinion on this subject. Revelation, even now, gives an anticipated view of those scenes, both of transport and of terror, which the natural eye sees not. In its light I beseech, I adjure you; and, ere you enter on the world, make up your mind, and with God, and heaven, and hell, and judgment, and eternity before your eyes, decide for yourselves, whether it be not better to suffer affliction with the people of God, than to enjoy the delusive, degrading, damning pleasures of sin for a season; and as you decide, so act. Time is short, eternity is at stake, and the moments are on the wing that will decide your fate for ever.

Oh, God! look down with pitying eye on this group of beings now to be dispersed; and, wheresoever they may wander, so guide their inexperienced steps that they may meet in heaven. Do this for the Redeemer's sake, and to thy great name shall be the glory.

X.

DELIVERED ON SUNDAY EVENING BEFORE COMMENCEMENT, 1814.

[Instability of all earthly Things.—Motives to early Piety.—Filial Love and Gratitude.—Parental Affection.—Anxiety of Parents to promote the Happiness of their Children.—Christian Parents.—Instructions of Solomon.—Early Piety interesting in itself.—Leads to Happiness.—Joy of Christian Parents in pious Children, in Life and in Death.—Example of a pious Child.—The Good on Earth and the Angels in Heaven rejoice over Souls converted from Sin to Righteousness.—Union of Parents and Children in Heaven.]

THERE is something awfully impressive in the rapid and perpetual flow of time. To eternity this stream is ever tending, like a river to the ocean. Individuals, families, nations float upon its surface, and are borne away and lost in that absorbing gulf, whose dimensions no eye can measure, and on whose misty surface no wreck is seen.

Nothing here is stable, nothing permanent. The noblest specimens of genius, the proudest monuments of art fade, decay, and disappear.

Even society itself continues only by succession. The species is preserved, but the individual perishes. The relations of parent and child, of brother and sister, of neighbour and friend, are indeed perpetual. Not so the persons who sustain those relations. They were, but they are seen no more! Transient as the cloud on which the sunbeam of the morning played has been the glory of the preceding age, nor will that of the present or of the following be more abiding. All the virtue and talents, all the goodness and greatness that now exalt and adorn society, will soon vanish from the sight, nor leave a trace behind.

To a reflecting mind there is something deeply affecting in this idea. Life is naturally dear to us; we cling instinctively to the passing scene; but we cannot even check, much less arrest its flight and ensure its perpetuity. For us a shroud is weaving, for us the bed of death is spread. The grave waits to receive our ashes, and the church bell will soon have tolled our funeral knell. As individuals, we must die, nor can we continue to live upon the earth except in our successors. That, indeed, is only an ideal life; but still the thought of it is precious.

Were the race of men to become extinct when we ourselves expire, the darkness of death would appear still more dark; more desolate the desolation of the tomb. Standing on the verge of that abyss which has swallowed up our ancestors, and in which we ourselves are about to be ingulfed, how grateful is the idea that to us also there will be successors; and that whatever of learning, of virtue, and of piety the living world possesses, will survive us, and be perpetuated by those who will constitute posterity.

We ourselves must quit this theatre of action and of interest. We must resign our places of responsibility and of usefulness. The time will soon have arrived when, for our friends, for our country, for the church, for the world, we can do nothing more. Both the opportunity and the ability of effecting good and of effecting evil will be transferred to other hands. How solicitous should we be, then, to improve the virtues, to correct the vices, and to fix the habits of those to whom, under God, are to be intrusted the future destinies of mankind?

The motives to early piety are too numerous to be presented in an address like this. In the most elaborate discussion a selection would be necessary; and even then, on the topics selected much would remain unsaid. Among these motives is *filial gratitude*, on which I am about to insist this evening.

The sympathies subsisting between parents and children are reciprocal, and in nothing are the wisdom and goodness of God more manifest than in the bestowment of those sympathies, which, like so many ligaments, bind in perpetual amity those groups of beings, who, dwelling beneath the same roof, constitute the family.

The parent naturally commiserates his infant child; the child early feels a glow of affection towards his provident and attentive parent; these mutual sympathies are strengthened by indulgence; and from their habitual exercise springs no inconsiderable part of the bliss of life. Cold and comfortless indeed would human intercourse become, if paternal, filial, and fraternal affection were suspended. Not all the pomp and pageantry of courts, not all the formal and studied courtesies of fashion, could compensate for the loss of that heaven-appointed solace, *domestic friendship*. Beneath the paternal roof disguise is banished, and heart meets heart in amity: here nature operates, and there, and only there, man speaks and acts without dissimulation.

Partial, however, would be our view of Providence, did we consider these sympathies as if implanted merely to solace human misery and sweeten human intercourse. True, indeed, they do serve to tranquillize our passions, to soften our asperity, and to compensate at home for that tasteless, shallow courtesy practised on us abroad with unmeaning assiduity by those trained to the deceptive arts of a faithless, fashionable world.

But they have still a higher office. Time is the commencement of eternity. *To the due performance of these duties, filial and parental sympathies are alike conducive.* The one sweetens all the cares and softens all the sorrows incident to the nurturing of children. More than this: it secures, or, at least, tends to secure the exercise of those cares and the patient endurance of those sorrows. That man should not desert his infant offspring like the ostrich, that lays and forsakes her eggs upon the sand, his Creator has bound him to that offspring by ties which he cannot sunder without doing violence to his nature and ceasing to be man. The other sweetens submission, and renders even a state of tutelage not only supportable, but pleasant. More than this: love to parents often prompts to the endurance of restraints, to the practice of virtues, and to the formation of correct habits at a period when, to a thoughtless youth, no other motive would be availing. To this cause may be attributed much of that decency and decorum of manners which are usually observable in well-regulated families even among children naturally the most frivolous and wayward.

But the Christian moralist is not satisfied with mere decency and decorum. It behooves him, therefore, to co-operate with the Deity in his benevolent intentions; and, seizing on juvenile tenderness and filial affection, to endeavour to direct their influence to the accomplishment of the high purposes of revealed religion. When, amid the levity and thoughtlessness of youth, other motives prove unavailing, it becomes him to touch that string which for ever vibrates, and to constrain, if it be possible to constrain, to the love of God by the love of parents. And why may it not be possible? Why may not affection, as well as any other natural endowment, be sanctified; and thus the whole heart, through this as a medium of operation, by the efficiency of the spirit, be regenerated unto righteousness?

Nothing on earth is dearer to a parent than the happiness of his children; nor is anything more grateful to a dutiful child than to contribute to a parent's joy. And to a Christian parent, what joy can be compared to that which springs from seeing his children progressive in the path of righteousness, and adorning, by deeds of early faith and charity, the doctrines of God their Saviour?

To have been born and educated in a Christian land is the honour and privilege of the youth I now address. Some of you, I trust, have the still higher honour of being descended from parents who are Christians indeed: parents who bore you in their arms to the altar of your God in infancy, imploring on you his paternal benediction; and who, during your riper years, have never ceased to intercede in your behalf, when presenting their evening and morning supplication before the mercy seat: parents whose waking hours have been occupied with your wants, and in whose very dreams has mingled concern for your salvation.

Long as you may have been ungrateful to God, to your parents you have never ceased to be grateful. Though cold and callous to the love of Jesus, your hearts are yet susceptible of filial love. Though grace has never quickened you, nature has not yet become extinct. Dear is the name of parent, dear a father's counsel, dear a mother's care. In their welfare you feel an interest. You wish them blessed : wish that the evening of their days may be serene and cloudless, and that their gray hairs may ultimately descend, not with sorrow, but with joy to the grave. And do you really and from your hearts desire this? Does the idea of a provident father, of a vigilant and tender mother, excite aught of interest in your bosoms? Then, by the kindness they have manifested, by the anxieties they have felt and still feel, I adjure you to do homage to the Saviour whom they honour, and consecrate the first years of your being to the God whom they serve.

Solomon, that sagacious king of Israel, urges this motive with force and frequency. The relation which subsists between a parent and a child is introduced repeatedly, to give effect to those lessons of instruction imbodied in his proverbs. When the rising generation are addressed, the majesty of the king is merged in the tenderness of the parent. Then, not the monarch, but the father speaks: and how tender and affecting are his words.

My son, hear the instruction of a father, and forsake not the law of thy mother. My son, if sinners entice thee, consent thou not. Hear, ye children, the instruction of a father; for I give you good counsel, forsake not my law. He urges the interest which parents take in the well-being of their children, and describes in expressive terms the joy which their virtues excite, and the anguish which their vices occasion. *A wise son,* he says, *maketh a glad father; but a foolish son is the heaviness of his mother.* The same idea is elsewhere expressed, and in terms equally significant and appropriate. *Children's children are the crown of old men, and the glory of children are their fathers; but a foolish son is grief unto his father, and bitterness to her that bare him.*

In whatever situation we contemplate the parent and the child, the truth of the positions assumed by Solomon will be apparent. IN LIFE and IN DEATH, with equal justice may it be said that A WISE SON MAKETH A GLAD FATHER.

IN LIFE.—EARLY PIETY IS IN ITSELF AN OBJECT OF INTEREST. What a delightful spectacle is a family of docile and dutiful children living in amity; increasing in knowledge and in virtue as they increase in stature, and destined, after having adorned the earth, to be transplanted to the heavens. *Behold how good and how pleasant a thing it is for brethren to dwell together in unity; it is as the dew of Hermon, and as the dew that descendeth upon the mountains of Zion.*

EARLY PIETY IS IN ITS EFFECTS CONDUCIVE TO

HAPPINESS. *The work of righteousness shall be peace, and the effect of righteousness, quietness and assurance for ever,* saith Isaiah; a prediction verified by the experience of every Christian family in which charity is the bond of union; in which reciprocal affection reigns, and filial and fraternal duties are alike the business and the delight of life. How worthy of emulation is the condition of such a family! How pre-eminently blessed that parent whom God has placed at the head of it! All his joys are heightened, all his pains mitigated, and the most wearisome hours of his life are beguiled by the affection, the constancy, the cheerfulness, and the piety of those around him. Time thus occupied passes pleasantly away, and even eternity itself appears more rapturous in the contemplation, being heightened by the prospect not only of his own salvation, but that of his household.

To the parent thus highly favoured of the Lord, this is the consummation of sublunary joy. It is a joy already tinctured with the spirit of the heavens, and partaking of the tranquillity of the life to come. Even desire itself has ceased, because it is satisfied. It was not that his children might shine in honour or riot in wealth that he nurtured them with so much care, and supplicated for them with so much earnestness. Their salvation, more than any other concern, occupied his mind and pressed on his heart. Their salvation God has granted; of which their faith, and patience, and their labours of love are at once an evidence and a pledge. And this having been granted, desire ceases, and the cup of domestic bliss is full. Desire ceases because its chief object is obtained; and because, moreover, the Christian parent knows, that to them who have sought first the kingdom of God and his righteousness, all necessary good will be added thereunto. He knows that, whether his offspring, on whom such early grace has been bestowed, are destined to live in the obscurity of cottages or in the splendour of courts; whether they are appointed to turn the furrows of the field or to labour in the details of the workshop; whether they shall be called to preside in the counsels of the senate chamber, to fight the battles of their country in the field, or to defend, at the stake or on the scaffold, the faith once delivered to the saints, everywhere the God whom they have chosen and whom they serve will be with them, and qualify them for the duties, whether of action or of suffering, which, in their passage to glory, they shall be required to perform.

IN DEATH, a wise son maketh a glad father: a truth equally obvious, whether we consider the death of the *parent* or of the *child.*

OF THE PARENT.—If there be an idea which, more than any other, aggravates to a parent the dread of death, it is that of separation from his children. And yet even this idea, so full of anguish to the dying Christian, is also full of consolation. For, even in death, the pious children which he leaves behind him are his hope, his joy, and the crown of his rejoicing. Many a rapturous thought mingles in that melancholy train which at this momentous crisis occupies his mind.

Do the anticipated ills of orphanage present themselves to his view? He remembers who it was that said, *Leave your fatherless children with me, I will provide for them, and let your widows trust in God.* He feels that *they* cannot be accounted fatherless to whom God has become a father; nor destitute to whom an inheritance is bequeathed in heaven. The promises of the covenant occur to him, and he reposes his confidence upon the faithfulness of God. Vain, profligate young man, dost thou require a proof of the truth which is here asserted? Leave then thy banquet, and visit yonder habitation of expiring virtue, and thou shalt see with what tranquillity the parent of a pious offspring can leave the world. Dost thou sneer at the idea? Beware: that sneer may be the sneer of death unto thy soul.

But what proof of the truth which has been inculcated can yonder habitation of expiring virtue afford? Oh that I could faithfully exhibit to thy view the venerable father, like the dying patriarch, assembling his household to receive his benediction: a benediction which contains the only patrimony he is able to bestow. Enviable patrimony: the blessing of a dying and of a pious parent! More to be desired than all the gold that misers ever counted, than all the crowns that tyrants have bestowed. Oh that I could imitate the strain of heavenly eloquence in which he addresses the weeping auditors who stay his pillow and hang upon his lips. "Persevere, my children," he says, "persevere in the course on which you have entered; be faithful to the Saviour you have chosen, and continue to reverence the God of your youth, and I assure you, by the peace I now feel, by the joys I now anticipate, that, when you are old and gray-headed, He will not forsake you." Then, raising his eyes to heaven, he adds, " There I appoint to meet you; that, approaching the throne of mercy, and presenting you, my children, to my Saviour, I may say, *Lord, here am I, and those which thou hast given me.*" Here his voice falters; he smiles adieu, and the serenity of heaven beams from his countenance, as he closes his eyes upon this world, and in faith resigns up his spirit. *Oh death, where here was thy sting! Oh grave, where thy victory!*

OF THE CHILD.—It is not according to seniority that the king of terrors selects his victims. Often does the disconsolate mother weave her daughter's shroud, and often the bereaved father plants the cypress beside the tombstone of his sons. Even these sad services the parents of a pious offspring perform not without consolation, because they are performed not without hope.

Parental love seeks not its own, but the felicity of its object. Whatever loss it may be to the parent, to the pious child it is gain to die; and the more so the earlier he is called to do this. He who *tempers the breeze to the shorn lamb*, often takes away the children of his grace from the evil to come. At death the race ceases, the combat ceases, and joy is consummated. Disease no longer preys upon their bodies; no longer temptation assails their virtue. Hitherto they have been sinners on the earth; henceforth they will be saints in heaven. Before they were associated with men; now they have become companions of angels.

To have borne and nurtured children for the skies; to have seen them, even during their state of tutelage, accounted worthy to be transplanted there—what consoling, what triumphant reflections are these to a bereaved parent! True, he no longer enjoys the solace of their company. Their seat is vacant at his table; it is vacant at the fireside; it is vacant at the altar. A thousand afflicting incidents remind him that they are gone. But, as often as this saddening thought recurs, it is softened and transformed by the cheering recollection that they are gone to glory. And because they are gone to glory, the pang of separation is forgotten, and the full heart, almost disburdened of its sorrow, responds to the song of holy resignation:

"Why should we mourn departed friends,
  Or start at death's alarms?
'Tis but the voice that Jesus sends
  To call us to his arms."

Delightful idea! Supported by this, I have seen the parents of a much-endeared child sitting with composure beside his bed of death. They were parents familiarized with sorrow. Once they had been blessed with an ample fortune and a numerous offspring. But the hand of God had been upon them. Stripped of the one, bereaved of the other, they were left in the decline of life naked and defenceless, like the trunk of an aged oak, whose leaves and branches have been swept away by the pitiless storms that have beat upon it. One little son.

the child of their old age, alone remained to them. His brethren and sisters were dead, and in his life the life of his parents was bound up. Hitherto they had considered this son as a special gift of Providence, granted to solace their sorrows in age, to minister to their wants in death, and afterward to preserve their name and become their memorial among the living. He was, indeed, a lovely child; and what rendered him the more so in the eyes of his godly parents was, that he also feared God. Often, as he hung upon his mother's arm, or clambering his father's knee and stroking back his gray hairs, he would inquire of them so earnestly about death, and talk to them so sweetly about heaven and Jesus, that their hearts were overcome, and their lips had not the power of utterance.

Thus did this child increase in wisdom as he increased in stature: till on a day, like the child of the Shunamite, he cried out, *My head, my head!* Like that child, too, he was carried from the field unto his mother. But, alas! no prophet of Israel was nigh. No swift Gehazi ran from Carmel to lay the staff of the holy seer upon the face of the child. It was, indeed, a sickness unto death. His soul, however, was resigned; his faith in the promises immovable. "Do not grieve thus," said he to his aged parents, as they watched the changes of his countenance, and in pensive silence bedewed his pillow with their tears; "God will take care of you, and he will take care of me too. My body will be laid in the grave, where the body of my Saviour was laid. My soul will fly up to heaven, where I shall see my brothers and sisters, and Jesus Christ, and the angels who attend him. Have you not often told me that he is the friend of children? I have read, too, how he took them in his arms on earth, and I am sure he will bid them welcome to his arms in heaven." Thus early ripe for glory, this dear child, without a murmur and without a groan, drew his last breath, and fell asleep in Jesus. I saw, indeed, that his parents wept; but their tears were tears of joy. Happy, thrice happy parents, called to commit such precious dust unto the sepulchre, and to resign a spirit thus ripe for glory, unto God who gave it.

What a powerful motive to youthful piety does this address unfold? Oh that I were able duly to enforce it! Oh that I were able to revive in your minds the recollection of those numerous incidents by which parental kindness has been evinced, that unwearied care that guarded your wayward steps, that sleepless vigilance that watched the slumber of your cradle!

Do you not feel the obligation you are under to your parents? Do you not wish to make requital? Then break off your sins by repentance, and by faith make your peace with God. You remember how the filial gratitude of Ruth the Moabitess evinced itself towards the widowed Naomi. "The Lord do so to me, and more also, if aught but death part thee and me. For whither thou goest I will go, and where thou lodgest I will lodge: thy people," mark these emphatic words, "thy people shall be my people, and thy God my God. Where thou diest I will die, and there will I be buried." Lovely

Moabitess, thy vow is accepted, and thy faith shall save thee: thy posterity shall be numbered among the lineage of Jacob for the choice which thou didst make, and the spirit thou didst show evinces that thou wert worthy to become for ever the daughter of a mother in Israel.

Ah! would the youth who hear me—youth born and nurtured, not in Moab, but in Zion—make the same wise choice, what joy would it light up in many a heart in this assembly? How would that aged father exult to hear his sons openly declare for Jesus; and what raptures would thrill the bosom of that widowed mother, as her eye caught the first symptoms of contrition in that little group of beings that surround her, covered with those weeds which are at once a symbol of orphanage and a memorial of the dead. Yes, children, piety in you is lustre to a father's eye; it is balm to a mother's heart; it sooths the inquietudes of age; it mitigates the pains of sickness; it softens the gloom of adversity, and extracts more than half the anguish of the pang of death.

It was for this high purpose, that you should join yourselves unto the Lord, that they educated you with so much care, that they nurtured you with so much kindness. To Jesus Christ they have given you, his they have ever considered you; it was in his behalf that, with so many prayers and tears, they have fulfilled the duties of the parental office. Nor will they ever be relieved from the dread of failure, that burden which still oppresses them, till you ratify their vow, and by an act of faith *give yourselves* to Jesus. Nothing short of this—no other act can free your souls from the guilt of abusing parental kindness, because no other act makes requital for that kindness, and cancels the debt of gratitude which it imposes. And this does cancel it: in the eye of God, and in the eye of those who nursed and nurtured you, it cancels it. All this, and still more would they have done, and done cheerfully, for the sake of swelling Emanuel's retinue, and adding to the number of those who shall wear in heaven his livery.

"Oh that I were able," methinks I hear some sorrow-wounded heart exclaim, "oh that I were able to call back from sepulchral ashes the spirits of my parents. Could I do this, I would pour my tears into their bosoms if thus I might wash away the remembrance of those crimes of mine which disturbed their lives, and imbittered even their bed of death." Returning penitent, it is not at the sepulchre, but at the altar, that thou shalt do this. That marble tomb contains not the sainted spirits of those pious parents whom thy sins have grieved. They are either praising God in heaven, or sent from thence to execute some office of good-will to man. Perhaps they are even now thy guardian angels, commissioned to watch thy orphan steps by day, and to guard by night thy orphan slumbers. Be they where they may, thy return to God will not long remain unknown to them; nor will it less occasion joy because they have gone before thee into glory. There, in ecstasy they will receive the welcome tidings, or perhaps themselves will be the bearers of those tidings, shouting as they ascend, "Grace hath reclaimed another wanderer, and brought home to Jesus a child of ours!" Every redeemed spirit sympathizes in their joy, and every angel strikes on his golden harp with a bolder hand the deep-toned hallelujah, *because an immortal soul was dead and is alive again, was lost and is found.*

And well may the angels do this. The recovery of a soul from sin to righteousness is a splendid event. What a range of progressive glory opens before the young immortal; and what a train of rapturous ideas must spring up in celestial minds, as they see the heaven-bound pilgrim taking the inceptive step in that upward way that will conduct him thither! They know the issue; and, because they know it, dwell with ecstasy upon the growing number which the church on earth is nurturing up to fill their own thinned ranks and repeople their native mansions: mansions which, ere our race was made, sin had invaded, and apostacy from God depopulated.

But not the angels only—all other virtuous beings, the wise and the good of all nations, sympathize with your parents in their joy. Everywhere young converts awaken peculiar interest, because they add peculiar beauty to the church, which is God's moral husbandry. In this arid world, every spot of moral verdure attracts the eye. Especially does the verdure of the springtime of life attract it. We love to contemplate these *young willows by the watercourses; pleasant trees, the planting of the Lord.* The sun of righteousness shines benignly on them with his beams; the showers of grace water their tender branches, which already bud and blossom for the skies. Oh! how unlike those aged and barren trunks, which only encumber and deform the vineyard; and which, because they encumber and deform it, are doomed to destruction; and the axe and the fire become their portion.

Thus the angels of God, the saints in glory, and the church on earth, partake in that pulse of joy which dilates the parent's heart when his offspring incline to wisdom. Nor least, nor last, beloved pupils, does your *Alma Mater* partake in this. Ye also are her joy and the crown of her rejoicing. It is not the ignorant, the idle, or the profligate that she numbers among her blessings. These are names that pollute her records, and are spots in her feasts of love. She wishes to be known only as the guardian of youthful wisdom, the patroness of talents consecrated to God. In all your future plans of usefulness she will take an interest. She will delight to see this dim scene of earthly glory brighten as you enter on it. To see vice everywhere, awe-smitten by the dignity of your demeanour, hide its deformed head; and oppressed virtue, beneath your auspices, look up and triumph: to see the whole force of your example given unto righteousness, and the whole vigour of your minds directed to the rearing up of some monument for God.

In the hope of this requital it was that she opened to you her halls of science; that she delivered to you her lectures of instruction, and that she offered up, and still offers up, her evening and her morning prayers before the altar. And will you disappoint her hopes? Ah! in her paternal eye, what a glorious spectacle would it be to see the youth she had nurtured, clad in celestial panoply, everywhere breasting the storm, and breaking those bars of error and delusion which apostacy " has flung across man's obstructed way" to glory.

Seeing then, beloved youth, that ye are compassed about by such a cloud of witnesses, be entreated to *lay aside every weight, and the sin which doth most easily beset you, and to run with patience the race set before you, looking unto Jesus, the author and finisher of our faith; who, for the joy that was set before him, endured the cross, despising the shame, and is now set down at the right hand of God.* So even ye, if ye overcome, *shall set down with Christ on his throne; even as he, having overcome, has set down with his Father on his throne.*

What a glorious jubilee are pious children at once preparing for themselves and for their parents. Oh that I were able to direct your eye to those favoured groups of beings, which in yonder heavens grace will have brought together! Each redeemed child which the parent numbers in those realms of glory, will be by him accounted a distinct pledge of his Creator's goodness, an additional monument of his Saviour's mercy.

With what emotions will Abraham recognise among the multitude of the saved that beloved Isaac, whom, when a lad, with so many gloomy thoughts he led towards the altar upon one of the mountains of Moriah! With what emotions will Isaac there recognise that Jacob, whom his eyes, through dimness, saw not, when he came bringing savoury meat, and to receive his paternal blessing! And how will Jacob exult, when, presenting his offspring before his Saviour, he finds himself surrounded by the twelve patriarchs—all the heads of the tribes of Israel!

Nor less the joy of every other parent, who, missing no member of his household, dares to say, as he stands amid the convocation of the righteous, "Here, Lord, am I, and of all the children thou hast given me have I lost none."

Remember, ye youth who hear me, that it is only your impiety that can deprive your pious parents of such an honour, and prevent the bliss of such a meeting.

Great God! interpose by thy grace, and avert from our children the awful doom of final separation from thy people; and to thy name shall be the glory in Christ. AMEN

XI.

[Effects of the Apostacy.—Man vainly seeks for Happiness in Riches—in Power—in Wisdom.—Man's boasted Wisdom considered—in the Philosophy of Mind—in the Philosophy of Matter.—Chymistry.—The Microscope—Astronomy.—The Telescope.—The Fixed Stars.—True Wisdom consists in the Knowledge of God.—Pagan and Christian Theology, in their Character and Effects, compared.—The Bible the source of the most precious Knowledge.—To be truly Wise is to understand the great Truths which it reveals, and comply with its Requirements.]

On the morning of man's creation, the first object that met his eye was the God who formed him. If, with a sentiment of personal consequence, he then raised himself from his bed of dust, it was the dignity of his parentage that prompted that sentiment. He felt upon his heart, as it throbbed with life and gratitude, the ligament that bound him to a stable and an eternal throne. Little in himself, he was great as the offspring of the Almighty; and weak in himself, he was strong in God's strength.

Not so striking or so mournful was the change in Eden, when its flowers fell withered to the earth beneath the curse that smote it, as was the change in man, who, till now, had continued his song of praise and worn his robe of innocence. But when he deserted God he was deserted of him, and the decay of all his moral habits gave evidence of that desertion. Thenceforward his tone of feeling and his type of character were assimilated to those of the fell spirits, wandering from their prison, with whom he had become associated and joined in interests. The ties of filial affection broke bleeding from their hold; the aspirations of filial love ceased; even devotion ceased; nor did any inward sentiment lift up his soul towards the Author of his being. Bewildered amid the mazes and benighted by the darkness of his own depravity, on which ever side he turned him, the glories of the Godhead had faded from his eye, and the very recollections of his mercy were passing from his memory.

The desire of happiness remained; but it had lost its object, and a mighty void was felt in the bosom which hitherto God had filled. A substitute was sought. A substitute has been found, as the sinner fancies, in each successive object which excites his concupiscence; but all of them alike, in the end, fling back his hope unsatisfied, and only mock by disappointment his idolatrous devotion.

Sometimes it is RICHES that supplant God, and the sinner's heart fills with covetous desires. Avarice becomes the ruling passion; and in place of the *man*, erect in posture and with an eye directed to the heavens, the *miser* appears, inclined to the earth, picking from the kennel each shining particle, eking out his freehold by usurious purchases, or piling away in coffers, on which *mammon* has been stamped, his worshipped treasures. It was covetousness that destroyed Ahab; it was riches that beguiled Crœsus: since whose times there has lived unblessed, and died unwept, a race of wretches still more mean and more mercenary, concerning whom there is only this memorial left on earth, *that their God was gold.*

Sometimes it is *might* that supplants God : when a little creature, a few feet high and a few years old, may be seen walking in the pride of his strength and indulging in a dream of his independence. That haughty son of Anak, whom the sling of David humbled while in the act of his proud defiance, is not the only individual who has been the dupe of this illusion. It was in *might* that Nimrod gloried, that Belus gloried, together with those later and fiercer conquerors who wielded the Grecian phalanx, who prompted the movement and smote with the arm of the Roman legion : men who left, even in the eye of posterity, their bloody track upon the herbage of the valley and the glaciers of the mountains ; who indicated the place of their encampment by the desolation which surrounded it, and lit up the whole line of their march to hell by the fires of one great, frightful, continuous funeral pile.

Sometimes it is *wisdom* that supplants God : when a creature, religious by the very constitution of his nature, is seen giving those hours to study which belong to devotion, and those affections to knowledge which are a tribute due to goodness. It is among this group of intellectual idolators that we recognise the names of Ptolemy, of Archimedes, of Aristotle, of Plato, together with that lengthened catalogue of Athenian sages, by the fire of whose genius we enkindle our own, and in the light of whose intellect Athens is still visible at the distance of so many generations. And if there were anything but God in which it were rightful for man to glory, it should seem that wisdom were that thing. Its love is not sordid like the love of riches; it is not cruel like that of power. The groves of the Academy are tranquil, its pursuits are peaceful: alas! that they are not always holy.

For years you have joined in those vigils which are kept beside the quenchless lamp that philosophy hath kindled; and high in hope, and decked with classic honours, you are about to enter on the world. At such a moment, how chilling to youthful ardour, to literary enterprise, is the rebuke that meets you at the very threshold: "*Let not the wise man glory in his wisdom.*"

So spake not Socrates, so spake not Seneca, so spake not Cicero. The lecture-room conveyed no such counsel, the Lyceum contained no such oracle. No, it did not: this is not the language of Athens, but of Zion. We are not now among the groves of the Academy, we are not beside the seat of the Muses. Here, it is not the harp of Orpheus, but of David, that is struck, and the song it breathes is not in the manner of Homer or of Hesiod, but of Isaiah and Habakkuk. We are associated with the disciples of a Christian school; we have entered the vestibule of a Christian temple, where all that is splendid in intellect, as well as all that is splendid in fortune, is eclipsed by the intenser splendours of righteousness.

Never was counsel more timely or more pertinent than that which is now addressed to you from the hill of Zion, and by the lips of a prophet of the Lord. *Let not the wise man glory in his wisdom.*

And why should the wise man glory in his wisdom? After all the ostentatious eulogy that graceless learning, that unbaptized philosophy has bestowed on itself, what is there that should make a religious being, a being of moral capacities, glory in it? After all the enlargement of modern discovery, and sublime as the march of genius is said to have been during the last centuries of the six thousand years that have passed away, has the wisdom of the schools become either SO CLEAR IN ITS VIEWS, SO VAST IN ITS REACH, OR SO SUBLIME AND SPIRITUAL IN ITS NATURE, as to entitle it to such high distinction?

HAS IT BECOME SO CLEAR IN ITS VIEWS, SO VAST IN ITS REACH? Or, rather, does not human intellect, bewildered amid a mighty maze, and met and mocked at every turn with mystery, still look with weak, and wavering, and tremulous perception on a little span only; a mere hand's breadth, taken beside those bold and interminable lines of wisdom, the direction of which is so soon hidden in the distance which they run upon the great, measureless, untravelled map of infinite intelligence? Is it not even so? I put it to your own experience. You have passed your examinations in the lecture-room: take your last in the sanctuary and at the altar of your God.

Is it in the philosophy of mind that your wisdom is so clear and comprehensive? You have studied the philosophy of mind; you have noticed and named the more obvious acts of the soul within you and of the souls around you. Have you done more than this? If so, with all that more, can you inform me what the soul within you is? or what the tie that unites it to the body on which it acts, and by which it is acted on so wondrously? Whence that waking and that sleeping state it assumes alternately; those bewildering dreams that characterize the one, and the more orderly perceptions that predominate in the other? How do its volitions arise? How is its train of thought kept up? Or how, blind to the future as it is, does memory bring back with such acknowledge accuracy *the past?* Can you answer these inquiries? You know you cannot: nor can your teachers answer them. Such knowledge is too wonderful for us. Does glorying in it, then, befit you! David did not think so, when, struck by the sublime incomprehensibility of his own mysterious being, he uttered that humble and heartfelt note of homage, *I will praise thee, for I am fearfully and wonderfully made.*

I pass to the souls of others. Take those with which you are most familiar; the members of the families in which you have resided; the companions with whom you have associated; the class with which you have so often met. To say nothing of that great world of spirits above you and around you, do you understand and can you explain what passes within even this narrow limit; this bird's-eye field of vision? The eccentricity of taste, the peculiarity of temper, the diversity of talent, the variety of opinion, the secret motive of action, the sudden change of purpose, the transformation of habits, the revolution of character, the communication of feeling, the contagion of passion, together with all those varieties of action and reaction with which related beings are affected—do you see these things as God sees them? Or, rather, do not mysteries meet you at every step, and rests there not even on this select and frequented field, and on every part of it, a veil which no arm can lift, no eye but the Omniscient penetrate?

Is it, then, in the philosophy of matter that your wisdom is clear and comprehensive?

In chymistry there have been recent and great discoveries. With these you have become acquainted. You have familiarized yourselves with tables of chymical affinity; you have learned the names and become acquainted with the properties of certain agents. More than this, you have been within the laboratory, seen experiments in analysis and combination, and witnessed the action of electricity and of fire. But have you, as yet, detected that hidden agency that solves the solid in the crucible, or that causes in the liquid the elemental movement at the touch of the galvanic pile?

You have analyzed the air. Can you tell me why it renders percussion audible? You have separated the rays of the solar beam. Can you tell me why it renders visible the bodies on which it falls? You have analyzed the dewdrop. Why does it ripen the vintage? You have analyzed the spring shower. Why does it refresh the herbage, and brighten the verdure on which the eye so sweetly reposes?

Among all the processes of combination and analysis through which you have travelled, is there one step in either which you have comprehended? or did you ever discover, in a single instance, that unreveal-

P

ed connexion between your experiment and the result? You have been schooled to little purpose if you have yet to understand that here, emphatically, learning teaches the more effectually " to know how little can be known."

Let us leave these intricacies, these mimic processes of formation, and glance at the simpler and the lovelier forms of nature. Here, too, regarding only the visible and tangible qualities of bodies, how circumscribed is your wisdom! Even the eye, the most excursive organ and the richest source of knowledge, is confined in its information within humble limits. Above, and beneath, and around, there are elements too subtile, and bodies too near or too remote, too large or too minute, to be brought within its field of vision.

But you have surmounted this obstacle to universal science. You have remedied the defects of the natural eye by the intervention of artificial glasses. Still, even this expedient, which extends so wonderfully the range of human knowledge, only renders more direct and palpable the evidence of human ignorance.

Before this expedient was resorted to, the blossom that hung suspended from the fruit-tree was, in the eye of man, but a blossom; nor had it any other or higher use than to shelter the tender fruit which it enfolded. Now that blossom is seen to be the base of a vast and complicated system, and carries on its surface, and on every fibre of its surface, the ample habitation of many a living creature. Nor that blossom only. Every leaf of the forest, every flower of the field, every spear of grass in the valley and on the mountain-top, breathes beneath the microscopic lens with animation, and teems with life. A population as vast, a movement as constant and as hurried, and, for aught we know, as full of incident and interest, takes place on the surface of every new world thus brought forth to view from its obscurity, as takes place on the surface of that world the spectator treads on. Other, and still other, and yet other compartments are unfolded, and new races of beings pass before the eye, as glasses of greater, and still greater and greater magnifying powers are interposed. Indeed, the farther this downward track to nothingness is travelled, the farther seems to stretch the still untravelled residue. No glass has yet been found of power to reach quite down to non-existence. Not even the nether limit of creation has been fixed. That line is yet undrawn that marks creation's *minimum*—Jehovah's *ne plus ultra*. After all this reach with artificial means to littleness, that distant unknown point, that barrier to existence, still remains to be discovered, beyond whose fearful verge the atoms are too small for God to organize, the space too narrow for God to work in. Beneath us, as around us, all is mystery. There is a profound in littleness too vast for man to compass, too deep for man to fathom. Even here God's counsels are unsearchable, and His ways past finding out.

Let us turn, then, to larger masses and bolder lines. Astronomy is a more certain science. It is so. Still, even here, though there be many a lesson of humility, there is none of pride written on the firmament: at least there is none when read from the hill of Zion and in the light of the sanctuary. For, seen in this light, it is God's glory that yonder heavens declare. It is His handiwork which that firmament above us showeth forth. Of Him only, day unto day uttereth speech, and night unto night showeth knowledge. Even a royal observer, surveying the heavens which God has made, and the moon and the stars which are the work of His fingers, uttered, in view of them, only this submissive reflection, " *Lord, what is man, that thou art mindful of him? and the son of man, that thou visitest him?* But the astronomy of the schools is not the astronomy of the sanctuary. To the novice, instructed only in the latter, the earth, fixed and motionless, spreads out its ample surface, forming on every side the base which supports the arches of the sky, across which the sun, and moon, and stars, and planets, in undistinguished order, make their daily and their nightly marches. Even this is grand and awful, especially since God is seen to direct the movement.

You, however, are able to correct these vulgar errors. You can tell the novice, schooled in the sanctuary, and who has derived his notions of the dimensions of the universe, not from the measurements of Newton, but from the melodies of Asaph, that the earth is not a plane, as he supposes, but a globe; and a globe of secondary magnitude, hung in open space, measuring the day by a revolution on its axis, and the year by the circuit it performs around the sun, the common centre of the earth, and of those other related planets which, with their train of secondaries, constitute this system.

To confirm your doctrine and strengthen his conviction of your superiority, you adjust the telescope to his eye and point it to the neighbouring planet. With reverential awe he looks upon the hills and valleys, the morasses, and the plains that diversify yon silvery surface. His eye catches the illuminated summits that glitter in the sunbeam; and, thence descending, traces the lengthening shadows that stretch from the broad bases of the lunar mountains. You turn the instrument to another, and another, and another of those kindred planets, which hang, with their bright array of belts and moons, from the solar centre.

Amazed, he pauses and reflects upon this vision. The earth he trod on has sunk beneath him, and the heavens he looks at rise into greater majesty. A thousand interesting conjectures start up, a thousand anxious inquiries arise. And who so competent to answer them as he who, by his superior wisdom, unfolded the regions to which they relate? Proud of this distinction, and confident of your ability to maintain it, you proceed to reply. Naming the planets, you tell him their respective densities and distances, the inclinations of their axes, and the angles their orbits make with the ecliptic. You acquaint him with the seasons of Venus, the length of a day at Jupiter, and the duration of the year of the more distant Saturn. Elated with this success, and anxious to know still more of those worlds you have introduced to his acquaintance, he asks to be informed of what material they are composed, when they were created, how long they will continue, and what high purpose they were designed to answer. But you tell him not.

Again he demands, what is the nature of their soil, the kind and variety of their productions, the number of their inhabitants, the form of their governments, the character of their literature, and the deeds of glory recorded in their histories and celebrated in their songs. Has sin entered there? he asks; has death? or has salvation been proclaimed? Again you are silent. You answer not, because you cannot answer. No eyeglass has made visible the halls of justice or the temples of devotion on either of the planets; no turrets are seen, to indicate their cities of commerce or their seats of empire; nor has a sigh or murmur, or a single shout of triumph, ever yet been sent down to earth from yon distant conjectural population. Thus, even here, your boasted wisdom dwindles to a mere knowledge of the naked facts of distance, revolution, and dimension. But on every question of moral moment, concerning all that renders distance, and revolution, and dimension interesting, with all your parade of the measurements of Newton, you are as profoundly ignorant, nay, much more so, than that humble learner who has gathered his notions of the dimensions of the universe from the meditations of Job or the devotional songs of Asaph.

Nor, if we pass beyond the planets, will your wisdom be found more decisive. How much can you here tell the peasant from his cottage, or even the Indian from his thicket, which he before knew not?

You can tell him that those stars he sees, and which seem mere radiant points, are suns, and a million times larger than the earth he treads on. That their distance is so great, that, were they struck from existence, their continued light would fall upon the eyes of unborn generations; and centuries elapse before those rays they have already sent forth, and whose speed is the speed of lightning, would have travelled down from their amazing height to the little planet we inhabit!

You might, recurring again to the help of glasses, show him other and still more distant, and yet other and still more distant central orbs, till you had numbered millions; each a sun, filling its separate system with light and heat, and seen, even across the immeasurable space between us, in the blaze of its own unborrowed glory.

Here, at this last, farthest, extremest range of astral observation, vision ceases, and with it ceases all your information. But whether even this is creation's ultimate limit, you know not, nor does any other mortal know. For who can tell whether even the range of Herschel's larger telescope was the fixed radius to which Jehovah set his compass, when he swept on every side that mighty circle which divides the universe from chaos, and indicates the field within whose limits *His* infinite, eternal spirit broods and operates? Or whether other and still more powerful glasses would not unfold another and a vaster range of constellated glories, scattered with a bolder hand, and planted at a more awful distance? This vaster range unfolded, whether even this were all; or only some small province, some unimportant member of a yet mightier empire, whose limits and whose line of measure, reaching beyond the ken of angels, is only known to Him who governs it; and from some loftier height of which an eye looks down on us, and on those suns and planets which stretch across our firmament, as we look down upon the hidden glories which the microscope reveals suspended on the fibres of the vernal flower; and which suns and planets, if swept from existence, would be as little missed amid the mightier fabrics that still remained, as would be that flower, withered on its stem, among the varied, rich array of blooming nature.

Whether we take our stand beneath the seen or the unseen firmament, how insignificant is man! Surrounded by such an infinitude of objects—objects scattered through such measureless extension, what can a creature know of distance or of matter? Or, space and matter known, why should a moral being glory in that knowledge?

Ah! could you lift the Christian from the sanctuary up to ethereal heights, and plant before him, a fixed star its pedestal, some mightier telescope than Herschel's, and, turning from point to point its ample tube, show him the kingdoms of the universe (as Satan did his master the kingdoms of the world), how would one thought of God—that God he worshipped in the sanctuary, and whom, placed among the constellations, he still worships—how would one thought of God, even amid this boundless, this glorious prospect, dazzle into darkness all that is bright, and sink into insignificance all that is great! Descending from his empyrean height, and re-entering the sanctuary, how would he sympathize with yet profounder humility in the sentiment of the prophet now addressed to you : *Thus saith the Lord : Let not the wise man glory in his wisdom; but let him that glorieth, glory in this, that he understandeth and knoweth Me; that I am the Lord, who exercise loving kindness, judgment, and righteousness in the earth.*

Whatever else we may know, it is the knowledge of God—no matter whether obtained beneath the ceiling of a temple or the ceiling of the firmament—on a globe of earth or a sun of fire—it is the knowledge of God which alone gives value and character to all our other knowledge. It is the recognition of his great mastering spirit amid the elemental movements—disposing the atom, balancing in air the vapour, guiding down to earth the sunbeam, sending forward to the shore the billow of the ocean, darting forth from the tempest-driven cloud the lightning, shaking the mountains amid the earthquake, staying the constellations in their places, binding the planetary masses to their centres, and propelling the blazing comet along its elongated orbit—it is the recognition of his great mastering spirit amid these elemental movements that strikes the silent awe, that wakes the solemn interest! Ah! you may measure the distance of the stars; you may subject to analysis the elements; but in God only will you find that energy by which they act, that immensity in which they move.

Mind has a higher majesty than matter; the

knowledge of it is sublimer knowledge; and of this knowledge, that of the eternal mind is immeasurably the most sublime. There is an inward sentiment in man which renders reasoning on this topic useless. A false and feverish spirit of devotion, even where God has been rejected, prompts the deluded worshipper to seek a substitute. The territories of pagan Rome were endeared by their imaginary genii, and the rivers and fountains thereof were consecrated by their nymphs and naiads. It was not the form of Ida nor the height of Olympus, but the gods who frequented them, that caused those hills of Greece to be so intensely interesting. Even Homer has flung additional enchantment over the conflicts he describes, whether of the elements or of armies, by the sublime agency of those superior beings made by his creative fancy, and so admirably marshalled and governed through all the varied incidents of his imperishable song.

But oh! what deeper interest, what loftier feeling is excited when, not the Jupiter or the Mercury of Homer, but the Elohim of Abraham, the Jehovah of Moses appears: seated, neither on Olympus nor on Ida, but enthroned amid his own immutable perfections—filling with his eternity all duration, and all immensity with his omnipresence!

Taste, as well as morals, is infinitely indebted to those richer views of goodness, those bolder lines of wisdom, and that loftier march of power, which from the hills of Zion the holy seer has rendered visible along the whole course of Providence, and throughout every field of nature.

That juster and sublimer theology of Moses and the prophets, of Christ and his apostles, has banished not only the hero gods of the poets from our altars, but also that profane and countless rabble of crawling, purring, mewing, bleating, barking, hissing divinities from our fountains and our rivers, from our fields and our forests.

The walk of friendship is far more sweet, as is the walk of contemplation far more intellectual, when only the one almighty, universal God is seen, exerting everywhere his wakeful vigilance, and throwing around each little being the arms of his protection, than when the bewildered wanderer is met at every turn by the factitious agency of demons, smiling in the dewdrop, scowling in the December cloud, sighing mournfully through the forests in the mountain breeze, or shrieking angrily from the billow in the ocean tempest.

Nor the walk of friendship only: a richer colouring, a sublimer aspect is given to the whole of nature, and a loftier train of associated grandeurs rise in prospect, when her incomprehensible phenomena are held in contemplation, in connexion only with that one great, all-pervading Spirit whom the Bible reveals.

Ah! how are the horn of Ceres, the arrow of Mercury, the trident of Neptune, the thunderbolt of Jupiter, with whatever other pagan symbols of divinity glow on the canvass, breathe from the statue, or rise in bold relief from the pages of the poet—how is this diminutive, contemptible machinery blotted from the fancy by the august conception of that awful Being, of whom the prophet amid the grandeurs of Sinai saw no similitude, and of whom the awestruck Israelite, dropping from his trembling hand the instrument of his art, attempted none! For, being once possessed with the grand idea of the self-existent Spirit, he felt upon his heart, as the disciples of the same school now feel upon theirs, a deep conviction that, however pagans might paint and mould the humble idols of their devotion, the real and the living God is not like anything that may be drawn upon the canvass or hewed from the marble: nay, that, being himself the maker of all things, he is not like, and therefore may not be profanely likened, either in sculpture, in painting, or in song, to anything which he has made, whether in heaven above, or in the earth beneath, or in the waters under the earth.

It is not with Homer, or Virgil, or Lucretius, but with Moses, and Job, and David in his hand, that the man of taste should contemplate the scenery of nature. In the heavenly light which revelation throws over the wonders of creation, oh! how I love to mark the blaze of noonday, to catch the breeze of evening, to watch the shadows lengthening from the mountains as the sun descends behind them, to survey the fading landscape beneath the lingering twilight, or raise my wondering eye up to the grandeur of the midnight firmament! All is significant, all is replete with interest; for it speaks the watchful and active presence of a spirit infinite, who sees even me, marks out my path amid this mighty movement, and shields my being from the crush of yon uplifted worlds.

But it is not in the knowledge of God, as the all-powerful Governor of the material elements—though this is knowledge more sublime than any which blind, but proud philosophy imparts—it is not this knowledge, but THE KNOWLEDGE OF HIM AS THE RIGHTEOUS GOVERNOR OF A MORAL UNIVERSE, AND OF EVERY PART OF IT, that we are this day called to glory in.

With this knowledge we associate neither Ida nor Olympus, hills of Greece, but Carmel and Sharon, hills of Palestine. For here it is not the poets of Athens, it is not the philosophers of Athens, but the prophets of Judah, fishermen from the Sea of Galilee and the Lake of Gennesaret who are our teachers.

Here the Bible is our only text-book. To it all appeals are made, from it all deductions are drawn. Its doctrines are Jehovah's declarations. These are *truth itself.* All we gather elsewhere is only ornament or illustration. The learned and the unlearned, on the subject of religion, are all alike shut up wholly to the faith. No eyeglass of philosophy reaches quite up to heaven or down to hell. Astronomy affords no tables that assist to calculate the soul's duration. Chymistry has not yet revealed the analysis of death, nor taught her proud disciple how to recompose the body once turned to dissolution. We have heard, indeed, of the perfectibility of man's physical as well as moral nature. We have heard of the progressive triumphs of medicine over disease, and of the prospect of its ultimate triumph over death itself. But no facts corroborate this boastful theory. As yet, the march of science has not kept pace with the march of death. While the limit of knowledge has been extending, the limit of life has been contracting, and it is even now reduced to a span. Methusaleh lived nine hundred and sixty-nine years; neither Newton nor Halley lived a century : all their compeers in wisdom have already forsaken us, and the locks of Herschel, their disciple, are whitening for the sepulchre. No astronomer has yet been able to trace a practicable path from mortal up to immortality, nor has the tomb of any alchymist, like that which contained Elisha's bones, quickened his remains enclosed within it. The time is far distant when the druggist shall vend an antidote for death, or the chymist, by any subtile process, revivify the ashes of the urn.

All of moral moment that we know on these high subjects God has told us. And all that God has told us is written in that authentic record of his will and revelation of his purposes, *the Bible.*

Here we learn, what philosophy teaches not, or only indistinctly teaches, that material pomp and splendour do not constitute the only or the principal exhibition of the Godhead ; that matter, and magnitude, and distance are no more than his theatre of action ; that, amid this outward movement of numerous worlds, and the conflict of mighty elements, he is carrying forward a vast, continuous, and eternal plan of wisdom and of goodness, which embraces not only the armies of heaven and the legions of hell, but all the dwellers that are upon the earth.

Wide as his empire extends, and countless as are the worlds which spread their wants before his eye and present their claims upon his attention and his mercy, how welcome the message assuring us that God, rich in the resources of his own exhaustless attributes, has time and goodness to *exercise loving kindness, judgment, and righteousness,* in this inconsiderable province of his immeasurable domains. Cold to gratitude must the heart be, and dead to virtue, which does not respond to that annunciation of the angel to which the heavenly host responded, " Behold, I bring you glad tidings of great joy, which shall be to all people ; for unto you is born in the city of David a Saviour, who is Christ the Lord." Were a wandering planet, that had been driven by some convulsion from its orbit, brought back to move in it again, or were the fires of some quenched sun rekindled in the firmament, would philosophy behold such renovation with indifference? And was it, think you, an incident of minor interest, when the light of virtue again broke forth from the dark disk of the moral world, driven by apostacy from its sphere of duty, and wandering away from its centre, God ; but now brought back, to move, and shine, and harmonize, a redeemed member in the one great and changeless system of love and righteousness? So thought not the angels. Ah! what an hour was that, when on the strings of a thousand harps there trembled this note of exultation, Alleluiah, *For a world was lost, but is found : was dead, but is alive again.*

It is the exercise of God's loving kindness on the earth which has made it the theatre of scenes that excited the highest joy in heaven, and awoke in angelic minds the deepest emotions. True, in dimensions it is a little world, but its interests are vastly important in the plan of Providence. It is the world where Adam once lived in innocence, and where the posterity of Adam will be raised in power. Defaced as its beauty has been, and rebellious as its inhabitants have become, it still retains many an impress of mercy on its surface, and many a beacon of hope rises along the entire line of its duration.

At no period of its history has it been completely abandoned. Even in its antediluvian age, Enoch walked with God, and Noah preached righteousness. Thereafter a covenant was made with Abraham, and many a subsequent message was conveyed from heaven to earth, through the ministry of angels or the inspiration of prophets. In the record of its history we read of the ladder of Jacob, the chariot of Elijah, and that bush of Moses which burned, but consumed not; and, after the revolution of so many ages, there may yet be pointed out upon its map that Sinai where the tables of the law were given, and that Moriah on which the temple of Jehovah stood. But its tenderest memorials of the past, its surest tokens for the future, are its manger of Bethlehem, its Garden of Gethsemane, its Hill of Calvary, its rock of Joseph, and its top of Olivet.

These are points of vision on which the eye of a sinner, nay, of a seraph, rests with more rapturous hopes, gathering more sublime associations than from the radiant orbs in that mighty range of constellated glories which the telescope reveals.

Not without reason did an angelic messenger

congratulate the shepherds on that night when the heavens resounded with Christ's natal anthem. The tidings which he bore were indeed glad tidings, and to all people: tidings of justice vindicated, of heaven reconciled, and of sin forgiven. Oh, how the moral night brightened when the Star of Bethlehem broke upon it! Since which, this earth has been advancing with every revolution towards the dawn of a more effulgent day: this earth, comparatively insignificant in its physical dimensions, but great in its moral consequence, as being the centre of a glorious plan of redemption, and distinguished among the planets as the theatre of God's loving kindness and the birthplace of his Son.

It is the knowledge of this system of redemption, in which such mighty interests are concentred, such conflicting claims harmonized, such matchless glories brought to light: it is the knowledge of this system, and of God in Christ acting by it, that sinks and degrades all other knowledge, and becomes itself exclusively the sinner's ground of hope and cause of glorying. Even Paul, brought up at the feet of Gamaliel, and deeply instructed in the learning of the Rabbins, counted his attainments but loss for the excellency of the knowledge of Christ Jesus his Lord.

And how is it with you? You have been studying the works of God and the Providence of God. You have been exercising your intellectual powers in the analysis of matter and of mind. With what success have you done this? Among all the relations you have discovered and traced, have you yet discovered and traced that great moral relation which binds you to your Creator's throne; which makes allegiance obligatory; which makes sin heinous, and hell just? While you have been solving the body in the crucible, or gazing on the firmament through the telescope, has the conviction fastened upon your hearts that, as the sovereign of the universe, God deserves the homage of the moral beings who inhabit it; and that, as being rebels against him, your damnation has slumbered only because He *exerciseth loving kindness*, as well as judgment and righteousness, on the earth?

Of this loving kindness of God, what has been your own individual experience? I speak not now of your creation, or of the protection and defence you have found in his Providence. I speak not of the preservations of infancy; of your recoveries from sickness; your rescues from danger; your hair-breadth escapes during so many years, and in the midst of such mighty desolations: desolations which have already swept away more than half the human beings who were on the earth when you began to exist; while you, surrounded on every side by the remains of the dead, and walking among their sepulchres, yet continue companions of the living and monuments of sparing mercy. I speak not now of these things; but I speak of that *loving kindness* of God, by which the soul of a sinner is regenerated and redeemed.

You are each of you acquainted with at least one wanderer from virtue, one rebel against God. What do you know of grace having followed that wanderer, and what of his submission and return? What reception did he meet with, and was it a father's welcome that he received? In one word, have you, who have heard so many lectures and studied so many sciences, have you yet acquired that saving knowledge by which you are enabled more and more to die unto sin and live unto righteousness? Do you feel in your souls the hope of sin forgiven, and do you find there the evidences of renewing mercy? Has God shed abroad his love in your hearts, restraining your appetites, subduing your passions, purifying your desires, elevating your affections, and carrying forward, by the indwelling influences of his spirit, a work of sanctification so progressive, so holy, so tinctured with the temper and the humility of heaven, that you dare to hope He purposes you shall enter it. If so, your education, though not complete, has been begun aright. Its elements are pure and durable. You have laid your foundation deep and broad, and you may build upon it a superstructure which no shock shall overthrow, and which shall rise in those heavens where no telescope can reach.

But if you have not acquired this knowledge, with all your boasted attainments you are fools, and the day of judgment and the bar of God will prove you so. Yours will be no common destiny, and you are even now weaving its fearful web. As there are degrees in guilt, so there will be degrees in retribution. The servant who knows his master's will and does it not, deserves to be beaten with many stripes. It were better to sink into perdition from the cities of the plain than from the hills of

Zion; and Sodom and Gomorrah will have less to answer for in the day of judgment than Chorazin and Bethsaida: nor only than Chorazin and Bethsaida.

To be driven from the halls of science to the prison of demons is to be doubly damned. Ah! how many sad associations, how many agonizing contrasts will rush upon the mind of the lettered reprobate, doomed to the confinement of convicts and the companionship of the finally impenitent!

Accustomed to all that is tasteful in art, or sublime and picturesque in nature, how will he endure the privations and the disorder of that abode of horror which light never visits, and where salvation never comes. In hell there are no temples of science any more than of devotion, no walks of contemplation or fields of verdure; no Ida, or Parnassus, or Vale of Tempe. All is dark and sombrous, as well as impious and guilty; and the smoke of torments endless overhang that starless firmament, across which no healthful planet moves, no bow of promise stretches.

It is in other and holier regions where taste as well as devotion finds its object and receives its consummation. Heaven is as replete with beauty as it is secure from evil. There is the tree of life, and there the river of salvation. There the cherubim chant their pæans, and the harps of angels give forth their notes of melody. There God for ever reigns, seen in the light of his own uncreated perfections, and filling the realms of paradise with his peculiar glory. There his redeemed children obey and worship Him. At home in every province of their Heavenly Father's empire, swiftly and securely they fly from world to world, to bear his messages, to admire his wonders, and adore his majesty. Ah! who would not inherit heaven! Who does not shrink appalled at the thought of hell!

Oh! if a guardian's fondness, if a father's love could move you, how would I pour out my full heart in expostulation and entreaty. But expostulation and entreaty fall powerless on souls which grace has never quickened. Oh! thou Maker of these immortal beings, guide them to the knowledge of thyself, and bring them to thy kingdom, and to thy *ame shall be the glory.

XII.

[Absolute Independence predicable only of God.—The Relations between Parents and Children.—A foolish Son a Grief to his Father.—Sin the greatest of all Folly.—The Sinner's Character and Course described.—The Effects of Sin.—Children growing up in Sin.—The Prodigal Son.—The Anguish occasioned to Parents by dissolute Children.—Their Affliction in leaving such Children behind them.—Their Hopelessness in the Death of such Children.—David and Absalom.—The Petition of Dives.—Future State of the Wicked.—Close of the Argument.]

ABSOLUTE independence exists not except in God. Through the whole line of created intelligences, being acts reciprocally upon being. Between the individuals of different races the influence of this action is felt. Not the angels themselves are unaffected by those changes that affect the destinies of men. There is joy in Heaven over the repentant sinner on earth. This action increases as the relation between beings becomes more intimate. But no relation is more intimate than that which subsists between the parent and the child; none more indissoluble, and, of course, none more fruitful in pleasures and in pains.

Of this, Solomon, that sagacious observer of human society, was duly sensible. Taught both by experience and observation, he asserts not only *that a wise son maketh a glad father*, but *that a foolish son is a grief to his father and bitterness to her that bare him.*

It is not the folly of idiocy, however, but the folly

of sin, to which the wise man here alludes. God may, and in his inscrutable wisdom sometimes does withhold intelligence from children; or, having bestowed it, he suffers it to be impaired by disease or disaster, and, it may be, even to be utterly destroyed. A human being destitute of intellect is, indeed, a pitiable spectacle, and doubly so in the eye of an affectionate and anxious parent. But even in such an eye it is not the *most pitiable* spectacle. The sight of it occasions sorrow, it is true, but not the most poignant sorrow; not sorrow inconsolable, because, with reference to eternity, it is not sorrow without hope.

Death, which crumbles down the body, at best a prison, may remove the veil that has so long obscured the vision of the mental eye, and pour upon the idiot's soul, as it escapes from the confinement of material organs, the radiance of intellectual day. And even though it should be otherwise; though death should bring no relief, and the idiot in eternity should be an idiot still, neither the parent nor the child would be responsible; neither would feel compunction, neither suffer reproach.

Idiocy is the act of God. It displays his sovereignty who in a thousand ways teaches us that He is the potter and we the clay; clay which He moulds at-pleasure, and for his own glory, into vessels of honour or of dishonour.

The withered intellect of an immortal being is, indeed, a mystery which reason cannot comprehend, and which can be solved by faith even only by referring it to that awful Being who sometimes pleases to cover himself and his ways with darkness from the scrutiny of man. Providence, as well as creation, has its shades; but in both alike they are only shades, which relieve the picture of good, and soften the blaze of mercy.

It is not, however, with foolishness as opposed to intelligence, but as opposed to virtue, that we are at present concerned. The folly of *sin* is a folly which transcends all other folly, and wrings into the cup of parental misery that wormwood which no ingredient sweetens or can sweeten.

This is not a constrained interpretation of the words we are now considering. *Folly* and *wisdom* are expressive of *sin* and *righteousness* on numerous pages of the sacred volume. Says Job, *Behold the fear of the Lord that is wisdom; and to depart from evil is understanding:* says David, *The fear of the Lord is the beginning of wisdom: a good understanding have all they that do his commandments:* says Solomon, *The fear of the Lord is the beginning of knowledge; but fools despise knowledge and instruction.* It was the FOOL whose soul was required of him in the midst of his revelry; it was the FOOL *who said in his heart there is no God.*

Nor is this a perversion of language. Sin is the most consummate folly, and the sinner is pre-eminently a fool. Not the idiot, slavering out his nonsense, furnishes so foul and disgusting a spectacle of folly as the sinner muttering his imprecations, hymning in secret his obscenities, or belching forth in public his deep-toned blasphemies. What! shall that man be deemed rational who insults the God above him, who resists the conscience within him, who prostitutes the mercies around him, and, outraging reason, outraging faith, outraging decency, breaks down before him all the barriers of truth, of justice, of temperance, of chastity, and transgresses at every step of his bewildered course those eternal rules of action which are sanctioned by wisdom, and which constitute the boundary between sanity and madness? Shall the man who does this—who does this without relenting, and in spite of admonition, in spite of warning, in spite of entreaty—the man who does this, not casually, but habitually, and who persists in doing this from his cradle to his sepulchre—shall this man be deemed rational? Ah! beloved pupils, to drink poison one's self, or to cast among others firebrands, arrows, and death, and to say, " Am I not in sport?" are not indications of sanity, but of madness. Yet such are the indications which the life of the sinner furnishes.

True, the sinner may be endued with natural talents. So may the maniac. Sallies of wit, flights of fancy are occasionally discoverable: even the fire of imagination sometimes sparkles, and coruscations of genius glare amid that ungoverned and ungovernable train of thought which he pours forth during the paroxysms of his phrensy. Yet the maniac is not a reasonable creature: so neither, with all his love of arts, with all his talents for excelling, is the sinner.

The wicked man, accomplished and erudite as he may be, is, notwithstanding, a deranged man. That intellectual order which God ordained is subverted, and all within is anarchy. Reason is prostrate, lust predominant, and conflicting passions agitate his bosom, and wring and rend his soul. Like the ship dismantled and rudderless, and at the mercy of the elements, he is driven about by every wind that blows, and turned from his course by every surge that rises. What port he shall arrive at, or on what shoals be wrecked, he neither cares nor calculates. He takes no observations, he keeps no reckoning, he shapes no course: neither chart nor compass is regarded: he is impelled by accidental causes and in opposite directions, and his whole voyage is a voyage at random.

This is not exaggeration. Whatever else the sinner possesses, he possesses no discretion: at least he exercises none. He acts according to no fixed rules, he lives in conformity to no established plan. His intermissions in excess, his changes from crime to crime, are wholly capricious; so that whether he becomes less profligate or more so, the act is not deliberative, but, as it were, instinctive. And, even when he seems to deliberate, the means he chooses are mischosen, and have no relation to the end he aims at. All is wild, and fanciful, and erratic.

Neither is this exaggeration. If you think so, mark the sinner in his bewildered and delirious course. His fortune is squandered, his constitution destroyed, his honour sullied, his conscience defiled, and his soul sacrificed—heaven sacrificed—immortality sacrificed. And for what? For nothing. He deliberates not, he makes no calculation; but is hurried on, as if lashed by demons, from play to gambling, from gambling to the dramshop, from the dramshop to the brothel, from the brothel to the madhouse or the prison, and from thence to—hell.

Again I ask, can such a man be deemed rational? No, he cannot. As we have said, sin is the most consummate folly, and the sinner pre-eminently a fool. With truth and reason, therefore, Solomon calls a wicked son a foolish son; and with no less truth and reason, he affirms of such a son THAT HE IS A GRIEF UNTO HIS FATHER, AND BITTERNESS TO HER THAT BARE HIM.

Mark these emphatic words. Solomon does not say that a foolish son is grievous, but a *grief* unto his father: not bitter, but *bitterness*—the very gall itself—to whom? TO HER THAT BARE HIM.

Who would have expected such an issue? Behold with what anguish the mother bears, and with what constancy she nurtures that infant at her bosom. All her other cares are laid aside, all her other pleasures are forgotten. She tends and caresses it by day, and by night she watches the slumber of its pillow. She is ever vigilant, ever active, and never weary in performing the humblest and most tender offices in behalf of that little being.

So strong is the maternal instinct, so true, so steady to its object, that, when the prophet sought an image to illustrate the ever-wakeful and never-failing faithfulness of God, among all that assemblage of related beings which surrounded Him, no ties were found so tender, so indissoluble as those which bind a mother to the tenant of her cradle. Hence he significantly asks, as being the least probable of all things, and because he could seize on no stronger instance of kindness and of constancy, *Can a mother forsake her sucking child?*

And can it be possible that this child, whom, before its countenance has been lit up with intelligence and smiles—even from the first moment of its being the mother forgets not—can it be possible that this child, now the source of so much happiness, the object of so many and such delightful hopes, will hereafter become the source of the most aggravated and unmitigated misery?

Yes, even this is possible. Sin subverts the order and destroys the harmony of all God's works. It poisons the very fountains of felicity, and causes pain to spring from the soil where pleasure alone might be expected to grow. It sunders the ties of friendship, and renders the ties of nature even, which it cannot sunder, galling and corrosive: so that the very bond which binds a mother to her offspring binds her to the object of her misery: a misery which the partner of her bosom shares, but without alleviating; for it is a misery which admits not of consolation, and which division even lessens not. Thus it may be said emphatically *that a foolish son is a grief unto his father, and bitterness to her that bare him;* FOR HE IS SO IN LIFE, HE IS SO IN DEATH—NAY, EVEN AFTER DEATH—IN THAT ONLY WORLD WHERE POSTHUMOUS MISERY IS POSSIBLE.

IN LIFE. Of all the wounds inflicted by one human being on the peace of another, none are so deep, so lasting, so incurable as those which sin inflicts : nor is there any object so noxious, so hateful, as the agent who inflicts those wounds. Other causes may deface the beauty of the body, but sin deforms the very soul of man. It renders even that deathless inhabitant of the bosom vile and polluted, as well as guilty and hideous. Not the most odious object that meets the eye is so offensive a spectacle as the soul of man in ruins : the soul degraded by appetite, defiled by lust, and infected throughout with the leprosy of sin. Such a spectacle, so loathsome even to the eye of strangers, what must it be to the eye of kindred : what, especially, to the eye of virtuous parental affection !

With what emotions must a father, a mother, look upon such a child, upon such children : children, the objects of their tenderest love, and of their earliest and most anxious care ! Children whom they have warned and counselled by day, and borne upon their hearts to the throne of grace by night !

With what emotions must those parents, who themselves feel an habitual horror of sin and dread of the displeasure of the Almighty—with what emotions must such parents witness the broils, the recriminations, and contentions of children, whom they have taught so long, and with such assiduous care, to live in amity! Ah! with what dissonance must oaths and imprecations grate on the parental ear, from lips whose first accents were prayer and praise ; but whose later and hoarser tones have filled even the hallowed retirement of the domestic circle with the clamour and the ribaldry of demons !

To see the members of a family ripen in sin as

they ripen in years; to see them trampling on authority, breaking through restraints, and, finally, tearing themselves away from those withered arms that would have still led them back to virtue; or, if this were quite impossible, would at least have kept them for a season from perdition; to see them tearing themselves away from those arms, and, in the spirit of fiends, entering on the world only to corrupt and curse it—mere outcasts, forsaken of God, despised of men; to see this downward course, this surrender of prerogatives, this sacrifice of prospects, this perversion of talents, this prostitution of reason; to see this in the person of a child, already diseased in body as well as in mind, and literally corrupting in anticipation for the sepulchre; to see this as a parent sees it, especially as a mother sees it, and, at the same time, to remember, and to be obliged to remember, that the object of all this guilt, and misery, and disgust, and pollution, *is bone of her bone and flesh of her flesh*—oh! this, this it is that drains from the very wormwood its dregs, and gives to the bitterness of maternal misery its consummation. *The spirit of a man may sustain his infirmities; but a wounded spirit who can bear?*

When Brutus raised his treacherous arm in the Roman senate-chamber, the heart of Cæsar sunk; and, concealing his face beneath his mantle, without resistance he received in his bosom the parricidal stab, and fell. And yet Brutus owed not Cæsar so much as children owe their parents; nor did that parricidal stab of his inflict so deep or so unnatural a wound on Cæsar's bosom as children by their crimes inflict on the bosoms of their parents.

Eli's was not the only priesthood that has been dishonoured, nor were *his* the only gray locks which have been brought, by the profligacy of sons, with sorrow to the grave.

You remember that prodigal, whose crimes and whose repentance have been rendered memorable by the record which Jesus Christ has left of them. What, think you, was the father's anguish, when this his younger son, impatient of restraint and incapable of submission, demanded his portion, and, deserting his home, commenced his rash and ominous career? What was his anguish when he saw this son, gradually receding from virtue, changing the habits of his childhood, and, finally, relinquishing both character and conscience, giving himself up wholly to debauchery? What when he saw him deserted by the good, a companion of the vile, surrounded by harlots, and squandering even the last remnant of his patrimonial inheritance in wanton and riotous living? What, finally, must have been his anguish, when he saw that son, once perhaps so amiable, so respectable, so promising, and still to a parent's aching heart so dear—what must have been his anguish when he saw that son, deserted and despised even by the wretches who had feasted on his bounty, at length reduced to beggary, a keeper of swine, and driven by hunger to feed, in common with the herd he tended, upon husks? Let that burst of parental joy which welcomed the first homeward movement of this repentant, returning prodigal, answer our interrogation.

Vile, and wretched, and covered with rags as he

was, his exulting father waited not for his arrival; but, flying to meet him, in ecstasy he fell upon his neck and kissed him. The best robe was instantly ordered to be put upon him, shoes upon his feet, and a ring upon his finger. The fatted calf was killed; the festive board was spread; and the note of joy was again heard within the so long sad and silent mansion.

It was meet it should be so. Why? A father's heart declares the reason for this domestic jubilee: *Because this my son was dead and is alive again; he was lost and is found.* To conciliate the elder brother returning from the field, and offended at the welcome the prodigal had received, the same reason was repeated: *This thy brother was dead and is alive again; he was lost and is found. It was meet, therefore, that we should make merry and be glad.*

It was, indeed, meet they should do this: never was festivity more rational. The very angels sympathized in it; for *there is joy in heaven over one sinner that repenteth, more than over ninety and nine just persons that need no repentance.*

Ye parents, ye afflicted parents, whose hard lot it is to have ungodly children; who in the bitterness of your souls have said, and still say, in the closet and at the altar, oh! that God would recall another wanderer, and cause that abandoned son of mine to relent and to return; parents whom not death, but sin—more cruel than death—has robbed at once of your peace and of your children, what solace can I offer you? what words of consolation address to you? None: for none would be availing. These are mis-cries which solace reaches not, and which words of consolation only aggravate. Ah! who can comfort those whom the God of heaven has not comforted? Sorrow is yours by His appointment; and to Him, therefore, you can only lift up your hearts and weep. Peradventure, even as respects that prodigal of thine, His mercies are not quite gone, and His wrath will not burn for ever.

Pity, oh God! we beseech thee, our guilty and erring children. Pour out thy spirit upon them, and they shall be renewed. Turn them from the error of their ways, and they shall be turned.

But if a foolish son be a grief to his father, and bitterness to her that bare him *in life*, how much more is he a grief and bitterness to them *in death:* and this, whether respect be had to the death of the parent or of the child.

The death of the parent.—Can the mind of man conceive a thought (except, indeed, it be the dread of damnation for one's own sins)—can the mind of man conceive a thought so full of terror, of anguish, of all that can distract the soul, as the thought of dying, and leaving behind a profligate and ungodly child—a family of profligate and ungodly children; children with whom all the means of grace have proved unavailing; children whom no kindness could conciliate, no counsel influence, no tears soften, no motives move; but who, in despite of parental love and parental virtue, have remained obstinately impenitent; and who are now about to be deprived of those abused mercies they have hitherto enjoyed, and to be left orphans as well as profligates in the midst of an insidious and treacherous world? I repeat it, what other thought is there, except it be the dread of one's damnation, which can plant so sharp a sting in a parent's bosom, or press upon his heart in death with such a tremendous weight?

To be surrounded, when dying, by impiety and impenitence, by intemperance and debauchery; to be deprived even of the hope of being forgotten when dead; to foresee that one is to be remembered only through the profligacy of children who are left behind, to nurture, it may be, other children still more profligate than themselves, and who, in their turn, shall nurture others, thus transmitting guilt and misery through a race of immortal beings, and sealing reprobation, perhaps, to a remote posterity— what ideas are these! ideas rendered still more dreadful by the remembrance of these tremendous words: FOR I, THE LORD THY GOD, AM A JEALOUS GOD, VISITING THE INIQUITIES OF THE FATHERS UPON THE CHILDREN, UNTO THE THIRD AND FOURTH GENERATION OF THEM THAT HATE ME!

Miserable comforters indeed are wicked children around the pillow of a dying parent. What an afflicting prospect to the eye! What sad forebodings does it press upon the heart! My God, deliver me in that hour from the bitterness of such a scene. Oh! grant that the hand of filial piety may wipe the cold dew from this forehead and close these eyelids. Then shall thy servant die in peace, when his eye shall have seen thy salvation in the person of his children.

The death of the child.—Ah! how hard, how

very hard to a pious parent to give up for ever an unrepenting and incorrigible child. David had such a child : but mark how he loved him ; even after he became his enemy, how he loved him.

Though he had alienated from his father the affections of his people, wrested from his hand the sceptre, and seized by violence on his throne, Absalom was still unsatisfied. With the ingratitude of a demon he pursued that father, who, bowed with age, fled before his son over Kedron into the wilderness, as a doe flies to the thicket before the tiger. Yet, even in this exile so afflicting, so unnatural, David, forgetful of himself, remembered only Absalom, and pitied him. Yes, even *there* nature asserted her empire in the heart of the deposed monarch; and the compassion of a father, in all its tenderness and strength, returned. Gladly would he have stayed the arm of retribution, and snatched this intended parricide from the vengeance he deserved. Thus, even at the hazard of his kingdom and his life, in opposition to himself, he interceded for the traitor. All were strictly charged, for the *father's sake*, to spare his son, though in arms against him. To the captains of Israel, even to Abner, Abishai, and Ittai, as he sent them forth to the battle, he said, *Deal gently, for my sake, with the young man; even with Absalom.*

When the messengers, Ahimaas and Cushi, arrived in succession with tidings from the camp, though his crown and kingdom were suspended on the issue, the first anxious inquiry which David addressed to them was not, has Abner been victorious? but *is the young man Absalom safe? The enemies of my lord the king*, replied Cushi, *the enemies of my lord the king, and all that rise up against thee to do thee hurt, be as that young man is.* Not the tender and flattering terms in which this triumph was announced could render it acceptable. The voice of Cushi, joyful to every other heart, conveyed no joy to the sorrow-stricken heart of David. Far from it. *The king was much moved, and went up to the chamber over the gate, and wept: and as he wept, thus he said, Oh! my son Absalom! my son, my son Absalom! would God I had died for thee, oh Absalom, my son, my son!*

Nor is David the only father who has felt this sentiment, and spoken this language beside the bier and at the grave of his son. There is a sorrow far more inconsolable than that of Rachel's, who filled ancient Rama with her lamentation, and who refused to be comforted; because there is a thought far more distressing, even to a mother's heart, than the thought that her *infant children are not.* The wicked lives of children, their unforgiven sins, ah! this it is that robs the mourner of the mourner's consolation, and changes, even in the maternal hand, the cup of death, always bitter, into *bitterness itself.*

Ah! ye unnatural children! ye murderers of your parent's peace, in what language of remonstrance shall I address you? Alas! there is no language of remonstrance of power to reach and quicken a bosom dead to every ingenuous feeling—dead even to filial gratitude. That is the last throb felt by the seared conscience; the last sentiment of hopeful omen that forsakes the indurating heart. But remember, scoffer, though dead to virtue, you are not dead to suffering. From the habitation of your mother, made wretched by your profligacy; from the tomb of your father, slain by your ingratitude, your sins cry aloud to heaven against you. Forbearance has its limit; God is just as well as merciful; and wo unto that sinner on whom at once rests his parents' blood and his Maker's malediction. *The eye that mocketh at his father and despiseth to obey his mother, the ravens of the valley shall pick it out, and the young eagles shall eat it.* These are awful words. Let them sink into thy heart, profligate young man; thou rebel at once against nature and against God.

But to return from this digression. Not even the wickedness of parents invalidates the truth of the position we have been attempting to illustrate and enforce. Profligate as your father or mother may be, they are not so profligate but that your sins will aggravate their misery. Yes, even profligate parents wish the happiness of their children. In *their* hearts so obdurate, there is still one cord that vibrates in unison with nature.

But, even were it otherwise; though they had lost the parental instinct, and become as selfish and as reprobate in their feelings as the damned, a foolish son would still be a grief and bitterness to them. Sin mingles its poison in the cup of the wicked, and carries its woes into their families as well as into the families of the righteous. A wicked son, therefore, even to wicked parents, must be *a grief and bitterness.* He must be so in life, so in death;

and so after death, IN THAT ONLY WORLD WHERE POSTHUMOUS SUFFERING IS POSSIBLE.

When Dives lifted up his eyes in torments, and saw Abraham afar off, and Lazarus in his bosom, he addressed to the patriarch two petitions, and but two; the one respecting himself, the other his kindred. Sweltering beneath his Maker's wrath, and finding no rest, *he cried and said, Father Abraham, have mercy on me; and send Lazarus that he may dip the tip of his finger in water and cool my tongue; for I am tormented in this flame.* This denied him, he added, *I pray thee, therefore, father, that thou wouldst send him to my father's house; for I have five brethren; that he may testify unto them, less they also come into this place of torment.*

Whether this petition was prompted by a dread that the presence of his brethren would aggravate his misery, or whether the sympathies between kindred on the earth find place in hell, is not material to inquire. It is enough for us to know that Dives thus prayed. And be it remembered, this is the only form of prayer we have any knowledge of having ever been offered up in those regions of dark despair which mercy never visits, and to which deliverance never comes. Methinks I hear the same mournful cry repeated in behalf of children by every ungodly parent that has joined Dives in his abode of misery.

Since it is so—since not even Lazarus may be permitted to administer to our relief, though but one drop of water, oh! that it were granted that he might go to yonder world, where mercy is still admissible; that he might go to the houses we once inhabited; to the children we have left—left, corrupted by our counsel, ensnared by our example—oh! that it were granted that some messenger might be sent to warn them, lest they should also come to aggravate our doom in this place of torment.

Nor is it strange that the anticipated dread of such a vengeance should extort, even from damned spirits, such a note of supplication. For, among all the forms of retribution which incensed justice has in store for sinners, what damnation is there so doubly to be deprecated as the meeting of a parent with a child—in hell! Ah! what mutual curses and recriminations will be exchanged between the malignant, fiendlike offspring, and the no less malignant and fiendlike author of his being and his misery; who, having inherited on earth his father's crimes and fortunes, has come to share in hell, and to aggravate by sharing, the torments of his reprobation.

Imagine such a meeting. Oh! how the cavern deepens! how the darkness blackens! while from the gulf below is heard a groan of more, more deep-toned misery. But I forbear. Let the veil rest which covers a scene by living men not conceivable. As yet, thanks to Almighty God, we know not its terrors. May He grant that we shall never know them.

I have now reached the consummation of my argument; and, in view of all that has been said, are you, who have heard me, willing to take, with a life of sin, its consequences? Art thou willing, thou gowned fool—thou fool even from the halls of literature and from the vestibule of science—art thou willing to sacrifice at once thine own peace and the peace of those whose happiness is identified with thine, bone as thou art of their bone, and flesh of their flesh? Are ye willing, ye profane young men, who, with all your learning, have yet to learn that the fear of the Lord is the beginning of wisdom—are ye willing to become the assassins of your godly parents on the earth, or the executioners of eternal vengeance on your ungodly ones—in hell?

By all that is touching in a parent's misery—by all that is dreadful in the Almighty's malediction—by the terrors of the hour of final separation, and the deeper terrors of an after-meeting to the wicked, doomed to become, and to continue through eternity, tormentors of each other—I adjure you to renounce your folly, and, ere the guardianship of the spirit is withdrawn and the temple of mercy shut, betake yourselves to acquiring that heavenly wisdom which will abide the coming of the Son of Man, and be availing in the day of judgment and at the bar of God: a wisdom which the Academy teaches not, and cannot teach. It is not from Socrates or Seneca that we learn to know God and Jesus Christ, whom to know aright is life eternal: a knowledge, in comparison with which the learning of the schools is folly, and the boastful possessor of it, untaught in purer doctrine and by a holier teacher, is, and will remain throughout eternity, *a fool.*

Oh God! this wisdom from above is thy hallowing, hallowed gift. Bestow it on these youth ere they depart from around thine altar, lest they return to their homes the harbingers of discord, and carry into the domestic circle, and to their parents' hearts that deep misery for which, grace apart, there is neither antidote nor remedy.

Hear this our prayer in their behalf. Confirm the wise in their wisdom, and turn the heart of the fool from his folly. Do this, thou Author of our being, thou Father of our spirits and object of our hopes, for Christ's sake, and to thy name shall be the glory.

S

XIII.

[All wish to Die with the Assurance of Happiness hereafter.—As Youth is the most important, it is also the most dangerous Period of Life.—Religion only can guard against the Temptations incident to this Period.—The Example of Josiah.—All Men mean to repent of their Sins.—Danger of delaying Repentance—from the uncertainty of Life and of the continued possession of Reason—from the hardening effects of Perseverance in Sin—from being left to a Reprobate Mind.]

Let me die the death of the righteous, and let my last end be like his, exclaimed the son of Beor, when summoned by Balak to curse the Israel of God. Lives there a man who does not sympathize in this sentiment of the prophet, or who would not appropriate his language?

Could we travel round our world, and, visiting all the dwelling-places of its guilty inhabitants, collect their various opinions, adverse as we might find them on other questions, on this they would be found to harmonize in one common and fraternal sentiment, *Let us die the death of the righteous, and let our last end be like his.*

Let me die the death of the righteous is articulated by the tongue of the miser, as he appropriates the dower of the widow, and throws his remorseless fangs over the orphan's patrimony.

Let me die the death of the righteous trembles on the lips of the drunkard as he mingles his cup, and in the intervals of his execrations. Even from the hall of youthful revelry might be heard, were the language of the heart audible, that prayer, their only prayer, *Let us die the death of the righteous, and let our last end be like his.*

Much, however, as all desire to die the death of the righteous, few are disposed to live *his* life; and yet the one is not to be expected without the other.

To urge the immediate adoption of the life of the righteous cannot, therefore, be impertinent at such a time and before such an audience.

If piety be desirable at all, early piety is desirable. *Youth is at once the most important and the most perilous period of man's existence.*

It is the most important, because it is the first; and, as such, leaves its own impressions on all those other periods that follow in an endless series.

Man enters on existence ignorant and impotent, but pliable and docile. The first impressions on his heart are the deepest and the most abiding. Thus, at the outset, and during the inceptive process of moral agency, a cast is given to his tone of feeling and his type of character. Secondary impressions of a similar kind only deepen the preceding, and carry forward the process of formation. Soon his taste receives a bias; soon his pleasures are selected, his companions chosen, and his manner of life settled. Thenceforward he advances, I do not say under an absolute necessity of being, but strongly predisposed to be, for ever after what he hitherto has been. Habit renders pleasurable what indulgence has made familiar. Hence the sentiments cherished, the maxims adopted, the modes of thinking and acting practised in youth, cleave to the man with the tenacity of a second nature; and thus the web of life runs on uniform in its texture, and woven of the same material to its close. All, therefore, that is either grand and glorious, or mean and miserable, in ceaseless being, is contained in embryo in life's first act. And every step which the actor takes on earth is a step of destiny; for it is a step towards hell or heaven.

As youth is the most important, so it is *the most perilous period of man's existence.*

It is the period of fancy, of imagination, of passion; the period when the world appears most gaudy, and pleasure is most enticing. Reason, as yet, has not detected the sophistry of sin, nor experience revealed its bitterness. Even that worldly prudence which age imparts is not yet acquired; and all the avenues of the heart are left open and unguarded to the assaults of every invader.

Now it is that health nerves the arm, ardour fires the bosom, and insatiable desires prompt to action. Now it is that a field of ideal glory presents itself, rich in objects of interest, and replete with scenes of gratification; a field where every evil is disguised, every danger concealed, every enemy masked; where vision follows vision, and phantom succeeds phantom. Wealth, honour, pleasure, each big with promise, but faithless in performance, courts his attention and solicits his choice. Forms of beauty flit before his eye, songs of melody enchant his ear, streams of bliss invite his taste; and, before a creature who is to die to-morrow, a long life rises up in prospect; while from the banquet of bewildering folly a voice is heard to say, "Rejoice, oh young man, in thy youth, and let thy heart cheer thee in the days of thy youth; and walk in the ways of thine heart and in the sight of thine eyes;" but that voice adds not, and the deluded victim knows not, that it remains to be added, "Know thou that for all these things God will bring thee into judgment?"

At such a moment of danger, at such a crisis of being, ah! how needful the eye of faith, the anchor of hope, and the monition of the Spirit.

Religion, at the very outset, places her votary on the vantage ground in this warfare of the soul. To him, in anticipation, she unmasks the world, exposes its vanity, discovers the sting which sin conceals, and detects the poison which pleasure mingles in her chalice. When temptation assails, when passion impels, when companions invite, she interposes eternal sanctions, sheds prophetic light on the eye turned heavenward; and God, who sees, is seen by it: the spell breaks, the vision vanishes, and the child of promise, recovering his decision, shrinks back, and drops the fatal cup, untasted, from his hand. His patrimony is spared, his constitution spared, his honour spared: life still remains a blessing, and heaven is still attainable.

What but piety preserved Joseph in the house of Potiphar? What but piety sustained Josiah on the throne of Israel? You remember the history of this enviable youth? Descended from a libertine parentage, nurtured at a licentious court, he succeeded at a tender age to the sovereignty of a mighty empire. But even on this giddy height, and compassed by every allurement and seduction, the young Josiah stood secure; and, though he had no example to copy, no friend to counsel, no monitor to warn, still he continued inflexible, and to the end resolutely maintained his integrity. More than this, he breasted the torrent of national corruption, gave a new tone to public sentiment, and brought back a whole community to the practice of virtue and the worship of Jehovah.

And what was the cause of this singular felicity? Religion. His heart had been early imbued with the spirit of piety, and he entered on his reign in the fear of the God of his fathers. It was not the battles he fought, it was not the desolation he occasioned, but the deeds of goodness he performed which endear his memory, and will continue to endear it to a thousand generations.

Adventurous youth, just entering on the world, need you not that shelter which Josiah needed? Are you quite sure that no temptation will prevail against your virtue? no sally of passion pollute your honour? no deed of rashness wreck your hopes? Go, then, daring adventurer; go unsheltered to the combat, and without thine armour. Thy very confidence is ominous, and presages naught but danger. Now, as formerly, *Quem vult Deus perdere, prius dementat.*

But, apart from the virtue it secures and the safety it affords, it were wise to become religious *in youth,* because of the uncertainty of becoming so thereafter.

Whether you desire at all to become religious is not now, nor has it ever been, a question. Live as he may, no man means to *die* a sinner. Each one who hears me has already offered up the prayer of the son of Beor; and you all intend to put yourselves in an attitude for receiving its fulfilment. Yes; you all intend, ere long, and before the summons shall have gone forth, *Away, sinner, away to judgment*, you all intend to break off your sins by repentance, and by faith to make your peace with God.

But when? Perhaps in meridian life—in old at farthest. But know you not that the meridian life, the old age on which you calculate, and on which such mighty interests are to hang suspended, are quite uncertain? Has mortal man any claim upon the future? Or lives there one who is certain of tomorrow?

Rash neglecter of present opportunity, who art thou? or what was thine origin, and what will be thine end, that thou shouldst court such hazard, and stake thy soul on a mere contingency?

On repentance that is future thou art relying for the expiation of present crimes. But when is that repentance to be performed? Where is it to be performed? On earth? Hast thou, then, made a covenant with death? Hast thou entered into a league with hell? Are the ministers of wrath shut up, or is the arm of Omnipotence chained back, that folly should presume on sufferance, and treason rely upon impunity?

Behold, *saith the high and lofty One that inhabiteth eternity, whose name is Holy, your covenant with death shall not stand; your agreement with hell shall be disannulled. When the overflowing scourge shall pass through, then ye shall be trodden down of it. Judgment also will I lay to the line, and righteousness to the plummet; and the hail shall sweep away the refuge of lies, and the waters shall overflow the hiding-place*—of sinners.

Preposterous youth, and are thy powers of action at the outset to be perverted, and thy first years of being to be filled up with sin? How durst thou, even for a moment, make God thine enemy, and set thy Maker at defiance? When he but wills the sinner's overthrow, every agent in the universe becomes a messenger of evil, and every element of nature a minister of death. Now, as formerly, there is a destroying angel that walketh in darkness, and a pestilence that wasteth at noon day.

Be your intentions what they may as to a future reformation, what assurance have you of a future opportunity? How know you that God will proportion his mercy to your misery, and spare you until age, that you may bewail the crimes of youth: crimes deliberately committed, and with a view to be repented of?

A fearful uncertainty overhangs the future. Youth and age, strength and imbecility, bow alike before the King of Terrors. That young man, devoid of understanding, whom Solomon saw from the casement of his window, presumed on future penitence. Imboldened by this presumption, he yielded to the voice of flattery, and hastened to that banquet whence he returned not; for suddenly a dart passed through his vitals. Thus goeth the sinner to his pleasure, as the ox goeth to the slaughter, or the bird to the snare, and knoweth not that it is for his life.

Indulge not the vain dream of a future opportunity. In the counsels of God no such opportunity may ever be granted. On the contrary, many of you will die; will have appeared at the bar of God; will have received your doom, and passed onward to that state where the unrighteous are unrighteous still, before that period shall have arrived which you are now presumptuously appropriating to a preparation for these dread events.

Do you ask for proof of this? The monuments in every cemetery furnish it. There it is written on many a marble tablet, with the iron pen of death. Have you not beheld those mounds where youth and beauty lie interred? Have you not read the prophetic lessons there inscribed? The testimony of the dead is decisive testimony: sustained by which, we announce to you who hear us, that many a living youth is marked for the sepulchre, and will prematurely reach it. The decree has passed; the designation for early death has already been made in heaven; and time will reveal the order of that succession which will conduct you severally to your unlooked-for dissolution. How dangerous, then, delay! Hopes built on future opportunity, how fallacious! Know, oh man! that now is the accepted time, now the day of salvation. By embracing religion now, you make God your friend, and secure the prize of immortality. By neglecting to embrace it, you put your souls in jeopardy, and leave the question of ultimate salvation suspended on contingency: a contingency how full of peril! since more than half of all who yet have lived have died before maturity. And, knowing this, will the living still procrastinate? Or, if they do, will not death, that finds them without preparation, find them also without excuse?

But death is not the only contingency which renders dependance on future penitence fallacious.

Those mental powers, without the exercise of which repentance is impossible, are held by a precarious tenure. God, who withdraws his spirit and the heart indurates, touches the nerves of the brain and reason departs, foresight departs, reflection departs, and all the attributes on which moral agency depends, and which give to being all its value, as if blotted from the soul, cease to be manifest; or, if manifest, appearing only in conflict, like the troubled elements of nature when the laws which govern them are disturbed or suspended.

Have you not read of that king of Babylon, exiled by mental malady from the society of man, who ate grass like the ox, and was wet with the dew of heaven till his hair became like birds' feathers, and his nails like eagles' claws?

Have you never seen a fellow-creature bereft of reason, chained in his cell, or fearfully ranging in his liberty? And felt you not the withering influence of that glance which he cast upon you? Felt you not the spell of that piercing shriek which he sent forward to your ear? That unhappy being once possessed talents; once indulged in dreams of happiness; once formed plans of reformation. Wretched wanderer, what avail him now those plans and purposes!

Can he pray? Can he believe? Can he repent, or make aught of preparation for death, for heaven, or for judgment? Ah! no. Whatever of guilt was on his conscience, when from the Almighty this blight came over him, he must carry it unrepented of, and therefore unforgiven, to the bar of retribution.

His fate, presumptuous young man, may be thine own. Minds of the finest texture and the highest cultivation are peculiarly exposed to mental malady. They who think most are most in danger of losing the capacity of thought. It is from the halls of science, from among the votaries of the muses, that lunatic asylums receive their most regular and constant accessions. Oh, then, serve God now. Hereafter thou mayest not have the ability to serve him; or, if the ability, not the disposition.

You imagine reason permanent, death distant; and that ample time remains to be appropriated to religion. Suppose it were so: does it follow that that time will be so appropriated? Having despised God in youth, are you sure that you will be disposed to render, or he to accept the services of age? It is not quite so clear that sin indulged conduces to the renunciation of sin; or that the dregs of life are the most acceptable offering which man can present to his Maker.

It is not said of those who seek God late, but of those who seek him early, that they shall find him. Wherefore, ye young, turn at his reproof. On you he will pour out his Spirit: to you he will make known his words. Reason allows of no delay: religion allows of no delay. The language of both is, *Remember now thy Creator in the days of thy youth, before the evil days come, and the years draw nigh when thou shalt say, I have no pleasure in them.* Now is the time for decisive action; *now,* not to-morrow. God is found of them who seek him early:

> " Now is the time he bends his ear,
> And waits for your request;
> Come, lest he rouse his wrath, and swear
> You shall not see my rest."

But if you neglect to secure salvation in a season the most favourable, is it probable that you will secure it in a season that is the least so? Will crime, think you, appear more odious the more it is familiarized? Or will the love of God fall with greater power upon the heart the longer it casts contempt upon that love?

Ah! no; though you were to live as long as did Methusaleh, if you embrace not religion in youth, it is not probable that you will afterward embrace it. *As the twig is bent the tree is inclined* throughout the whole extent of God's moral husbandry. Exceptions, indeed, there may be, but they are only exceptions.

Far be it from me to detract from the power of grace, or to set limits to the Holy One of Israel. There is a bolt by which the cedar of Lebanon is riven, a blast before which the oak of Bashan bows. But not like these are the ordinary visitations of the Spirit. It descends, not like the tempest in its strength, assailing the aged, and subduing the confirmed in sin, but like the shower upon the new-mown grass, the dew upon the tender plant, causing the young to hearken, and out of the mouths of babes and sucklings perfecting praise.

I repeat it: if you do not in youth embrace religion, it is not probable that you will ever afterward embrace it.

Among the multitude by crime rendered memorable, can you name one sinner whom age has reformed? It was not Cain; it was not Ahab; it was not Jezebel; it was not Herod: no, nor was it any of their profane coadjutors. But, waving the record of by-gone days, where is now its reforming influence?

Look into the world. Do you not see the miser still hugging his treasure, and the drunkard still revelling in his cups, though both are gray with age, and bending to the tomb? Even these wretched outcasts, now so dead in sin, so callous to reproof, once seriously intended to devote the evening of their days to God.

But have they done this? No: nor will they. In the attitude you see them now, death will find them, and, with their sins upon them, they will appear at the bar of judgment.

Age reform the sinner? Ah, no! Age has no reforming power. As well might the Ethiopian change his skin or the leopard his spots, as that they who have been accustomed to do evil should learn to do well.

But you imagine that with you it will be different. That, unlike those miserable men who have lived before you, you will love sin less the more you practice it; that you will think of God more the longer he has been forgotten; that, having first secured this world, you will be all attention to secure the next.

Were it even so, still your salvation would be uncertain. Wearied and worn out in the service of Satan, what assurance have you that you will be admitted to the service of God? The vigour of youth exhausted in dishonouring your Creator, is it certain he will accept the dregs of age—the valueless tribute you have the audacity to intend offering him?

When the frosts of threescore years shall have passed over you, withering all your joys, and extinguishing all your hopes; when, having reached the verge of life, and standing on the brink of eternity, you shall turn your affrighted eye to heaven, and try your unpractised voice in supplication unto God, are you quite sure that he will hear your cry, that he will answer your petition? May he not then say to you as he said to Judah, *Go now, and cry unto the gods to whom you have offered sacrifice?* May he not say unto you, Go, sinner; go to the world—to its pastimes and pleasures: these have been thine idols; let them save thee.

There is a state, in regard to which God says of the wicked, *they shall cry to me, but I will no answer.*

The spirit of God is indispensable to your conversion. That spirit now offers you its aid. Behold, I stand at the door and knock. Hitherto you have refused it admission. Even now you say, Depart from us: we desire not the knowledge of thy ways. Taken at your word, that spirit may depart from you. Know you not who it was that said,

My spirit shall not always strive with man? Wo unto that sinner, abandoned by the Spirit, concerning whom it shall be said, as it was said of Ephraim of old, Let him alone; he is joined to his idols.

Oh God! interpose thy mercy, and avert from us so frightful a doom; and to thy name shall be the glory. Amen.

XIV.

ADDRESS DELIVERED BEFORE THE BIBLE SOCIETY, 1819.

[Character and Design of the Bible Society.—Christian Communities do not sufficiently appreciate their indebtedness to the Bible.—Nearly all that is pure in Morals or kindly in Feeling derived from it.—In the first Ages of the World, God's Communications to Man were direct, and were perpetuated and extended by Tradition.—The early Longevity of Mankind favourable to this —The Traditions and Institutions of heathen Nations coincide with and confirm the sacred Records of the Jews.—Divine Revelation and the Speculations of human Reason, as exhibited in their different Effects.—Dreadful Moral Corruption of the heathen World.—Influence of Christianity in ameliorating the Condition and Morals of Mankind. —Unspeakable importance of Divine Revelation in regard to a future State.—The duty of Christians to extend it to all Nations.]

Go ye into all the world, and preach the gospel to every creature, said the risen Saviour to his astonished disciples. Obedient to his mandate, and renouncing their humble occupations, they began to publish the GLAD TIDINGS.

What was said to them is, in effect, said to us, and to all who have received the doctrine of his resurrection. Though not evangelists ourselves, it is our duty to become *helpers* to those who are. And this we may do extensively, and, if God please, efficaciously, by aiding to translate, to print, and to distribute THE BOOK in which that gospel, commanded to be preached to every creature, is contained.

The speaker's voice is evanescent: this printed record permanent. The speaker's voice is erring:

this printed record is truth itself; the pure, unmixed, unadulterated word of God.

I address the members of this society, not as a few isolated individuals, associated for the purpose of giving a Bible to each one of their destitute acquaintance (though this were laudable), but as an integral part of a vast association: an association which stretches across the ocean, and compasses both continents; an association which concentrates the influence of distant nations, and is grasping the mighty object of preaching by the printed word, in all languages, the gospel of their common Lord to every creature. An association, in behalf of which saints on earth offer up their prayers; on which angels in heaven look down propitious; and which shall, as we trust in God, continue to exist long after its present members are forgotten; nor remit its exertions till every family under heaven possesses a BIBLE, and each member thereof has read or listened to its contents.

In contemplating such an association, with what force do the prophetic words of St. John rush upon the mind! *And I saw another angel flying through the midst of heaven, having the everlasting gospel to preach unto them that dwell on the earth; and to every nation, and kindred, and tongue, and people.*

If the most splendid triumphs followed the first proclamation of *the glad tidings* by the living voice, what may we not hope for from a second proclamation of the same tidings by the written word! And who knows but the reappearance of that primitive catholic spirit, which is forcing into union sects so adverse, and giving a moral organization to the commonwealth of Christendom—who knows but this spirit is the welcome harbinger, and this organization the honoured instrument destined to introduce the church's jubilee—mankind's millennium?

To justify the formation of a society, it is sufficient that its object be a rightful one. But if the public patronage be claimed in its behalf; if the community are called upon to embark in its design; if the rich are required to contribute their riches, the powerful their influence, and the pious their prayers, then is it incumbent on its advocate to show, not only that the object proposed by it is rightful, but that it is also important; and that great exertions are not called for without an aim commensurately great.

In behalf of the society in whose name I now address you, great exertions are called for; and I trust it can also be shown that its aim is commensurately great; equally *great in point of goodness and of magnitude.*

To attempt this before a Christian audience may by some be deemed unnecessary. Alas! that it were not so. We eulogize the Bible, but how much of this is from habit. We boast of our advantages; but are they not merely words of course? Do the people generally realize—does the statesman realize—does even the Christian at the altar of his God realize the supreme felicity he enjoys, or feel the eminence of that moral elevation to which the Bible has exalted him. Basking in the sunshine of gospel ordinances, and having never groped amid that frightful darkness which elsewhere overshadows the nations, we measure not the distance which separates the pagan from the Christian, nor appreciate what a wretched, friendless, hopeless world this earth had been without the light of Divine revelation.

To this light is owing whatever of benignity of manners, whatever of elevation of character, whatever of sublimity of morals or purity of faith the world exhibits.

In travelling along the track of ages, scarcely a monument of mercy or a deed of glory appears to rescue from infamy the fame, and from oblivion the memory of successive generations, which is not directly or indirectly referable to the influence of *that revelation imbodied in the Bible.* By the revelation imbodied in the Bible, I mean all the communications made by God to man, from the first intimation of his law in the Garden of Eden, to the last splendid discoveries of his grace in the island of Patmos.

Late, indeed, were inscribed the first pages of this sacred book: a book which, amid the wrecks of art and the revolutions of empire, it hath pleased God to preserve entire. The commencement of its inscription, however, was not the commencement of the revelation which it contains. An era of oral communication preceded that of the written word. As the human race was in its origin confined to a single family, and the first revelations were made to the heads of that family, the direct benefits thereof were coextensive with the race itself. As, again, its members increased and spread, they each became a medium of conveyance through which these then unwritten oracles of truth were carried to distant regions, and handed down to succeeding generations.

The longevity of man in the first ages favoured this method of transmission. Few, indeed, were the links in that chain of descent which connected the family of Moses with the family of Adam. A single individual might have communicated the sayings of the senior inhabitant of Eden to the senior surviver of the flood. With each of these venerable personages, it was the lot of Methusaleh to have lived contemporary; and thus an authentic history of the world could have been furnished, reaching through a lapse of more than seventeen centuries: during which period, and through faith in God's unwritten testimony, Enoch was translated, and Abel crowned with martyrdom.

Even amid that wide-spread dissoluteness of manners and abandonment of principle which preceded and produced the deluge, the true religion was preserved by Noah and the pious of his household. Those infidels, his contemporaries, who had lost the knowledge and forsaken the worship of the God of their fathers, were swept from the earth as one brushes dust from off his garment, and the race was again reduced to a solitary family: a family, however, instructed in the events of antediluvian history; made the depository of early and sacred tradition, and retaining within itself a knowledge of the origin and end of that multitude who had so miserably perished.

To receive this family, the Mountain of Ararat

lifted its head above the waters; whence, as from another Eden, Shem, and Ham, and Japheth went forth to repeople the desolate earth, and to re-establish the worship of the true God upon it. From one or the other of these favoured individuals, the millions now alive have derived their being. The Gentiles, therefore, must have been originally conversant with revelation—with the same revelation that we now possess; and which, after being enlarged and perfected, was imbodied in the Bible: a revelation competent to make, and which has made as many as have preserved and obeyed it, wise unto eternal life.

To what extent the true religion was thus spread, or how long, and in what degree of purity it was preserved, we know not. But we do know, that as late as the time of Abraham, the courts of Pharaoh, king of Egypt, and Abimelech, king of Gerar, retained the knowledge, were familiar with the institutions, and acknowledged the authority of the same invisible Being who was worshipped by the father of the faithful. And we also know, that when he returned from the pursuit of Chederlaomer, even in the vicinity of Sodom, he passed through Salem, a city of righteousness, and there received the benediction of a priest of the most high God. How many such cities of righteousness the world at that time contained, we are not informed; nor, considering the brevity of sacred history, is it to be expected that we should be. But we may well suppose that the unwritten revelation which had accomplished thus much may have accomplished much more; for, as we have said, there were but few links in the chain of descent between the first man and the first inspired writer; and those links are all known. Thus Moses might have conversed with Kohath; Kohath with Jacob; Jacob with Abraham; Abraham with Shem; Shem with Methusaleh, and Methusaleh with Adam.

Had the genealogy of other nations been kept with the same exactitude, and reported with the same fidelity, doubtless many additional channels of traditionary knowledge, and, perhaps, equally unexceptionable, had been afforded.

It is evident, therefore, from the longevity of man and the condition of society in the first ages, that, whatever just ideas of God were entertained, whatever hallowed sentiments of devotion were cherished, whatever acts of practical goodness were exhibited, all these may have resulted from revelations made to Adam, repeated to Noah, and transmitted to his descendants.

But if, from the longevity of man and the condition of society in the first ages, this may have been the case, *from other indubitable facts it is obvious that it must have been so.*

Similarity of ceremonies and institutions, of points of doctrine and forms of devotion, between the Israelites and the other ancient nations, evinces not only a common origin, but that they all derived the great constituent parts of their worship, as well as the essential articles of their belief, from the same pure source—the revelation of God.

Nor is this mere assumption. That the world was created in six days; that the human race sprung from a single pa r ; that their primeval state was holy and happy ; that they apostatized from God ; that misery followed, and that their whole posterity, with the exception of Noah and his family, were destroyed by a flood : these are truths of revelation with which the records of all antiquity are replete. They are replete, too, with direct and solemn recognitions of the institution of marriage, of the Sabbath as a day of rest, and of sacrifice as a propitiation for sin.*

* The ancient Hindus, according to Strabo, declared that the world was made; that it will have an end; that God made it; that he governs it; and that he pervades the universe. The ancient Chinese, Egyptians, Phœnicians, Greeks, and Romans held nearly the same doctrines.

In the Orphic Hymns it is thus written : " Regard steadily the Maker of the world. He is one ; he is self-existent : from him all things sprung. Surrounding the whole universe with his present energy, no mortal sees him : he alone sees all things."

Maximus Tyrius declares that it is the universal opinion of mankind that there is one God ; and Sophocles, that God is one, and only one, and that he made all things.

"The Spirit of God moved upon the waters," says Moses. "The world was all darkness, undiscernible, undistinguishable, till the self-existent God dispelled the gloom," says Menu, son of Brahma.

Sanchoniathon styles the wind which breathed on the original chaos *the voice of the mouth of Jehovah.* Thales says that the night was older than the day ; and Ovid, that at first, when chaos existed, the sun was not, nor the moon.

Sanchoniathon asserts that the first parents of mankind sprang from the earth ; being one male and one female.

Homer and Hesiod agree that man was formed from the earth ; and Euripides adds, that the spirit returns to heaven, whence it was derived.

Plato says, " In the days of old there flourished a divine nature in the first man ; and the likeness of man to God consists in this, that man be holy. After the father of the universe beheld his work, he rejoiced therein. He willed that all things should be good. It was not fitting that he who is the best good, should make anything but what was perfect. Then God fed and governed men himself, as men now feed and govern themselves. They fed on the fruits of trees, as the earth spontaneously sup-

Whence had the Gentiles these things? Did different nations, and kindred, and tongues, and people, plied them without culture. They were naked also, and passed their time in the open air, reposing on the verdant herbs." The cause of vice, he adds, is from our first parents.

Eurysus says that God made man in his own image; and Catullus affirms the corruption of the race, after they had lost their original righteousness, to have been generally believed.

Hesiod declares that the first mortals were of a serene and quiet spirit; that the next generation or sort of men were of a bad moral character; that they destroyed each other by acts of violence, and that Jupiter hid them.

Berosus, the Chaldean, says that there were ten generations before the flood; and he states, as do also Manetho, Hieronymus, and Hesiod, that in the first age the life of man was a thousand years.

An ark, in allusion to Noah's preservation, was introduced into the religious rites of many pagan nations. The dove, which announced the subsiding of the waters, was held to be a sacred bird; while the raven, which returned not, was accounted a bird of ill omen.

The bow, the token of the covenant spoken of by Moses, was revered for ages. To this covenant Hesiod alludes: he calls it the great oath, and says it was placed in the heavens as a sign to mankind.

Berosus, the Chaldean, affirms that, at the time of the flood, men fled to the top of a mountain in Armenia; and Abidenus, that birds were repeatedly sent out of the ark, and that, the third time they returned, their feet were marked with mud.

Three generations after the flood, says Melo, Abraham was born; and he had a son Isaac, whom he was about to sacrifice, when a ram was substituted in his place.

Hesiod says the seventh day is a sacred day; Homer the same; and Theophilus of Antioch affirms that it is a day which all mankind celebrate. Porphyry states that the Phœnicians consecrated one day in seven as holy; Linus, that a seventh day is observed among holy people; Lucian, that the seventh day is given to boys as a holyday.

Eusebius asserts that almost all philosophers and poets acknowledge the seventh day as holy; Clemens Alexandrinus, that the Greeks, as well as the Hebrews, observe the seventh day as holy; and Josephus, that no city, either of the Greeks or barbarians, can be found which does not acknowledge a seventh day's rest from labour. Plato affirms that the seventh day is a festival to every nation; Tibullus, that the seventh day, which is kept holy by the Jews, is a festival to the Roman women; and Sue without concert and without motive, stumble on the septenary division of time? Did the inhabitants of the world, by mere accident, all concur in resting from their labours on the very day on which its Maker rested from his?

The institution of sacrifice also forces upon the mind a similar interrogatory. Sacrifice, so frequent, so extensive, whence did it arise? Was it the effect of chance? Was it from caprice? Or did speculation, in regard to everything else so changeful and so contradictory, in this, uniform and universal as the laws of nature, guide nations of every temperament, and inhabiting every clime, to the same grand result, THE HOPE OF EXPIATING THEIR SINS BY THE BLOOD OF VICTIMS SHED IN SACRIFICE?

Had the solemnities of the altar no assignable origin? Had they no intelligible significance? Or did they not rather originate in the mandate of Jehovah, and express as a symbol, and contain as an envelope, that great mystery hid for ages—the mystery of godliness—God manifest in the flesh? which envelope was removed when the veil of the second temple was rent; and the significancy of which symbol was announced when the cross of Calvary

---

tonius states that Diogenes, the grammarian, used to dispute at Rhodes on the Sabbath-day.

The ancient Celtæ, the Hindus, and the Arabians computed time by weeks; and Dion Cassius affirms that all the world learned thus to reckon time from the Egyptians. Isidorus states that the ancient Romans computed time in this way; and Herodotus asserts that this method of computation was very ancient.—(See Panoplist for 1810-11, Shuckford's Connexions, and Asiatic Researches.)

U

was lifted up, imbued with the blood of the last great sacrifice—*the Lamb of God, that taketh away the sins of the world.*

That these institutions existed among the nations is undeniable; and if they did not exist from the beginning, and the commandment of God did not give rise to them, when were they first introduced, and what was the object of their introduction? The records of what historian indicate the one? the dogmas of what philosopher reveal the other? Of no one. Here antiquity is silent, or speaks only to confess its ignorance. If you doubt this, let the ancient sages be consulted. They will tell you that it was neither reason nor the authority of the wise, but tradition, which gave to them their doctrines and their institutions.*

Thus did revelation, even while unwritten, restrain and guide the researches of the wise, direct towards heaven the hopes of the humble, and for ages pre-

* Plato, in his Philebus, says: "The tradition which I have had concerning the unity of God, his essence, and the plurality of his perfections and decrees, was from the ancients, who were better than the Grecians. The Grecians received their learning from the ancients, who lived nearer the gods."

What is Plato, exclaimed Numenius, on reading his works, but Moses speaking in Greek? Plato had learned the unity of God from Pythagoras; the immortality of the soul from Therecydes. But these revered sages, as well as Orpheus, and Linus, and Musæus, if we may believe what is said of them, rested the truths they delivered upon tradition, and not upon the deductions of human reason. And, so long as the light of tradition was followed, mankind entertained more just ideas of God and of duty than prevailed among them in later times: ideas in many respects accordant with the sacred writings. The history of the ancient Greeks, of the Persians, of the Arabians, of the Chinese, and of the Hindus, proves incontestibly this surprising truth.—See Panoplist for July, 1810, p. 62

serve from atheism and idolatry no inconsiderable portion of the human family.

The articles of ancient faith, while they were traditionary, retained something of the unction of that Spirit which dictated to the progenitors of mankind the original creed from which these articles were derived. Although the systems adopted were in many particulars fabulous, still, amid their fable, some grand truths were apparent; some traces of wisdom and sublimity, which sufficiently distinguish these venerable compilations from those degraded and degrading theories which mere human reason has since palmed upon the world. For, no sooner had philosophy extinguished the lamp of tradition, than an impenetrable gloom settled over the temple and the altar, through which there has since gleamed only a portentous light, which, like the meteor's glare, has everywhere " led to bewilder, and dazzled to blind."

This claim, set up for the exclusive influence of revelation in the production of whatever there has been of sublimity of faith or purity of morals among the nations—is it disputed? Let facts then be appealed to ; and facts are not wanting : facts which bear directly and conclusively on the point in question; for, in process of time, the whole world, the Israelites alone excepted, lost the knowledge, and disregarded the sanctions of revealed truth. Out of Judea, where the sacred traditions were imbodied and their records deposited, the human race were no longer influenced by them. Here, then, mere human intellection found an opportunity to display its resources and exert its strength. Mark the issue. Be it what it may, it definitively settles the comparative merits of faith and reason, of revelation and philosophy.

Where are those productions of human intellection to be found which may be put in competition with the sacred oracles? What system of ethics is there so pure in its doctrines, so sanctifying in its influence as that of the Law and the Prophets? What nation can boast a faith so sublime, a worship so spiritual, as that which signalized the land of the patriarchs?

Is it Egypt? Egypt is, indeed, renowned for her sages and philosophers, her arts and literature. Greece even borrowed letters from the schools of the Nile. But *her religion.* To say nothing of the spotted calf at Memphis, or the sacred ox at Heliopolis, regarded as divinities, what think you of an erudite and polished people paying religious homage to cats, to dogs, to wolves, and to crocodiles? What think you of pools and pastures kept sacred to their accommodation; of a tithe imposed for their maintenance; of a priesthood set apart for their religious rites? And, finally, what think you of death inflicted for the smallest insult offered to these four-footed deities, these fleecy wanderers of the fields, or finny monsters of the waters?* My God! is it possible? It is. Such was ancient Egypt. Her history, her antiquities, her temples, her pyramids— the very monuments which attest her intellectual glory, preserve the evidence also of her moral degradation.

* Ant. Univer. Hist., fol., vol. i., book i., chap. iii.

Is it Phœnicia, then? Ah! it was at Phœnicia where were heard the shrieks of children sacrificed to Saturn! At Carthage, then? Here, too, the grim Moloch stood, extending his burning arms to enfold the immolated infant.

Where next? India, perhaps, will afford a more benign prospect. We have heard of the wise men of the East. But they are not at Orissa; they are not in Bengal. The ghastly visages of the famished pilgrims assembled there, evince that the temple they frequent is the abode of some malignant demon, and not the temple of the God of mercy. No; it is not in India that a pure faith and a spiritual worship are to be found. From the coast of Malabar to the banks of the Ganges, the flame flares terrific from the widow's funeral pyre. Graves open to swallow up the living, not the dead; and even the sacred Indus, along whose margin so many devotees assemble—even this sacred river bears away to the crocodiles and the sharks many a shrieking victim whom an accursed superstition consigns to its waters.* At Thibet, too, a no less detestable superstition reigns; and the fact that, in the single city of Pekin, more than three thousand infants are annually exposed to die, sufficiently acquaints us with the moral state of China.†

Let us, then, visit Greece. The Greeks were a polished nation, and yet not even barbarians were more barbarous in regard to religion.

* Ryan on Religion, p. 54; also Researches in Asia, by Claudius Buchanan.
† Gibbon's Rom. Empire, chap. xv. Puffendorf, de jure nat. et Gen., lib. vi. Ryan, sec. iii., p. 253.

History informs us that Themistocles sacrificed his Persian captives to conciliate the favour of the gods. At Salamis, a man was immolated to the daughter of Cecrops; one also at Chios, another at the temple of Diomede, and three at the temple of Juno. In Arcadia, even, there stood an altar to Bacchus, on which young females were beaten to death with rods.

Achilles butchered twelve Trojan captives at the funeral of Patroclus. A similar act of devotion was performed by the far-famed Æneas of Troy to the manes of Pallas. Indeed, it was a common custom of the Greeks, before a war, to propitiate their gods by human sacrifices. On one of these occasions Aristomenes offered three hundred human victims to Jupiter; and Italy was supposed to have been visited by calamity because a tenth part of its inhabitants had not been sacrificed to the gods.*

In the worship of the Greeks—nay, in pagan worship generally—obscenity forms as prominent a feature as cruelty: obscenity so gross, so public, so brutal, that the delicacy of a Christian audience allows only of its being alluded to. And how could it be otherwise? Is it to be expected that the worshipper should be less cruel or more chaste than the divinities he worships? But let the veil rest on this loathsome and detested part of pagan devotion.

What shall we say, then, to these things? Or where else shall we fly, to find among the Gentiles a temple in which the worshippers assemble apart from

---

* Plutarch's Lives. Hom., Il., xxiii., 175. Virg., Æn., x., 520. E sebei, Præp. Evan., lib. iv., chap. viii. Ryan, 247, 8.

scenes of licentiousness and blood? Not the tired dove that went forth from the window of the ark, so vainly sought, amid the waters of the flood, a resting-place for her foot.

Again I ask, what shall we say to these things? Or how comes it that, amid this universal degradation of the species, the Jews were not degraded? How comes it that, while so many nations were wandering in the darkness of this moral midnight, the inhabitants of Palestine, as if separated from the rest of mankind by a wall of fire, enjoyed light? For nearly two thousand years after the world had become idolatrous did this favoured people preserve the knowledge and worship of the true God. So stood Mount Zion as age after age rolled away; so stood Mount Zion amid the moral desolation, as another Ararat amid the deluge of waters. And whence this proud pre-eminence? Whence? From the ark of God's covenant resting on its summit. It was not the pagan talisman, but the sacred oracles, which shed a bright radiance around this hallowed eminence.

Mount Zion boasted no superiority in refinement or in arts. She produced no philosophers, no orators, no tragedians. Neither the Lyceum, nor the Academy, nor the Forum, nor the Theatre was hers. But hers (ah! enviable distinction), hers were the oracles of God; hers the Shekinah that overhung the mercy-seat; and hers the perpetual fire that burned upon the altar. Hers, too, was the hope of Messias, and the temple of Jehovah, whither the chosen tribes repaired to hear his law and to celebrate his worship.

The facts that a sublime morality was inculcated, a spiritual devotion practised, and the unity of God preserved in this chosen spot during so many ages of calamity and darkness, sufficiently evince the illuminating and hallowing efficacy of those sacred oracles from which alone were derived these admirable results.

Ah! had Judea been destroyed before the diffusion of mankind's last hope, the Bible, the sanctions of duty had ceased; the purity of worship had ceased; the example of the patriarchs had been lost; the history of the antediluvian world had been lost; nay, the history of creation itself had been lost, and all correct ideas of the great God had perished; and, unless restored by a second revelation, had perished for ever. Not the needle points the eye of the mariner more steadily to yon polar star, than does the finger of history the mind of the moralist to the hill of Zion. The hill of Zion is, as is shown by every page he reads, and by every monument that he inspects, the source and centre of all that is pure in faith or sublime in morals. The rays which enlighten the firmament proceed not more obviously from the natural sun, than do those which give light to the nations from the Sun of righteousness.

Thus far the effects of the written word in the land of the patriarchs and among the countrymen of the prophets.

But let us take a wider range. With the coming of Messias (whose coming was as the lightning of heaven) a new era commenced. Other oracles were added to those already given; God completed his revelations to man; and the Christian church was made the depository of the authenticated record in which they were imbodied. Truth now quickly flashed across that mighty empire of which Judea was a province. More than this: beyond its limits—even in the cold regions of the North, hearts were warmed and softened, and the distant islands of the sea, in the light of the Son of Man, saw light.

But what was the condition of these unbaptized nations when revealed truth was first promulged among them? To begin at Rome:

Rome had succeeded to the arts and the erudition of Greece. Alas! that we should be compelled to add, she had succeeded to her superstitions also. Over this vast empire—an empire where so many sciences were taught, where so much genius was elicited, where so many philosophers reasoned, where so many poets sung—over this vast empire, polytheism, with all its pollutions and all its cruelties, maintained undisputed dominion. A proof unanswerable, if such proof were wanting, that *the world by wisdom knew not God.*

These things are not lightly said. Plutarch affirms, that on the event of a war in Gaul, both men and women were buried alive, in obedience to an oracle. Porphyry states, that in his own time human sacrifice was offered at the feast of Jupiter. More than this: in their own blood the priests of Bellona did homage to that terrific goddess; and the Druids, who continued to the reign of Tiberius and Claudius Cæsar, added torture to murder, sometimes crucifying their victims, and at other times burning them alive upon the funeral pile.*

But not to the temple and the altar were the enormities of Roman superstition confined.

A funeral was not solemnized without carnage; the theatre was not attended without carnage; nay, in process of time, all Italy, and the empire itself, were filled with carnage and steeped in blood.

That the dead required the same accommodation and attendance as the living was one of the absurdities of ancient paganism. When a distinguished citizen died, wine and food were buried with him for his sustenance; and his wives and slaves were massacred to attend upon his manes. Besides these, one friend presented his servant, another his wife, and a third his son or daughter, as a token of respect to the deceased, and to swell the number of his retinue in another world. All these fell together, and one grave received their remains.†

This barbarous and most unnatural superstition, with the detestable practice founded on it, was adopted by the Romans; a practice modified, indeed, during the latter periods of their history, but so modified as to lose nothing of its cruelty, since the victims now fell by their own hands, instead of falling, as before, by the hands of the executioner.

On this murderous practice another still more murderous was founded: that of the gladiatorial shows, which became so general, and were so de-

---

* Plutarch's Life of Marcellus. Leland, part i., chap. vii. Tooke, part ii., chap. ix. Ryan, page 56.
† Ryan, p. 215.

lightful to the Roman people. I say delightful, for, incredible as it may appear, these furnished the favourite amusement of the populace, the magistrates, and even of the imperial Cæsars.*

On a single occasion Julius presented before the public three hundred and twenty pairs of gladiators; and at another time a thousand pairs were exhibited by Trajan. Even Titus solemnized the birthday of his brother by a show, in which two thousand five hundred human beings perished; and the birthday of his father was commemorated by a similar tragedy. "No wars," says Lipsius, "ever made such havoc of mankind as these games of pleasure, which sometimes deprived Europe of twenty thousand lives a month." Indeed, this passion for blood became so ardent and so universal, that not only senators and knights, but even women, turned gladiators.

The moral state of the other heathen nations furnishes no milder views to soften the horrors of this dismal picture. Everywhere human limbs might be seen bleeding on the altar, or human entrails quivering beneath the eye of the haruspex.

This is no exaggeration. The Gauls offered human sacrifice; the Thracians offered human sacrifice; the Germans offered human sacrifice; and, to add no more, the Lithuanians offered human sacrifice, and imagined that they could only please the devil whom they worshipped by torturing their victims before they killed them.†

* Ryan, p. 249.
† Ross, Religion of all Nations, sect. v. Ryan, p. 53.

How was it in Britain? in Britain, where now so many alms are distributed, where so much philanthropy is displayed, where so many spires now pierce the skies, pointing the eye of man to heaven, and his hopes to immortality—ah! precious fruits of the Christian dispensation!—how was it in Britain before the Bible entered there? Go to her temples of cruelty—to her altars of blood, and ask. Ask of her ferocious priests, and of her still more ferocious Druids. Approach her images sending forth flames, and listen to the victims within as they shriek and expire. Take the dimensions of that domestic felicity where children are articles of traffic; where marriage is unknown; and where whole clans herd together like the cattle of the stall.*

That such was the state of Britain before the Bible entered it, I appeal to Collier, to Guildas, to Jerome, to Tacitus, and to Cæsar. Great God! and did we descend from such parentage? and are these the miseries from which the Bible has redeemed us? Ah! Book of Life! henceforth, if I forget thee, let my right hand forget her cunning: if I do not prize thee above my chiefest joy, let my tongue cleave to the roof of my mouth.

But enough of this Eastern polytheism: the heart is sick with contemplating it. Let us quit these bloodstained temples, and cross the ocean. Perhaps in the Western wilds we shall find some sequestered spot where a purer faith is cherished, a less sanguinary worship maintained. Alas! though we cross the ocean, we only change, we do not es-

* Ryan, p. 251, 252, 253. Cæsar, De Bel. Gal., lib. vi.

cape the scene of misery. What the Eastern continent was, the Western is, excepting only where the Bible has reclaimed it—covered with idolaters. The sun, and the moon, and the stars, and not the Being who created them, receive the homage of the wild man. Even the infernal gods, so conspicuous in Grecian fable, are here acknowledged and honoured. The natives of Canada, of Virginia, and of the Floridas, literally worshipped the devil, to whom they sacrificed children to quench, as they affirmed, his thirst in blood.

Through all the regions of the North, false ideas of God have imparted to human nature a strange ferocity. The infant savage learns revenge from the sacred rites of his father, from the nightly orisons of his mother. Cruelty grows with his growth, and strengthens with his strength; until, at length, he inflicts torture as coolly, and drinks blood as greedily as the imaginary demons whom he worships.

As we descend along the isthmus towards the south, we discover monuments of art, but none of mercy.

In New-Spain the hearts of men were offered to the sun, and youths of both sexes drowned, to bear this idol company. When the corn first vegetated, young children were slain to ensure its growth; and it was afterward twice watered with the same blood before the harvest. Here, too, the domestics of a chief were interred in the same tomb with their master; and the manes of a prince were followed to the other world by a still larger retinue.*

* Ross, sec. iii. Ryan, p. 200, 216, 222.

On the event of the King of Cholulah's death, a human heart, riven from some living bosom, was by the high-priest offered to the sun; and for the ordinary sacrifices of this place alone, and for a single year, five thousand children were deemed insufficient.*

Mexico presents a still more bloody spectacle. Here every captive, without exception, was sacrificed. New wars were undertaken to obtain new victims; and in a time of peace, their gods were said to be perishing with hunger. As late as 1486, sixty-four thousand and eighty human beings were sacrificed by Ahuitzol, king of Mexico; and the ordinary victims of the altar cost the empire twenty thousand lives a year.†

Even the Peruvians, the mild and amiable Peruvians, sacrificed the subject for the health of the sovereign while living, and, when dead, an ample retinue was supplied to attend upon his manes. Their children they offered up to the ghosts of departed kindred, and often the son was slain to procure a respite from death for the father.‡

---

* Acosta's Hist. Ind., book v., chap. xx. Ryan, p. 256.

† At the feast of Quitzalcoult, the heart of a slave was presented by the merchants of Mexico to that idol; and ten to the same idol at Cholulah. And, as if this were not enough of cruelty, they added the ceremony of drawing blood from their own tongues and ears: a ceremony surpassed in madness only by that of the kings of Malabar, at the jubilee of the twelfth year; which jubilee the sovereign commenced by cutting off his nose, ears, and lips, and closed by cutting his throat in honour of the devil. Ross, sec. 3. Robertson's America, book vii. Raynal, vol. ii., book ii. Ryan, p. 220, 221, 223. Broughton, art. Quitzalcoult. Acosta's Hist. Ind., book v., chap. ix. Ryan, p. 255

‡ Ryan, p. 226. Robertson, book vii. Ross, sec. 3.

But we have proceeded far enough—perhaps too far already, and yet but a glimpse of this abomination of desolation has been taken. Other, and still other, and other rites, both of licentiousness and of blood, remain untold, which deserve yet severer execration, and which could be mentioned only in accents of deepest-toned horror. I might conduct you to the temple in which—but I forbear. As has been already said, let the veil rest on these enormities.

And now, over what a wilderness of crime and folly we have travelled : a wilderness which, for centuries, revelation has, step by step, been penetrating. And what have been its effects ? It has everywhere shed the light of truth on the temple and the altar ; and along its whole line of march has left its sacred impress on the moral map of nations.

Never were materials more stubborn and refractory than were those on which, at the commencement of the Christian era, revelation was called to operate. But these materials, hard and unyielding as they were, it melted, it refined, it remoulded. The temper, the manners, the habits, the pursuits, the institutions—nay, the very texture of society, was changed in every city, and province, and kingdom into which the Bible entered.

It allayed the thirst for conquest ; it diminished the carnage of conflict ; it infused a milder spirit into the law of nations. Extermination was no longer identified with victory ; the vanquished were acknowledged to have rights, and these were respected ; nor were prisoners of war thenceforth subjected to the dire alternative of massacre or vassalage.

Ancient slavery it abolished; modern slavery it is fast abolishing; and the trade itself—that accursed traffic in the muscles and the blood of man—is verging to its close, and will, ere long, cease to be the reproach of Christendom.

By one wise statute it terminated polygamy, with its broils and its vigils; and suddenly the chains fell from the mother and the daughter, and half the species emerged from the vilest degradation. By another, it put an end to the exposure of children, their desertion by parents, and the abandonment of the poor in their hovels of wretchedness and want, and on their beds of sickness and death. No sooner had the gospel law of charity touched the heart, than mercy flowed from it. The members of the infant church, though few in numbers, everywhere stood forth the defenders of orphanage, the relievers of want, the moral heroes and the almoners of nations.

It banished those gladiatorial shows which had so long piled the theatre with carcasses; those human sacrifices which had so long defiled the temple with blood. It banished, too, the worship of demons; the worship of heroes and of harlots, of images and of shrines.

No victims now bleed (with thankful exultation be it spoken)—no victims now bleed on European altars; no widows now burn on European pyres. The oracles which required such sacrifices are hushed; the altars on which they were offered, and the gods they were intended to propitiate, have sunk together in the dust, and the spiritual worship of the unseen Jehovah occupies their place.

The mummery of the haruspex has ceased; the mummery of the magician has ceased; the games, the festivals, the vigils, the lustrums, all have ceased. The entire machinery of the altar and the temple, the oracle and the response, the groves and the high places; the whole of that gigantic and tremendous fabric which fraud, and folly, and superstition, and cruelty had for ages been rearing, at the approach of the Bible, as if struck by the lightning of Omnipotence, fell to the dust, and has been swept by the breath of Heaven from the face of Europe. On the very site of these abominations, schools of education, asylums of mercy, and temples of grace suddenly arose; and these have everywhere been the results of the Gospel dispensation: proud monuments, announcing in every part of Christendom *that the reign of demons is past, and the kingdom of Messias come.*

What a comment is this upon that song of the angels which burst on the listening shepherds on the night of the Saviour's advent: *Behold, I bring you glad tidings of great joy which shall be unto all people; for unto you is born this day in the city of David a Saviour, who is Christ the Lord.*

Glad tidings indeed they were, and *to all people;* for, far as their annunciation has reached, the state of things has been changed. With every enlargement of the church's limits, the boundaries of the field of moral beauty have been extended. Examples of piety and patience, of charity and fortitude, have been multiplied. The character of man has assumed a new majesty; for his soul, loosed from

X

the bonds which once confined it, and the alliances by which it was degraded, has become animated by a heaven-directed principle, progressive in its nature, which, advancing in the track by Emanuel pointed out, has so raised Christian nations above the level of the rest of the species, that they seem as though descended from a different ancestry, and belonging to a nobler race.

As many centuries have shed their influence on Asia and Africa since the commencement of the Christian era as on Europe. When revelation was first promulgated in the West, Europe, in a moral view, was no less degraded than Asia—perhaps we might say, than Africa itself. How happens it, then, that while in Europe human nature has been progressive, and the march of mind has advanced with the rapidity of lightning, in Asia and in Africa it has remained stationary; or, if there has been any movement, that it has been only retrograde? How happens it that, even at this late day, the grossest idolatry and the most cruel superstition pervade those entire regions where revelation has not yet penetrated; that the whole mass of pagan population, the uncounted millions of the East and of the South, of the continents and of the isles, still grope in the profoundest darkness; still grovel in the most brutal degradation?

What is it that has elevated the Gaul, the Belgian, the German, and the Briton; that has given a generous impulse to the Dane and the Swede, and raised the Russian, even amid his snow-clad forests, so much above the wandering Tartar, who removes his gods as he does his flocks; or the unhappy negro, who worships the very vermin, and even the trees which grow upon his native hills of Africa?

There is but one answer. The whole world knows that it is the Bible only which has done this. The line which separates the light and shade in an eclipse is not more distinctly drawn on the disk of the sun, than is the line which separates Christianity from paganism on the map of nations.

In the light of the Sun of Righteousness Christendom enjoys light; while the rest of the earth is as one vast Valley of Hinnom, over which a darkness broods that is all but tangible. The very race is degraded; and the sons of God, ignorant of their origin and regardless of their destination, bow down to the earth and lick the dust.

If the view of the world here taken be correct (and where is the evidence that it is not so?), apart from those nations which the Bible has reclaimed, is there a single exception to this moral degradation? Not to speak of empires, or even provinces, is there a town, or village, or hamlet—nay, is there a family on which no ray of revealed truth has fallen, that retains the knowledge of God, that cherishes a rational faith, and offers to the Ruler of the universe a spiritual homage? I know not of such a family: *the civilized world* is ignorant of such a family. If it exists, its residence is in some sequestered spot to which no traveller has yet penetrated; its history is written in a language which no philologist has yet read. Beyond a doubt there is no such family;

and if there be not, then the view we have taken *is correct;* and, being correct, the proposition with which we commenced this discourse is fully established: *That whatever of benignity of manners, whatever of elevation of character, whatever of sublimity of morals or purity of faith this world exhibits, is owing to the Bible.*

From whencesoever these oracles were derived, the present state of the world—nay, the history of its condition in all past ages, clearly evinces, that they, and they alone, have power to sanctify on earth or qualify for heaven. And, though no retributive justice awaited the guilty, if mankind are to exist after death, and in circumstances at all correspondent to their earthly tempers and habitudes, then must the future condition of the Christian transcend that of the Mexican or of the Hindu, as much as the exquisite touches of St. John, in his portraiture of the New Jerusalem, transcend the coarse daubings of the false prophet on those pages of the Koran which he defiles with his gross picture of the Mussulman's paradise, devoted to licentiousness, and crowded with harlots.

The Bible is the world's first, last, best, and only hope. Much it has accomplished already, but much more remains to be yet accomplished by it.

Idolatry, with its impious, cruel, and lascivious rites, has been banished from the civilized states of Europe, and from all the settled portions of the Canadas and the United States. Even the Mexican temples, those Golgothas that swallowed up such multitudes, are demolished in the valleys; but blood, ay, human blood, even now trickles from the cliffs where those idol temples still stand among, the mountains of the South. In the forests of the West and of the North the worship of the devil is still maintained; and Africa, India, Thibet, Tartary, and the millions of China, to say nothing of the islands of the sea, what is their condition?

Ah! could I transport you to those regions of darkness; or, seizing the painter's pencil, could I but sketch a faint outline of the scenes of horror there acted; could I show you, at Calcutta, the son applying, with not even an averted eye, the lighted torch to the funeral pile of his living mother: at Giagas, the mother pounding her infant in a mortar, and smearing her body with the horrid ointment, to propitiate the demons that ride upon the wind, and shriek for the blood of children in the tempest: could I show you, on the banks of the Ganges, the father struggling to force into its depths his little son, still raising his supplicating eyes, and still clinging to the marble bosom of his parent—ah! hapless boy! in pagan hearts nature has left her seat, nor can the note even of filial anguish excite one pulsation of compassion there: could I show you, at Sumatra, the son whetting his knife, and adjusting his festive board beneath the shadow of some death-boding tree, at the foot of which a decrepit father, shaken from its top, is about to be devoured by his assembled children, who, as their sire descends, join in this precomposed chorus, " *The fruit is ripe and must be eaten:*" could I show you, at Juggernaut, the wretches crushed beneath the car of that dread

Moloch; or at the feast of Ganga, that terrific queen riding amid her quaking worshippers, with many a living victim literally spiked to her triumphal seat: could I show you, at Pekin, the infants whose brains bestrew the streets, and whose unburied bodies choke the very gutters; in the numerous cities of populous India, the poor that crowd the pathway of the traveller, in vain supplicating mercy, and trodden down as if they were dying weeds instead of dying men *—ah! could I show you these things, my purpose would be accomplished. You would pour out your wealth in alms: more than this, you would pour out your hearts in prayer, *giving God no rest until he establish and make Jerusalem a praise in the earth.*

Even though there were no day of judgment—no hereafter—and heaven, and hell, and eternity were chimeras, still reason, humanity, every motive that can touch an enlightened and ingenuous mind, should impel us to send to these benighted pagans the Bible, that we may rescue them from the bondage under which they groan, and terminate the miseries they suffer. But, great God! if there be an hereafter, if there be a day of judgment, and if heaven, and hell, and eternity be not chimeras, but reality— here my tongue falters, my heart overflows, and thoughts press upon me too solemn and too big for utterance.

On other occasions of charity I have wept, I have

---

* Mod. Univer. Hist., fol., vol. vi., chap. xiv. Ryan, p. 214, 219. Buchanan, Res., p. 144, 145. Broughton, Art. Ganga Gramma. Quar. Review of Baptist Mission.

entreated. On this I can do neither. The subject is too awful for tears, too authoritative for entreaty: and if its own inherent claims, its own tremendous importance does not interest, does not overwhelm you, nothing can. Tears would be vain, entreaties vain. I should tremble less for the poor pagans whose cause I advocate, than for the petrified audience—the hearts of stone which I address. For then, oh! thou Avenger of abused mercies, it would be manifest that we had been enlightened by thy gospel, and tasted thy rich grace for naught.

The signs of the times indicate that the chariot-wheels of the Son of God are approaching. It is rumoured among the nations that the Bridegroom cometh. Millions of supine Christians have suddenly awoke from their slumbers. The church has arisen, and is girding herself, that she may hasten to prepare the way of the Lord, and make his paths straight. No matter in what region we reside, nor whether the first object of our compassion be Jew or Christian, Mohammedan or pagan. The cause is one, the object is universal. It is the union of the redeemed of all nations, rising in the strength of their Lord and Saviour, to extend the limits of his reign, and multiply the subjects of his mercy.

Those missionary invaders of the kingdom of darkness whom the benevolence of Christendom is sending forth, not, like the promulgators of the Koran, clad in armour, rely on the omnipotence of truth and of the Spirit alone for success. Their weapon is the incorruptible word : at once the symbol and the seal of peace, which they carry with them to the nations.

Already, since this great effort began, has *the covenant of mercy* passed by translation into many a pagan tongue, and to many a worshipper of idols has it been distributed.

These achievements mark the commencement of a new era; and if the first beams of the millennial morning fall so benignly on the borders of the wilderness, how resplendent will be the *noonday glory*, when those entire benighted regions shall be reclaimed to virtue and flooded with light! Ah! thou church of the living God, cherish the spirit which at length inspires thee. Let no expenditure exhaust thy bounty; no divisions damp thy ardour. Still multiply and send abroad impressions of this life-giving record, till every nation, and kindred, and tongue, and people are supplied, and the whole earth is filled with the salvation of God.

But what can *we* do to help forward this vast, this gigantic undertaking? What? As much, at least, as did that poor widow who cast her willing mite into the Gospel treasury.

Every drop of water that distils from the distant mountain top, mingles with some rivulet which descends to swell the deep and broad river that rolls its mighty mass into the ocean. So every copy of the Word of God, whether written out with the pen or struck from the press, causes that hallowed stream to flow in a wider channel and with a more resistless force, whose waters are destined to heal the city and the country, and to make even the desert blossom like the rose. And how cheering the thought, that the very volumes purchased by our money or distributed by our hands may chance to fall, like the dews of Lebanon, on some barren spot in God's moral husbandry, and convert it into a spot of fruitfulness and verdure.

Let us, then, cherish the spirit and emulate the example of our brethren in the East. Let us bestow our property as cheerfully, and bend our exertions as steadily to the advancement of the glorious enterprise in which, with them, we are engaged. Let us strive to erect a monument to the Redeemer of mankind on this side the ocean, no less sublime than has been erected by his disciples on the other; nor leave to the seagirt isle alone the expense and honour of sending the Gospel to all nations.

Let us, at least, endeavour, by a more general distribution of these heaven-descended records, to console our own mourners, to prepare our youth for living, and our aged for death. Let us endeavour to purify our towns; to purify our villages; to raise the standard of our public morals, and exalt still higher our national character. In a word, let us endeavour completely *to Christianize* these United States, that the condition of our citizens may be more blessed on earth, and our whole population made meet for an inheritance in heaven.

What a lofty hope! and how welcome to the bosom of the patriot Christian! And shall we, having tasted the preciousness of this hope, lightly relinquish it? Ah! no. Necessity is laid upon us. We have sworn, and may not repent; we have lifted up our hand to God, and cannot go back. And let the thought animate us, that, by supplying our own destitute brethren, we are indirectly aiding to supply the destitute pagans. Yes, every Bible we distribute here is, in effect, a Bible distributed in Arabia, in Egypt, in India, or in the islands of the sea; for every Bible we distribute here spares the price of it from the common fund of Christendom, and leaves the same to be expended in some heathen country.

Let us, then, freely put forth our exertions and bestow our charities; and, though the morning dawn not, let us go forward confidently to our work, remembering who it was that said, *Surely I come quickly.* Even so, come, Lord Jesus.

XV.

ADDRESS DELIVERED BEFORE THE PHI BETA KAPPA SOCIETY OF UNION COLLEGE.

[Difference in the Intellectual and Moral Condition of Individuals and Nations.—Ignorance and Knowledge the principal Causes of this Difference.—Advantages of Associated Efforts in promoting Science.—Intelligence and Happiness capable of being vastly extended.—First crude Discoveries in Science contrasted with the Progress since made.—Present State and future Prospects of Scientific Research.—Chymistry.—Astronomy.—Mineralogy and Botany.—Meteorology.—Electricity. — Medicine. — Political Science. — Popular Governments.—The United States.—Anomaly of domestic Slavery, in its Origin, &c., considered.—Ameliorations in our Institutions and Laws in regard to Debtors—to Criminals.—Religious Freedom.—Multiplicity of Religious Sects not incompatible with Christian Union.—Science and Religion reciprocally aid each other, and should never be disunited.]

OF other worlds than our own, and other races of moral agents than ourselves, our knowledge is extremely limited. These are subjects on which reason is silent, or speaks only in conjectural accents. Revelation, even, gives but a few brief notices of the existence or habitudes of unimbodied spirits. From these brief notices, however, it would seem rather probable than otherwise, that the original condition of moral agents generally has not been fixed, but contingent; and that all have been permitted, under God, to weave the web of their own destiny, and severally to form, by a series of individual actions, their ultimate and unchanging character.

But whether this be generally so or not, that it has been so with terrestrial moral agents is undeniable : for, though the elements of a common nature are apparent in the entire posterity of Adam, those elements have been so modified by circumstances, so transformed by education, as to present the extremes of vice and virtue, of dignity and meanness in the human character. Nations there are whose march for ages has been onward and upward; and other nations, again, who have either remained stationary, or whose movement has been retrograde. Individuals too there are who seem approximating towards the perfection of angels; while other individuals are degraded almost to the condition of brutes, or even of demons.

Various and inscrutable as may be the causes which have contributed to these opposite results, it is sufficiently apparent that ignorance is wholly incompatible with improvement, and that everywhere alike knowledge is power. Were God, even, not omniscient, he would not be omnipotent; or, if omnipotent, he could not, as now, display his glorious attributes in those marvellous phenomena which constitute the universe, and which stand forth as the august expression of his joint wisdom and of might.

It is knowledge which makes the mighty difference between man and brute—between man and man. The unlettered savage of the forest is more muscular and fleet than the polished premier who wields a nation's energies, and from his closet sends forth a controlling influence over realms he has not so much as visited.

It was knowledge which gave, and it is knowledge which upholds the dominion of man over so many orders of beings, superior to him in numbers as well as in agility and strength: a dominion extending with every extension of science, not only over animals, but over the elements, and bringing Nature herself into greater and greater subjection.

But the duration of human life is too short, and the range of individual observation too narrow for the acquisition of that profound knowledge, and the arrival at those grand results, for which faculties, in their nature progressive and immortal, had otherwise qualified their possessor. To remedy, therefore, the defects which necessarily spring from the brevity of human life and the locality of human residence, and to prevent the loss of triumphs actually achieved, a moral organization has been resorted to, and isolated individuals, distant from each other, have united themselves into societies, supplying the want of personal ubiquity by the distribution of their members, and of immortality by their continued succession. By such organization remote and scattered agencies have been combined, and the wise and good of different nations and ages, who otherwise, perhaps, as to any permanent effect, might have lived in vain, have become fellow-labourers with one another; nor is it too much to say, fellow-labourers with God, in carrying forward his grand and beneficent designs.

As an integral portion of such an association—an association whose aim it is to increase human knowledge and perfect human virtue, which has extended its ligaments across the ocean, and the influence of which is felt in both hemispheres—as an integral portion of such an association I now address the members of this society.

Without indulging in Utopian dreams, and mindful of the nature of man, as seen in the light which revelation and experience have shed upon his history; without pretending to have ascertained the precise measure of intelligence or happiness possible to be attained by beings so constituted and so situated, it is surely neither presumptuous nor unphilosophical to anticipate the future existence of both these attributes through a greater extent and in a higher degree than they have hitherto existed. Nor can it be derogatory to scholars or statesmen to embrace this cheering hypothesis, and to combine their influence to secure to future generations its blessed reality.

In glancing even casually over the map of nations, it is impossible not to perceive that there is a striking difference in regard to everything which renders being valuable between the different branches of the human family. Neither man himself, nor his condition in enlightened Europe and America, can be contrasted with what they are in benighted Asia, or still more benighted Africa, without mingled emotions of exultation and pity.

But were it even the case that, in the former and more favoured states, human nature had received its highest finish, and human intellect put forth its utmost energy, most powerful motives would still exist to preserve and perpetuate among civilized nations the triumphs already achieved; and to rouse their barbarous neighbours to the achievement of similar triumphs, that the entire race might be raised to the highest standard of merit, and share the largest measure of happiness.

Nor will, nor ought the friends of science to remit their exertions until this shall have been accomplished; until the most degraded of the tribes of earth shall have become regenerate, and shall stand forth each one in the glories of its own Augustan age; until the hills and valleys, the lakes and rivers of other states, as well as of Greece, shall have been consecrated by the slumbering genius that remains in each to be yet awakened; until Attic wit and Athenian models shall everywhere appear; until Negroland shall have produced her own Granville Sharp, Abyssinia her Milton, Thibet her Homer, and the wandering Tartar's reed shall sound a note as tender as the shepherd's pipe, when, in olden time and in classic fields, the Arcadian Corydon and Thyrsis sung; until all that is gross, and vulgar, and revolting shall disappear, and not cities and provinces merely, or even empires, but the entire world shall exhibit through all its territories whatever is tasteful in art, recondite in science, or enchanting in eloquence and song.

True, we cannot reach directly the distant and scattered elements of ignorance and degradation, nor can we bring our influence immediately to bear on the process of their transformation. Still we may do both indirectly and remotely.

Every collegiate institution, with its associate alumni, is the source and centre of a mighty influence, which is sent abroad, not only over the scientific, but the unlettered public—an influence which reaches in its course every academy and school, and even every habitation—inspiring genius, stimulating enterprise, and supplying motives and means through many a town and hamlet for assailing ignorance, vindicating truth, and extending the empire of learning and refinement. So that the measures we are adopting, and the strength we are putting forth, may, after acting on successive individuals, reach to remote places, descend to future generations, and finally be felt to the extremities of the world.

Let us not deceive ourselves as to the amount, either of good or evil, which may be produced by a single scholar, especially by a society of scholars. It is wholly impossible to measure the power, to trace the connexions, or to fix the limits, either in duration or extent, of moral causes.

To the laboratory of Tubal-Cain, Europe and America may be indebted for their chymistry; to the harp and organ of Jubal for their instruments of music; to Noah for their navigation, and to Belus for the art of masonry. To the astrologers of Egypt or the shepherds of Shinar, mankind may remotely owe the calculations of La Place—nay, even the astronomy of Newton. But for the signs of the zodiac and other sidereal localities, so fancifully sketched by the first eager observers, the eye of this sublime inquirer might never have been directed upward, and the whole energy of his mighty mind might have been wasted, as had been the energy of so many other great minds, on essential forms and occult qualities.

Who can tell how much Athens was indebted to Phoenician voyagers, or how long the genius of Greece might have slumbered, but for the alphabet of Cadmus? or whether even Greece herself, dismembered and trodden down by her enemies, shall continue, as she has done, to form the taste of nations, and to send forth an influence to bear on the moral destinies of the world? And since Greece, dismembered and trodden down as she is, still struggles for existence, and science and the arts have pervaded or are pervading France, and Spain, and Portugal, and Italy, and Germany, and Russia, and Sweden, and Denmark, and Britain, and last, though not least, the young American republics; since commerce is furnishing a universal medium of intercourse, and the press is everywhere supplying facilities for instruction, is it extravagant to anticipate that a redeeming spirit may, and will, ere long, go forth from civilized nations of sufficient power to effect the wished-for deliverance of nations still in a state of barbarism?

This were a truly sublime achievement: though exertion here ceased and progression here terminated, this were a triumph possessing enough of goodness and of grandeur to stay the eye of hope and to stimulate the eagerness of enterprise.

But is there anything, either in the nature of man or in the history of the world, which favours the opinion that all which is attainable has been attained, even by educated nations? and that, to them, nothing remains but to retrace the circle already traced, by the landmarks planted by the pioneers of science as they have advanced along their adventurous and unbeaten pathway? Is it to be believed that even schooled reason has so soon come to know all of God that is knowable, and that the whole field of glories spread around him has been so quickly and so cheaply gathered? This appalling apprehension may, perhaps sometimes does, cross the mind of aspiring youth, as their eye glances on the heights already gained, and the distance already passed over in the march of science. But the illusion quickly vanishes; for it is perceived that everywhere the boundary recedes as the inquirer advances towards it, and that discoveries *made*, however great, have hitherto only prepared the way for discoveries still greater. The time is yet distant, it is believed, *when nothing will be left in religion to be purified; nothing in the remedial system to be improved; nothing in political institutions to be reformed, and nothing in the physical sciences to be acquired.*

Great, indeed, is the disparity between the conjectural alchymy of the middle ages and our present inductive chymistry, founded on actual and accurate analysis. The phenomena of light, and heat, and electricity, and magnetism, as well as of bodies gross and ponderable, are now incalculably better understood than they were formerly. Earth, and air, and water, once regarded as uncompounded elements, are now resolved and recombined at pleasure. New distinctions have been made, a classification more conformable to nature has been substituted, and a nomenclature more intelligible and significant has been introduced. More than this: galvanic electricity has been discovered, the alkalis have been analyzed, and the doctrine of chymical equivalents has been established.

Much, however, as science owes to Berzelius, to Davy, to Wollaston, to Guy Lusac, and their coadjutors, shall we be so weak as to imagine that they are the only wise men, and that wisdom will die with them? Who knows but that discoveries are now making which will cast a shade over even theirs, admirable as they are? Who knows but that some bolder and more fortunate experimenter is even now unsettling doctrines hitherto believed to be settled, and is displacing by solution from the rank they occupy, not only potassium and sodium, but the entire kindred class of metallic bases? Who knows but that a more condensed heat brought to bear upon the crucible, or the electric stroke from some more powerful battery, may not reveal to the sense of man still simpler elements and more subtile combinations, by which the artists of future times shall be enabled to approximate, in their humble imitations, nearer to those matchless fabrics which God produces in his vast laboratory? Nor will analysis have reached its utmost limits until all the elements which Omnipotence employs are known and named, and all the processes are revealed by which, in variety so changeful, he produces those endless forms both of utility and beauty, which perpetually succeed each other throughout the entire extent of a decaying and reviving universe.

Astronomy, indeed, so far as mathematics are concerned, is among the exact and certain sciences, and so precisely have the magnitudes and densities of the sun and planets been ascertained; so accurately have their paths been traced, and their motions noted; so exactly has the influence even of their reciprocal disturbing forces been computed, that their several revolutions and localities may be determined by *calculation* for ages to come with nearly the same precision that they have been by *observation* during ages that are past.

But these, perhaps, are neither the whole nor the most interesting phenomena which the heavens exhibit; and, after having become familiar with the bolder lines of their outward aspect, man still looks upward with an eager eye, under the influence of a vague presentiment that the firmament above him contains something more than a mere orderly display of magnitude and motion, and that the orbs which roll in it may perchance be the residence of some race of kindred spirits: spirits, it may be, whose acuter vision or more powerful glasses enable them to look down on us, regardful of our progress, eager to communicate their sympathies, and impatiently waiting for the time when our improved instruments shall enable us to recognise their signal, and to give back by telegraph from our sidereal watch-towers the signs of recognition.

Much that was once unseen, has been already rendered visible; and since the same light that falls on them is reflected upon us, and the light that falls on us is reflected back to them, who knows but some future and greater Herschel may construct an eye-glass of power to bring their habitations within our range of vision, and thus enable man to commence a correspondence with his sidereal neighbours? Who knows but that future generations, communicating with the nearest planets, and, through them, with planets more remote, may effect an interchange of tidings, passed from world to world with the celerity of light, and carried far as the sunbeam travels? and that thus successive glories may be revealed, till our race, improved in knowledge and purified in affection, shall be prepared to respond in a loftier sense to the sentiment expressed from every sun and planet, *Great and marvellous are thy works, Lord God, Almighty; in wisdom hast thou made them all.*

These may seem idle and extravagant conjectures, and yet be conjectures below the elevation of the subject, and short of that reality which futurity shall reveal.

Had the ascertained grandeurs which astronomy has made apparent been suggested to patriarchal man, who probably saw in the firmament above him only a spangled canopy, revolving at no great distance around this one fixed, central planet, would they not have seemed conjectures as idle and extravagant? And if, during the first six thousand years of their existence, the human race have found means to acquire a knowledge of the number, and distance, and dimensions, and localities of the planets which surround them, is it quite incredible that they should, in some hundreds of thousands of years to come, find means to acquire a knowledge of their zoology and botany, and of the condition and habitudes of the beings who inhabit them?

There has been, I am aware, a time when it would have been deemed impious to suggest that such might be the duration of the world, or such the destiny of the race inhabiting it; for there was a time when religion, unmindful of the apostolic counsel and of prophetic calculation, saw in the everyday appearance of the heavens omens only of immediate dissolution.

Philosophy, too, has given countenance to the same delusion, by asserting that the solar system contained within itself a principle of destruction, which was hastening its end by approaches that were visible. But that time has now gone by. Religion having purified her faith, and Philosophy corrected her deductions, Science no longer supplies arguments against even that endurance of the earth which St. John, in the Apocalypse, has been thought to predict: it having been shown in the *Mechanique Cœleste* that those apparent deviations which filled the mind with such gloomy presages were apparent only, and that the forces which produced them were so adjusted by the Maker of the universe as to compensate at intervals the irregularities they occasioned, and thus bring back the planets to the same relative position in a readjusted system.

Nor is it in astronomy only that room for new achievements and motives for new efforts remain. The downward series of combinations is, for aught we know, as continuous as the upward, and its nethermost limit as far removed from human observation. The minimum of nature is as difficult of ascertainment as the maximum, and perhaps as many wonders are yet concealed by nearness and minuteness as by distance and dimension.

After all that Linnæus and Jussieu, Werner and Haüy, have accomplished, mineralogy and botany are only in their infancy. Countries yet remain to be traversed, caverns to be explored, and beds of rivers and basins of seas to be examined, before the materials can be supplied for completing even the distribution of the genera and species. But is the completion of the genera and species all that remains to tempt and recompense the skill of the artist and the eye of the observer? No: nor will the triumphs either of art or intellect be complete in these departments, till the internal structure both of plants and minerals shall have become as familiar as their external aspects; till the true atomic theory shall be exhibited in experiment and verified by observation; till, by a more skilful arrangement of glasses and a more dexterous management of sunbeams, visibility shall be imparted to elemental particles, and the arrangement shown which they assume in all those tasteful and brilliant varieties of vegetable development, and the no less tasteful and brilliant varieties of crystalline formations.

With respect to rain, and snow, and earthquakes, and tempests, and the various meteorological phenomena, we possess little more than hypothesis. The observations remain yet to be made, the facts to be collected, and the conclusions drawn, by which anything can be arrived at deserving the name of knowledge. And yet the time may come when these various, and changeful, and apparently capricious phenomena shall be reduced to fixed and general laws; and their return, and duration, and degree shall be as capable of calculation as the ebbing of the tides or the changes of the lunar phases; so that the voyager and husbandman, relieved from uncertainty and no longer the sport of chance, shall pursue their occupations under the additional advantage of an enlightened prescience.

We have lived to see the lightning chained, and its dread stroke averted from the frail edifice reared for human habitation. We have lived to see the ship made independent of the breeze, riding triumphant on the billow, and breasting the tempest by the impulse of steam. We have lived to see inland villages converted into ports of commerce, and inland products floating on artificial rivers traced by human hands, and connecting distant lakes with the distant ocean. These are achievements which must ensure celebrity to individuals, and render memorable the age they lived in. But what farther achievements yet remain to be accomplished we know not; for who can set limits to science? or say that posterity will not employ still mightier agents, and obtain the mastery over elements which now only mock our efforts to control them?

In the healing art, nay, in the whole remedial system, progression is apparent.

For the relief of the deaf and dumb, a language has been invented and a system of education introduced, which, in a single age and during the existing generation, has produced the most admirable results. Suddenly has a portion of the human family, hitherto degraded by their ignorance, and nearly excluded by their condition from human intercourse, been raised to the rank of intellectual beings; introduced to the mysteries of science, to the mysteries of religion, and to a participation in the delightful sympathies and charities of social life.

This benevolent expedient, while imparting happiness, has evolved talent: talent under very peculiar circumstances, the remote effects of which cannot now be estimated; for the situation of *educated mutes*, insensible to the allurements of sound and incapable of interruption from it, must be eminently conducive to mental application, and especially to mathematical research; nor would it be surprising should they hereafter cancel, by their contributions to science, the debt which they at present owe to charity.

In the mean time, those schools, founded for their benefit, are diffusing the knowledge of a system of signs already extensively adopted, and which, from the number of mutes among the different nations, is likely to be still more extensively adopted. Even now voyagers and travellers profit by their use, as courtiers and statesmen hereafter may; so that an art, introduced by charity into the cottages of the poor, may come to dwell in the palaces of princes; and an expedient, devised by the benevolent Sicard to alleviate the ills resulting from deafness, may be employed to remedy the more diffusive ills that have resulted from the confusion of tongues at Babel; and thus a general intercourse may be established among the nations, trained to this new language of the eye: the only language which has any prospect of remaining uniform or of becoming universal.

Nor have the deaf and dumb alone shared in the distribution of new benefits: for the aged, eye-glasses have been provided; for the maimed, artificial limbs have been constructed; and to the diseased, appropriate remedies have been administered.

Maladies once deemed incurable have been cured. Neither vegetable nor mineral poisons, however virulent, are now uniformly mortal. Even hydrophobia is said to have yielded to surgical operation; and vaccination, introduced by the philosophic Jenner, has nearly removed the terrors of one of the most dreadful scourges of mankind.

The maladies of the mind, as well as those of the body, are beginning to be better understood, and to be treated more successfully than they formerly were. No longer is the lunatic bound in chains or scourged with thongs; nor is mental alienation any longer regarded as the most hopeless, because the most incurable of evils.

And here it is gratifying to remark, that American physicians have contributed to the introduction of those juster views and that more benign practice which are destined to bless the nations. With the wisdom of the sage and the benevolence of the saint, the late lamented Rush urged the substitution of kindness for cruelty in the management of the insane. But it was reserved for another and more highly-favoured individual to develop, by a series of patient experiments, the practical benefits of such a substitution.

This man, even yet unknown to fame, without fortune and without patronage, ventured to establish, and has for years continued to manage an asylum which, in its results, has surpassed, not only the asylums of other times, but of other countries; and from which there has been sent back to their friends and to society a larger proportion of patients restored to reason and to happiness than from any kindred institution now known on earth or recorded in history.

A design so benevolent and adventurous, executed under great discouragements, and with such incomparable success, needs no present commendation; nor will future eulogy be necessary to render the name of Chaplin hereafter as dear to fame as it is already to humanity.

To the increase of medical skill in Britain more than to any other cause, perhaps, is to be attributed that increase in the average duration of human life which has become of late a subject of remark.

And shall we suppose, in this conflict with mortality, because triumphs have been achieved by the disciples of Esculapius, that farther triumphs are therefore impossible? And that to the future practitioner it only remains to mark the diagnosis of dis ease laid down in his textbook, and apply the rem edies prescribed in his dispensatory?

There is no greater reason for believing the mortal maladies which remain *necessarily* mortal, than there once was for believing those to be so which now yield to the power of medicine. Here, doubtless, as elsewhere, and now as formerly, the field lies open; nor will the faculty have done all that man requires or that God enjoins so long as a disease remains to be healed or a pain to be relieved.

Brilliant are the successes of the past; but hope lights up the future with a prospect of successes still more brilliant, to be continued until, by a more perfect knowledge of disease, a more complete development of remedies, a farther augmentation of comforts, a wiser formation of habits, and a holier manner of life, Pandora's box shall again be closed, the vigour of primitive constitution reappear, and the longevity of antediluvian man return.

Let it not be deemed either visionary or profane to indulge such anticipations, since prophets divinely inspired have indulged them. Visionary or profane as we may deem it, the time approaches when *the age of man shall be as the age of a tree; and the inhabitants shall not say I am sick;* for the mouth of the Lord hath spoken it.

This may, indeed, be supernaturally induced; but it is not according to the analogy of Providence that it should be so. Means are the instruments in effecting man's *moral* renovation, and why should they not be in effecting his *physical* renovation also? From misery as well as from guilt, it is his, by the help of God, to accomplish his own deliverance and to work out his own salvation.

In political as well as in physical science, a like progressive development is apparent.

The older governments were reared, and they rest on the right of prescription. That authority is a sacred deposite in the hands of the few for the control of the many; that it is hereditary, and its possessor responsible to God alone for its exercise, has long been asserted by sovereigns and admitted by their subjects.

These ancient doctrines, for the continued maintenance of which such efforts are making on the one Continent, are to a great extent abjured on the other. Not merely new, but adverse doctrines have been promulgated : that national sovereignty is placed in the aggregation of individual volition ; that the people themselves are the original source and ultimate depository of human authority ; and that office is a trust from them, reclaimable at their pleasure, and to be executed conformably to their will.

These doctrines, once mere speculation, are now not only imbodied in form and adopted in theory, but millions of human beings, scattered over extensive territories, are carrying them into effect; and are making, on a mighty scale, and in behalf of the human race, the sublime experiment of practical self-government. Should this experiment succeed—and we trust in God it will—to say nothing of its reaction on Europe and Asia, nearly half the human race will probably, at no distant day, in America, participate in its blessed results.

And yet, even in the land where this experiment is making, its legitimate effects are but partially apparent; for even here slavery exists, and freemen are attended and served by slaves. This only institution of tyranny is a curse engendered in other times and under a different form of government. Had the opinions and wishes of the primitive colonists been consulted, such an anomaly as slavery, in any of its forms, could not now have had existence. Still its existence is not the less an evil on that account, and an evil that we seem doomed, for the present at least, to retain and to deprecate.

Thus has the most benignant form of government the nations ever witnessed brought no blessings with it to a multitude of wretched beings over whom Compassion weeps, but whom Compassion even cannot disinthral; and whose final disinthralment Hope sees only in distant and dim perspective, in the light of scme future jubilee, when domestic as well as civil oppression shall have ceased, and no print of vassal footsteps remain thereafter on freedom's soil, nor chain be worn beneath the sun of freedom.

I am aware that our domestic slavery is considered by many as merely a local evil; and that it has become fashionable to think and speak of it as though we at the North were no way implicated in its guilt, or liable to be affected by that ultimate vengeance it threatens to inflict.

Is it then forgotten that slavery was once legalized in New-England? or is it unknown that, till recently, it was legalized in New-York? Meet we not with the memorials of its once greater prevalence in those degraded menials that still carry about with them the print of chains, retain the manners, and speak the dialect of bondage? If the number of blacks and of slaves be less at the North than at the South, we owe this enviable distinction to our climate, not our virtue. It was neither the foresight nor the piety of the Pilgrims, but the good Providence of God, that traced the lines of their inheritance on this side the natural limit of negro habitation. If the planter of the South has long appeared in the odious charac ter of *receiver of stolen men*, the trader of the North has as long appeared in the still more odious charac ter of *man-stealer*.

It must be admitted—with humiliation indeed, but still it must be admitted—that with New-England capital slave-ships have been built, and with New-England seamen navigated. In New-England, too, have stood the workshops in which those yokes and manacles were forged that weighed on the limbs of the captive negro during his passage to bondage. On Virginia, at least, slavery was forced contrary to her will and against her remonstrance. Can as much be said in favour of all other and more northern colonies?

But, whatever may have been the comparative guilt of the parties concerned in making merchandise of men, the alarming consequence of their joint iniquity is sufficiently apparent in the existence among us of more than one million six hundred thousand slaves. This is an abatement of national prosperity connected with no alleviating circumstance; nor is there any softening light in which this feature in our condition can be viewed. Slavery, in all its forms, is odious; in all its bearings, hurtful. It is an evil gratuitous and unmixed; and equally an evil to the slave, his master, and the state.

Its existence bespeaks an unnatural state of things. In whatever society the few lord it over the many, the balance of energies is disturbed; and there will be a constant tendency in the system to weaken the preponderance of power and restore the equilibrium. Even in governments less popular than our own, this tendency is apparent. Roman slavery has long since ceased. Feudal tyranny has passed away from Europe, and the condition of the serfs of Saxony and the boors of Russia is ameliorating; and, though not free, they are gradually approximating towards freedom.

But there are causes that render the perpetuity of slavery here more difficult than elsewhere, and more difficult in the present than in former ages.

Domestic slavery is not abhorrent to the feelings of a community accustomed to political slavery, nor inconsistent in principle with governments founded on prescriptive and hereditary privilege. It harmonizes with the institutions of Tunis, Morocco, Algiers, and other provinces of Turkish despotism. Religion there even sanctions it; and it is felt to be as righteous as it is convenient, to compel the followers of Christ to become hewers of wood and drawers of water to the followers of Mohammed. With us it is otherwise. Slavery is here a perfect anomaly. It stands out by itself, an isolated institution, unsupported, unconnected, and at variance with all our other institutions. It is at variance with the spirit of our government; at variance with its letter. It is at variance with our political principles, at variance with our religious principles, revolting to our moral feelings, and crosses all our habits of thought and action. And can there be a question whether slavery, under such circumstances, in such a country, and among such a people, can be eternal? If villanage in Britain, and even in Gaul, has ceased —if the serfs of Saxony and the boors of Russia are rising in the scale of being, and there be even hope that the degraded Hindu will one day be disinthralled by the diffusion of science, and the slow but resistless march of public opinion, is there no hope of disinthralment for the African, who breathes the air, and sees the light, and treads the soil of freedom? Impossible! such an outrage cannot be perpetual. The constitution of man, of nature, of heaven and earth must change, or slavery be subverted. It cannot stand against the progress of society. Its doom has been pronounced already; and the forward movement of the world will overthrow it.

Is it forgotten that slavery was once sanctioned by even ecclesiastical authority? and that the cross and the crescent were alike arrayed on its side? Is it forgotten that the negro race have been solemnly consigned to perpetual bondage by the highest authority in Christendom, because they never attended mass, and were of the colour of the damned? And, thereafter, that centuries rolled away, during which Africa was considered as rightfully given up to plunder by Christian nations, who, without compunction and without regret, conspired to ravage her coasts and reduce her captive sons to slavery?

Nor was it till our own times that the spell which had so long bound the understanding and the moral sense of Christendom was broken. There are those now living who remember when the slave-trade, unassailed and without an enemy, remained interwoven with the policy and intrenched in the prepossessions of every Christian nation; when the king, and the Parliament, and the people even of Britain stood firm in its defence; when, in opposition to this array of opinion and of power, Granville Sharp first raised his voice, and Clarkson, and Wilberforce, and their coadjutors took their stand; and who remember, too, the contempt with which the first humble efforts of these men of mercy were regarded: efforts which were destined to shake, and which have already shaken, the system they assailed to its base, and changed the current of feeling throughout the world. The slave, of whatever cast or colour, has long since been declared free the moment he sets his foot on British soil; and the trade in slaves, already abolished by Britain, has been denounced by almost every Christian nation.

Everywhere, as discussion has increased, the friends of slavery have diminished; and results as memorable have been effected on this side the Atlantic as on the other. Time was when slavery sat as easy on the conscience of the Puritan of the North as of the planter of the South; when statesmen of the purest patriotism, and clergymen of the loftiest intellect New-England ever boasted, were found among its champions; and when, even there, men of every rank as much expected their slaves as their lands to descend in perpetuity to their children.

The slave-trade, however, has not only been abolished by the national republic, but slavery itself has also been abolished in the whole of New-England, New-Jersey, New-York, and Pennsylvania. In Delaware and Maryland it is waning to its close, and in Virginia, though it exists in strength, yet its existence is abhorred; while, by the rise of kindred republics in Spanish America, it has, through vast and contiguous territories, suddenly ceased to exist.

These are splendid triumphs which the march of public opinion has achieved. It is still on the advance, gathering momentum as it advances. And the posterity of those now so intent on sustaining slavery will not consent to its being sustained.

There are few enlightened patriots at the South who do not already abhor the system ; who do not regard it as an evil ; who do not desire its abolition. Our brethren of the South have the same sympathies, the same moral sentiments, the same love of liberty as ourselves. By them as by us, slavery is felt to be an evil, a hinderance to our prosperity, and a blot upon our character. That it exists to such a fearful extent among them is not the result of choice, but of necessity. It was in being when they were born, and has been forced on them by a previous generation.

Can any considerate man, in the view of what has been done and what is now doing, believe that, amid so many merciful designs, so many benevolent activities, the negro slave will experience no deliverance ? That the master will remain for ever undisturbed by the presence of stripes and chains, and continue without relenting, from year to year, and from generation to generation, to eat the bread, and wear the raiment, and export the staple produced by the tears and sweat of bondmen ? That the free and enlightened inhabitants of this proud republic will go on celebrating their Fourth of July, reading their Declaration of Independence, and, regardless of the groans of so many millions held in bondage, persist in the mockery of reproaching despots, of eulogizing republics, and holding up before the eyes of an insulted universe the ensign of liberty? It cannot be. To sustain such an abuse under such circumstances is impossible. There needs no domestic insurrection, no foreign interference to subvert an institution so repugnant to all our other institutions. Public opinion has already pronounced on it; and the moral energy of the nation will sooner or later effect its overthrow.

Already planted on the African shore is seen a beacon of promise. There an asylum has been provided, and thither the ransomed captives are beginning to return, reconveying to the land of their fathers both civilization and religion. These may be but the pioneers of a progressive civilization, to be continued until a continent has been reclaimed, and a race redeemed through the agency of our emancipated slaves.

True it is that neither the trader's manacle nor the driver's whip is the most obvious omen of national enlargement. It is, however, as much so as the yoke of Israel or the prison-house of Potiphar. Nor is the way to glory for Cush through bondage in America more circuitous and indirect than it was to Israel through bondage in Egypt. And since the Israelite has reached the one by making the circuit of the other, it will not be unparalleled in the history of the world should the Cushite also.

The civil jurisprudence of these states, retaining

whatever was consonant to reason and congenial to liberty in the Common Law—that matchless monument of wisdom—has silently accommodated itself to our new condition.

In most of the states the despotism of creditors has been abridged, and the prison limits of debtors enlarged, and enlightened and philanthropic statesmen are now employed in wiping from the natior, the reproach of making misfortune penal, and rendering to honest bankruptcy the retribution of imprisonment.

Our criminal code, by repeated revision, has been greatly ameliorated, and is still ameliorating.

Trial by battle has ceased; the practice of ridding society of felons by the summary process of the gallows is diminished, and, by rendering penalties *disciplinary* as well as retributive, a new principle has been introduced; a principle, the effects of which will then only be fully apparent when, by a more measured graduation of crime, a more judicious classification of criminals, and a more efficient administration of moral discipline, prisons shall have become retirements for contrition and schools of virtue, instead of being halls of ribaldry and nurseries of vice. Nor will farther revision be unnecessary until another principle shall have been introduced, and *prevention* as well as amendment rendered prominent in the system; for it is not only requisite that criminals should be reformed, but also that temptations to crime should be removed, facilities to crime diminished, and that the *children* of the republic, at least, should be so guarded and educated, that, though the aged should never be reclaimed, the state may, notwithstanding, be freed from the burden of maintaining either paupers or convicts, and society become purified from vagrancy and crime by the gradual production of a more industrious and virtuous generation. So that in this department, also, there remain new measures for policy to discuss, and fields untroddren over which patriotism may expatiate.

But there are improvements which owe their existence not so much to the wisdom of legislation as to the higher wisdom of forbearing to legislate. That undefined boundary where utility from regulation ceases and injury begins has not always been regarded.

Time was when even the homage man owes to his Maker was deemed a fit object for legal enactment and penal enforcement. The secret aspirations of the heart and the delicate workings of conscience were held to supervision by human inquest, and subjected to the rude discipline of terrestrial courts. Thought itself was regulated, opinion made penal, and fire and sword legalized in defence of faith. France and Britain, as well as Spain and Portugal, enforced uniformity by torture, and from dungeons and scaffolds addressed to dissent their rebuke. And, strange as it may seem, the land of those very Pilgrims who fled from martyrdom was itself stained with the blood of martyrs!

This most fearful of errors has at length been discovered and corrected. Cases of conscience have been dismissed from the courts, and penalties for unbelief blotted from the statute-book. Enactments against witchcraft have ceased, and prosecutions against witches have been discontinued: the learned disquisitions of divines on the nature of the crime, and the grave distinctions of jurists in trying the offence, as well as the vulgar tests of water and fire in discovering the offender, have all been alike disregarded. And it is satisfactory to add, that the crime of witch-riding, as well as the dread of being witch-ridden, have both disappeared with the disappearance of that pomp of inquest and execution which aggravated, if they did not even produce, the very evil they were intended to prevent.

These happy results have been effected, not by the doings of statesmen, but by their abstaining from action: an unostentatious method of conferring benefits, but not the less effectual on that account; and one by which still other benefits, perhaps, remain to be conferred: for, whether vagrancy and pauperism, as did witchcraft, do not owe much of their thrift and increment to the stimulus of legislation, is a problem that yet remains to be solved.

In religion, which has been the occasion of the purest virtues and the blackest crimes, of the keenest anguish and the holiest joys, though progress has been made, there is room for still farther progress.

As yet, even Christian nations neither fully know the merits nor feel the benefits of the Christian system. Nor is it strange that they do not. For no sooner did the church cease to be persecuted by the state, than she received the impress of its form, and became thereafter the subject of its policy.

The authority of priests was reared on the same base as that of princes. To regulate human action was the prerogative of the one, *to regulate human opinion that of the other.* They who might not think, need not read. Hence, to the vassal multitude, the Bible was prohibited. A dense and frightful darkness thereafter overspread the world, of which the darkness of Egypt, that could be felt, was but an emblem. In the mean time, the soul as well as the body of man, under this double despotism of the altar and the throne, became bowed to the dust.

Ages elapsed before the recoil was felt and the Bible restored; and even its restoration produced but a partial benefit. In Protestant Christendom, where liberty to read was granted, the book itself was rare; by many it could not be procured, while multitudes were incapable of reading it.

To meet this exigency, creeds and catechisms were compiled; and to these the people were sent, to acquire a summary knowledge of the contents of that restored and authoritative volume.

These manuals, though rich in doctrine, were yet abstract and unimpassioned in manner; addressing the intellect rather than the conscience, the affections, the imagination, or the heart. They contained the real, but *naked*, elements of the Christian system.

Truths, indeed, were thus communicated; but they were drawn up in form and stated with brevity: truths unaccompanied by that freedom of discussion, that variety of illustration, that freshness of colouring, that persuasiveness of motive, and general impress of divinity so apparent in the sacred writings. Useful as these helps might have been in the arrangement of Christian knowledge already acquired, they could never avail to an adequate acquisition of that knowledge; for they contained, at best, a mere skeleton of revealed religion, and not *revealed religion herself,* robed in beauty, glowing with animation, throbbing with life, and in the full array of those celestial glories which beam forth from the sacred canvass, on which her features are drawn with skill inimitable and by a pencil divine. And yet even children acquired their first ideas and received their first impressions from the study of lessons containing only formal propositions, systematically arranged in some chosen abstract of Bible truths; and not by the study of those simpler and richer, as well as diviner lessons of wisdom adapted to their years, addressed to their sensibility, and presented in forms so alluring, and in variety so attractive, on the pages of the Book of God itself.

Hence it happened that Luther, and Calvin, and Knox, and their revered coadjutors, while assailing the authority of Rome, silently established over many a mind a milder but a *paramount* authority; nor was it till a later age that the bearing of that great principle they had assumed was fully perceived, or that measures were taken to render its application universal.

An effort is at length making to give, not merely creeds compiled from the Bible, but the Bible itself, to every family in Christendom; nay, not only to every family, but even to every individual on the earth.

By the joint influence of the Bible and the Sunday-school, thousands of children are now exercising their understandings on the doctrines, treasuring up in their memories the facts, stimulating their consciences by the precepts, and staying their hopes on the promises of that blessed book which has power to make man wise unto salvation.

Already is the result beginning to be apparent in the excitement of Bible sympathies and the formation of a Bible character. Thus has an impulse been given to the juvenile mind training in these little nurseries of wisdom, which will be hereafter felt through all the ranks of society; which will even react on the sanctuary and the doctors of the law; not only inducing a holier life, but restoring to the universal church a purer faith and a sounder form of words: the words in which the great Teacher himself delivered *to mankind his oracles.*

It has been said that bringing the public mind into contact with the Bible, though it should unite opinion on obvious and important points, must, on points not obvious or important, call forth debate and ensure division. Be it even so. Is this an evil so greatly to be dreaded?

How much crime, and blood, and treasure, has the attempt to *coerce* uniformity cost the nations? How few have even yet attained it? And when attained, what people did it ever benefit? Has it anywhere either promoted industry, advanced science, or purified morality?

If it be so important that the train of *future* thought should be kept for ever within the limits of existing forms, it were as well to resume the ancient mould, and again subject the operations of the mind to the pressure of that great moral lever, the fulcrum of which has, for so many ages, been planted at Rome.

Apologies, indeed, have been offered for the variety of opinion in which freedom of thought has issued. But apologies were unnecessary. A multiplicity of sects, differing in faith and forms, and yet reciprocating kindness and dwelling together in unity, is among the fairest features that modern Christendom exhibits. How do the racks, and gibbets, and dungeons, and scaffolds, and fires, with which uniformity has for ages been surrounded—how do these compare with the mild, and tranquil, and varied array of different Christian communities, advancing side by side towards heaven, and provoking one another on the way only to love and good works!

And is it, then, to be dreaded as so great an evil that, under the more diffusive influence of the Bible, other and yet other Christian denominations may arise to quicken the labours and stimulate the zeal of existing denominations ; to correct, perhaps, their errors ; to check their declension, to augment their means, and co-operate in the execution of their designs of goodness ?

Notwithstanding the dogmatism of courts and councils, the fatal maxim that diversity of doctrine or worship is incompatible with social happiness and public safety has been at length refuted, and it is ours to share in the glory of its refutation. And who knows but, in the farther progress of Christian knowledge and the farther development of Christian principle, it may come to be universally apparent, that the unity of the church itself, and the only unity which God requires or of which he approves. consists not in that outward identity of aspect which persecution has for ages been struggling to impress, but in *an inward oneness of spirit:* a unity nowhere on earth more apparent than in the diveis Christian communities, each performing its appointed duty, each moving in its appropriate sphere, and all combined and harmonized in one common system of benevolent exertion, by the influence of that celestial charity which on earth, as in heaven, is the cement of society and the bond of perfectness; and which requires only to be cherished and extended to banish discord, and transform the world itself into a theatre of peace, in which nothing shall remain to molest or make afraid, *as in God's holy mountain.*

Religion is intimately connected with the best interests of the human race; and every advance made in the knowledge of its doctrines or in the administration of its discipline must be favourable to those interests. To religion, even under its pagan form, both art and science are indebted. It was the achievements of the gods that woke the harp of Homer; it was the statues of the gods that employed the chisel of Phidias; it was the portraitures of the gods that imbodied those touches of the pencil of Apelles.

Hunger, and cold, and nakedness may call forth mere physical energy, but the inspirations of genius result from sublimer stimuli, and require both motives and models from an incorporeal world. Those motives and models revelation furnishes, in a higher degree and of a holier kind than were ever elsewhere furnished; and the scholar is now encouraged in his efforts and in his anticipations by the indications of

Providence as well as the language of prophecy, since it is impossible for him not to see, in the light the Bible sheds upon his prospects, that great and benign results must follow from the operation of that moral machinery which is beginning to bear upon the world.

It has been truly said that science is the handmaid of religion; and it may be as truly said that religion, especially revealed religion, is the patroness of science; for, though its direct object is to make man holy, in effecting this it cannot fail to make him wise also. Without regard to rank or condition, the Bible furnishes both the means and motives to improvement, in whatever language it is read, and far as its editions circulate. Imbodying a system of history the most authentic and the most ancient, a system of morals the most pure, and of theology the most sublime, it carries this epitome of universal truth to every cottage, bringing its quickening and mighty influence to bear on the native elements of individual character, as they exist in all the varieties of a changeful and scattered population. Its specimens of composition are as finished as its maxims of wisdom are profound. The study of it, therefore, must tend to purify the taste as well as the heart, to fix the habit of investigation, and to sharpen the appetite for knowledge: nor is it possible that any kindred or nation should continue either ignorant or degraded among whom the Bible has been distributed, and by whom it is studied and revered; and it is now perceptible that the sphere it fills is rapidly enlarging, and that the influence it exerts is becoming more extensive and decided.

We pass onward, therefore, to encounter new difficulties and to achieve new triumphs with increased confidence, inasmuch as religion is bringing fresh auxiliaries to our aid, and experience supplying new proofs that God is on our side. It can no longer be a question whether the world is to be filled with other knowledge, since it is about to be filled with the knowledge of his word.

There was a time when priests alone were capable of reading, and when even many of them possessed not the Bible. Now its entire text is stereotyped in different languages, and the press in many a land is perpetually employed in throwing off new copies of the history of Moses, the dramatic compositions of Job, the Lyrics of David, the Proverbs of Solomon, the Prophecies of Isaiah, the Lamentations of Jeremiah, and the piercing rebuke of Zephaniah and Habakkuk; together with whatever else of wisdom and goodness, of grace and mercy, of beauty and grandeur, either the prophets or evangelists contain. Agents, too, are actively employed in scattering these productions among every caste, and wide as the race of men are scattered.

And is it to be believed that the Scriptures of both Testaments are to be read by the millions of the human family, and yet those millions continue to groan in bondage and grovel in ignorance? Where has the Bible ever entered that arts and science, that music, and painting, and sculpture, and poetry, and eloquence have not followed in its train? Nowhere: nor will it hereafter.

Within the limits traced by its circulation, even now is found all that renders life a blessing and being desirable; but cross those limits, and you leave behind you whatever is lofty and endearing, and you see around you only that which is debased and revolting.

To the Bible science owes a mighty debt, which the friends of science should be neither reluctant to acknowledge nor slack to pay. Nor is it only on account of the aid it gives to other science, but also on account of that science which itself alone contains, that we are called upon to array ourselves among its advocates and its defenders.

The advance of political science will, it may be hoped, ameliorate the sufferings, multiply the comforts, extend the privileges, and elevate the character of man. The world itself may perchance become a republic in government as well as letters. Progress in the arts may increase the efficacy of remedies, diminish the inveteracy of diseases, and prolong the duration of life. Still death will be not the less dreadful, since it will be not the less inevitable. There is a limit to everything but omnipotence; and, however skill may delay, it cannot prevent man's ultimate mortality.

The grave is, and, in spite of all our efforts, will continue to be, as appointed, the house of all living. No elixir that will render man immortal remains by future analysis to be revealed. Nor is there any hope that synthetic chymistry will, in its progress, reverse the process of final dissolution, recompose the ashes of the urn, and reproduce those fabrics demolished by death. In the mean time, shadowy forms satisfy not the fabled inhabitants even of Elysian fields; nor has philosophy been able to discover a more substantial residence, or song to inspire a less visionary hope.

After all, it is the Bible, and the Bible only, that meets the case, and supplies a remedy to the miseries of man. Its sublimer chymistry, distancing our puny efforts and dissipating our childish fears, reveals a process by which the desolations of a thousand generations shall in a moment be repaired, and heaven enriched with new forms of beauty, reproduced immortal from the ruins of the sepulchre.

Astronomy, indeed, has disabused reason of many a superstition, and extended to many an unknown orb the range of human vision; but no star which the telescope reveals casts so benign or cheering a light across a benighted sinner's pathway as the Star of Bethlehem; nor does any sun guide up the eye of man to a firmament so high, so holy, or so enduring, as that made visible by the Sun of Righteousness.

Let us, then, hereafter connect Jerusalem with Athens; entwine the ivy of Parnassus around the cedar of Lebanon; weave into the wreath of flowerets plucked from the Vale of Tempe, the rose of Sharon, and remember at our festivals that among the hills of Palestine there is a hill of tenderer interest and of higher hope than either Ida or Olympus. Yes: let us plant the banner of religion in the vestibule of science; nor feel that our object is accomplished till we shall have rendered her temple, already sacred to Truth, sacred also to Devotion.

THE END.

www.ingramcontent.com/pod-product-compliance
Lightning Source LLC
Chambersburg PA
CBHW031905220426
43663CB00006B/775